ILLUSTRATED
GUIDE TO
KNITTING
The Creative Way

ILLUSTRATED GUIDE TO KNITTING
The Creative Way

Exeter Books

NEW YORK

Consultant Editor: Sandy Carr
Editor: Janie Ryan
Designer: Liz Rose
Production: Dennis Hovell

First published in USA 1986 by Exeter Books
Distributed by Bookthrift
Exeter is a trademark of Bookthrift Marketing, Inc.
Bookthrift is a registered trademark of
Bookthrift Marketing
New York, New York

ISBN 0–671–08306–6

Photoset by Quadraset Limited
Printed and bound in Italy by
L.E.G.O. Spa, Vicenza

Contents

Introduction

In recent years knitting has shed much of its rather dowdy, old-fashioned image. Shops selling wonderful new yarns in fashion colors have sprung up everywhere; and there are lots more interesting patterns to choose from than there used to be. As a result, there are many people now who would like to learn to knit but are, perhaps, discouraged because it seems hopelessly difficult. Expert knitters seem to knit so quickly that it's impossible to see what they are doing and how. In fact, basic knitting skills are easy and the Knitting Skills section of this book will teach you everything you need to know to produce some highly impressive results.

Armed with this knowledge (and you don't need to know it all before you begin) you can try one of the forty-six patterns in the following pages – all right up-to-date and the work of some top knitting designers. There are garments for men, women, and children, for summer and winter; and besides main items like sweaters, dresses, and coats, there are accessories – shawls, gloves, socks, scarves, and hats – something, in fact, for everyone.

Knitting Skills

Knitting is one of the easiest and quickest crafts to learn. You don't have to be an expert to produce acceptable results and there is very little specialist equipment that you have to buy before you can begin – just needles and some yarn. The very basic skills you need are casting on and binding off, knitting and purling (see pages 14–18). Increasing and decreasing (pages 19–21) are also important for shaping garments. The other, more advanced, techniques such as bobbles and cables, you can leave until later.

Equipment and Materials

Knitting equipment has remained virtually unchanged for centuries, but there are wonderful new yarns to choose from every year.

The basics

Pattern It is best to use a commercial pattern when beginning to knit.

Yarn Buy one ball first to check tension, then buy or reserve enough to complete the garment to avoid any slight change in the dye. Note the dye lot number in case you need more.

Pair of needles For flat knitting along the rows. The knobs prevent the stitches from dropping off the ends. Use good needles: bent, uneven, or easily breakable ones spoil your knitting. Most are coated metal, plastic, or wooden for large sizes. They are sized by number, from the smallest, 0, to the largest, 15. You will also find some needles graded metrically, according to the number of millimetres in their diameter. The chart shows the metric equivalents for American sizes. The size of a needle relates to the gauge. For a tighter gauge use smaller needles and *vice versa*.

Additional equipment

Needle gauge For checking needle sizes, both American and metric.

Row counter For counting increased and decreased stitches; also rows.

Stitch holder For holding a number of stitches on any part of the work until they are needed later on.

Cable needle For holding stitches at the back or front of the work while twisting a cable. The cable needle size should be similar to the main needles.

Double-pointed needles For seamless, circular knitting.

Circular needles For flat or seamless circular knitting with a large number of stitches. Choose a suitable length for tubular knitting — about 2in less than the circumference of the work.

Scissors For cutting yarn.

Tape measure Choose one marked in both inches and centimeters.

Pins For checking gauge. Choose ones with big colored heads which will show up on thick yarn.

Press cloth Use a fine cotton fabric.

Sewing needles For sewing pieces together. Use a large tapestry needle, which has a blunt point, to avoid splitting the yarn and a large eye to take the thickness of the yarn.

Needles sizes			
American	Metric	American	Metric
0	2mm	9	5½mm
1	2¼mm	10	6mm
2	2¾mm	10½	6½mm
	3mm		7mm
3	3¼mm	11	7½mm
4	3½mm		8mm
5	4mm	13	8½mm
6	4½mm		9mm
7		15	10mm
8	5mm		

Types of yarn

Yarns are generally sold by weight in balls, hanks, or (for machine knitting) cones. They can be made from natural fibers, synthetics, or a mixture of the two. The yarn label will usually give guidance as to the most suitable method of cleaning and pressing; in some cases, a needle or hook size and gauge measurement are given.

Natural yarns

Wool Spun from the fleece of sheep; warm, resilient, the most versatile of yarns.

Cotton Available in many thicknesses, from very fine to heavy.

Silk A luxury yarn produced in a range of thicknesses and textures.

Mohair Fluffy goat hair yarn often combined with other fibers.

Angora A delicate, soft yarn made from rabbit fur.

Alpaca A slightly hairy yarn obtained from llamas, usually sold undyed.

Synthetic yarns

Acrylic, nylon, rayon, and polyester are among the synthetic fibers used in knitting yarns. They are most successful when used in blends combining the easy-care attributes of the synthetic with the texture of a natural fiber.

Smooth yarns

Fingering A lightweight yarn, usually spun from three plies, or strands.

Baby yarn A lightweight yarn, slightly bulkier than fingering.

Sport-weight yarn A medium-weight yarn, usually four-ply.

Knitting worsted A fairly heavy yarn, spun from four plies of wool. The term is also commonly applied to yarn of the same weight made from other fibers, such as acrylic.

Bulky yarn Considerably thicker than knitting worsted and very quick to knit.

Shetland A medium-weight, loosely-twisted wool yarn, dyed in soft colors.

Fisherman About the same weight as knitting worsted, or slightly heavier, most often used for Aran-style sweaters.

Icelandic A bulky, softly-spun wool.

Novelty yarns

Slub An unevenly-spun yarn which produces a soft, irregular fabric.

Bouclé A loopy yarn available in various thicknesses. It produces an attractive bobbly texture.

Glitter Metallic man-made threads in gold, silver, copper, and other finishes.

Imported yarns

Many European and some Oriental yarns are now available in the U.S. and are becoming more familiar to American knitters. (See the list of addresses on page 192.) Some of the terms used to describe these yarns, however, may be unfamiliar. Two of the most commonly-used are explained here.

Double knitting A smooth yarn, slightly lighter than knitting worsted. The term is also applied to European novelty yarns that knit up to the same gauge as this yarn.

Four-ply In Britain this term applies to a smooth yarn slightly lighter than a sport-weight yarn. The phrase "knits as four-ply" is applied to novelty yarns that knit up to the same gauge.

Some of the garments in this book have been designed for double knitting and "four-ply" yarns. In these cases, the required amounts of knitting worsted or sport-weight yarn are also given, along with the required amounts of the original yarn (in grams). Because the American yarns are generally thicker than their European counterparts, you may find it necessary to use a smaller needle in order to obtain the correct gauge.

Understanding Knitting Patterns

The shorthand used in knitting and crochet patterns is designed to avoid repetition and save space. To follow a pattern successfully you must have thorough understanding of the abbreviations

If you intend to use a pattern you should buy it before buying your yarn and read it through. If you are going to substitute another yarn for the one recommended in the pattern, pay particular attention to the size, gauge, and materials sections.

Abbreviations can vary considerably from pattern to pattern, so read and note them before beginning work. The abbreviations used in this book are shown below.

Size The "*to fit*" measurement is not intended as a precise measurement of the garment. The actual measurement is sometimes given after the "to fit" measurement or in a measurement diagram. Continually refer to this

diagram to check all your actual measurements. The "to fit" size is what it says: a body measurement. If it is a tight-fitting garment, there will be little difference between the "to fit" measurement and the corresponding measurement on the diagram.

The figures in the *brackets* are the larger sizes given in the pattern. Choose your size and encircle or underline all the instructions for that size throughout the pattern before beginning work. This way you will follow through the instructions consistently for your size.

The *length measurement* refers most usually to the length from shoulder seam down to the bottom of the garment.

The *sleeve seam measurement* is from the underarm join to the end of the sleeve.

Gauge This is very important, especially where you have chosen to substitute a different yarn, so always work a gauge swatch. Some patterns only give the number of stitches, whereas others also give the number of rows. For more information about gauge, see page 11.

Materials If you decide to substitute a different yarn, make sure you buy enough — weight is not necessarily an indication of length i.e. a 1oz ball of the substitute yarn may not go as far as a 1oz ball of the recommended yarn.

Main pattern To keep your place through the pattern it may help to cross off the rows with a pencil as you work them. Where a section of the pattern is to be repeated several times it is a good idea to use a row counter.

Never deviate from the *order of the pattern*. If you do, you may find that you are unable to finish the garment as instructed because the necessary stages have not been completed beforehand.

Where instructions are grouped together in *parentheses*, read just beyond them and you will see that they tell you how often to repeat the instructions in parentheses — for example, (K1, P1) to end, (rib 4, M1) 4 times. Sometimes instructions are grouped together in parentheses to indicate that they should all be worked into the one stitch, e.g. (K1, yo, K1, yo, K1) all into next st.

Always note *asterisks*. A single asterisk is usually used to indicate a repetition of the stitch pattern within the row. Double, triple, and quadruple asterisks usually indicate the repetition of larger areas of instruction.

Abbreviations

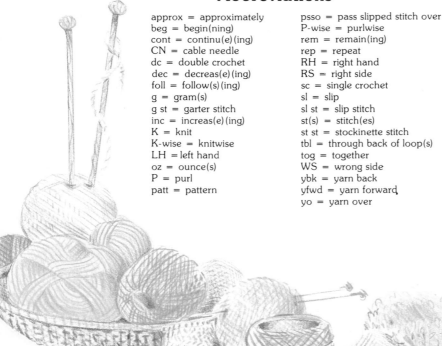

approx = approximately	psso = pass slipped stitch over
beg = begin(ning)	P-wise = purlwise
cont = continu(e)(ing)	rem = remain(ing)
CN = cable needle	rep = repeat
dc = double crochet	RH = right hand
dec = decreas(e)(ing)	RS = right side
foll = follow(s)(ing)	sc = single crochet
g = gram(s)	sl = slip
g st = garter stitch	sl st = slip stitch
inc = increas(e)(ing)	st(s) = stitch(es)
K = knit	st st = stockinette stitch
K-wise = knitwise	tbl = through back of loop(s)
LH = left hand	tog = together
oz = ounce(s)	WS = wrong side
P = purl	ybk = yarn back
patt = pattern	yfwd = yarn forward
	yo = yarn over

Gauge

Gauge is the most important single factor in the success of any piece of knitting. However imaginative the design, or beautiful the yarn, the final result will inevitably be disappointing if the gauge has not been carefully checked at the start and maintained throughout the work.

What is gauge?

At its simplest, the gauge of knitting is a measurement of its tightness or looseness. It describes the number of stitches and rows it takes to achieve a given width and length. Gauge is affected by four factors: type of yarn, needle size, stitch pattern, and the individual knitter.

Yarn

Yarns come in a wide range of thicknesses and finishes. The labels of some yarns nowadays recommend a gauge measurement. This is the gauge which, in the manufacturer's opinion, will produce the most suitable finish for that particular yarn. It is especially useful if you are designing your own garment or substituting a new yarn for the one specified in the pattern. Often pattern designers use the "wrong" gauge deliberately, to achieve special effects – a floppier or more rigid fabric, for example – so whatever the label says, always match your gauge to the one given in the pattern. In general, however, thicker, bulkier yarns must be knitted on larger needles than fine yarns, and produce a gauge of fewer rows and stitches to the square inch. Even yarn apparently of the same weight and thickness can display variations in gauge. Not all knitting worsted-weight yarns, for example, knit up to the same gauge.

Needle size

This has an obvious effect on knitting gauge. The larger the needles, the looser the fabric and the fewer the rows and stitches to the square inch. This is clearly demonstrated by casting on a given number of stitches and knitting in stockinette stitch for, say, 8in, using the same yarn throughout but changing to smaller needles every few rows. Work a purl row on the right side between each needle size. The width of the knitting and the distance between the rows will gradually decrease.

Stitch pattern

Different stitch patterns are designed to produce fabrics with widely varying surface textures, and properties. Some, like seed stitch, are tight, firm fabrics which hold their shape well. Lacy patterns are, by definition, loose and open, Rib patterns are stretchy, tending to pull inward widthwise. All these properties affect gauge measurement. The same yarn and needle size will result in widely differing gauge over different stitch patterns. For this reason you cannot substitute a new stitch pattern for the one specified and assume that the resulting garment will be the correct measurements. The gauge of the new stitch pattern must be carefully checked against the original one. Often it is not possible to match both row and stitch gauge simultaneously. In such cases you should use a needle size that will achieve the correct stitch gauge and follow the measurement diagram for length.

The knitter

The tension with which you knit has a direct effect upon gauge. It is almost as personal a thing as handwriting or fingerprints. It is therefore never advisable to allow anyone else to finish a piece of knitting that you have started. This is also the reason why you must adjust the gauge you obtain to that of any pattern before beginning work on it. The gauge of the pattern is that obtained by the designer, and the chances are that his or her personal knitting tension will be different from yours. You cannot adjust the gauge successfully by trying to knit more loosely or more tightly than you usually do. This will simply interrupt the natural rhythm of your knitting. It will be uncomfortable to work, and as you relax into your normal style it will almost certainly produce an uneven gauge over the whole garment. If the gauge you obtain needs adjusting you must change the needle size.

Checking gauge

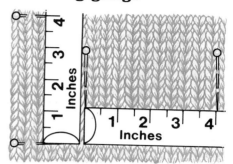

1 Knit a gauge sample using the same yarn, needle size, and stitch pattern specified in the gauge measurement (in this case 10 stitches and 14 rows to 4in), casting on a few more stitches and working more rows than given. Place a ruler along the width of the sample and mark off the measurement with pins at right angles to the ruler. Place the ruler vertically on the sample and mark off the measurement with pins. Count the stitches and rows between pins.

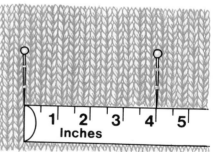

2 If there are too many stitches or rows your gauge is tighter than that of the designer. Knit another sample using larger needles and check it again.

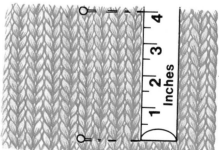

3 If there are too few stitches and rows between the pins your gauge is looser than that of the designer. Knit another sample on smaller needles and check it again.

Finishing

Bad finishing can ruin the most skillful knitting, so take plenty of time and extra care over blocking, pressing, and assembling the garment for a really professional finish.

Finishing — as the word suggests — is the final stage in making a crocheted or knitted garment. Perhaps because of this there is a tendency, even among otherwise careful knitters, to rush it; but poorly finished garments with lumpy seams look dreadful, however good the knitting itself. There are five basic stages in finishing: blocking, pressing, seaming, picking up stitches (for edgings, for example) and finishing (sewing on buttons, zippers, and so on). Some, but not all, of these stages are described in detail in the finishing section of patterns.

Blocking

First check whether or not the yarn used for the garment should be pressed. Sometimes the pattern gives pressing instructions. If not, they should be printed on the yarn label. If the yarn cannot be pressed, go straight to the seaming stage. If it can be pressed, each piece of the garment must be blocked to the correct shape and measurements before pressing. Use a thick ironing pad (a folded towel or blanket is ideal). Lay the knitting right-side downward on this, and begin pinning it out all around. Push the pins into the pad right up to the head and about half an inch apart, keeping the edge of the knitting straight and flat. Check the measurement diagram for the *actual* measurements of each part of the pieces and first pin out the widest point (usually the chest measurement). One of the advantages of blocking is that the knitting can be eased into or slightly stretched to the correct measurement if necessary. After the chest, pin out the rest of the basic shape — length, armhole depth, shoulder width, and so on — then fill in between these points with pins. Pin around the whole piece, except for the

ribbing which is never blocked or pressed. Place the pins along the top edge of the ribbing where it meets the main part of the back, front, or sleeves of the garment.

Pressing

The pressing instructions on the yarn label should tell you not only whether it can be pressed but also how — dry or damp, and hot, warm or cool. Always use a cloth; the iron should never come into direct contact with the knitted fabric. Press very lightly using up and down movements. Avoid ribbed sections and any knitted-in garter stitch or textured stitch patterns. Some fabrics, such as mohair and angora, are lightly steamed rather than pressed. Block them right side up and lay a wet cloth on the work. Hold a hot iron just over the cloth; the steam produced will be forced down into the fabric. The same method can be used to "raise" stitches that have been flattened by heavy pressing.

Blocking and pressing

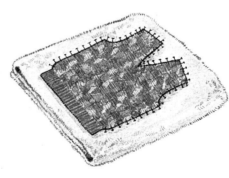

1 Place the knitted pieces right side down on a thick pad — a folded towel or blanket, for example — and block them out to correct measurements.

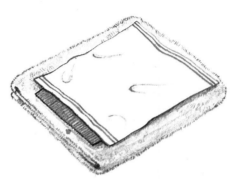

2 Cover the knitting with a clean cloth — dry or damp according to the instructions on the yarn label.

3 Using a warm iron, press the knitting with vertical rather than horizontal movements, lifting the iron off the knitting between each press. Keep the pressure even over the whole garment. Do not press the ribbing.

Seaming

The knitted pieces are usually joined together by seaming. In some cases they can be grafted together (see page 143) making a joining that is totally invisible. There are several seams suitable for joining knitting.
Backstitch seam Use this on shoulder seams, to set in sleeves, and for the main garment seams.

Flat seam Use this to join ribbed edges, to attach button and buttonhole bands, and on heavily textured fabrics.
Invisible seam Use this on straight-sided pieces worked in stockinette stitch, for vertical seams only.
Always use a tapestry needle for seaming. Use the garment yarn if possible. If it is unsuitable for some reason (it may be too thick or textured) use a matching finer yarn with the same fiber content. The order in which seams should be joined is usually given in the finishing instructions in the pattern. Generally the shoulder seams are joined first. There are several methods of setting in sleeves. They can

be joined before or after the side seams.
When joining sections of the garment that fold over to the right side (for example, a turtle neck collar) remember to reverse the seam at the appropriate point. Press completed seams lightly on the right side if the yarn is suitable for pressing. Darn in loose yarn ends.

Flat seam

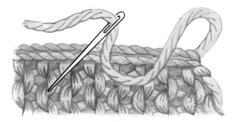

1 Use a flat seam when seaming heavily-textured fabrics. Place the two edges together with RS facing, and secure the end of the yarn with a double stitch.

2 Continue along the seam as shown, taking care to match rows or stitches on the two pieces of knitting.

Edgings and bands

Some edgings can be worked only after certain seams have been joined, so that instructions for these are usually included in the finishing section of the pattern. This applies to neckbands, armbands, collars, and sometimes button and buttonhole bands. Since these parts of the garment are usually worked in ribbing, it is not necessary to block or press them at this stage.

Invisible seam

1 Place the two edges side by side right sides uppermost, matching stitches and rows exactly. Secure yarn at bottom right-hand edge. Pick up stitch just opposite on left-hand edge. Pull yarn through and tighten. Pick up stitch in row above on right-hand edge. Pull yarn through and tighten.

2 Continue in this way moving from edge to edge, pulling yarn through and tightening after each stitch until the seam is completed. Fasten off. This seam produces a flat joining. It is particularly suitable for straight-sided seams in stockinette stitch.

Finishing touches

Depending on the type of garment, it may be necessary to insert a zipper, case a waistband, sew up a hem, make button loops, sew on buttons, and so on. Buttons that are likely to receive a great deal of wear can be reinforced by sewing a smaller button behind the button on the wrong side. Sew through the holes in both buttons at the same time. Finally, add any decorative touches – pompons, beads, cords, or embroidery.

Backstitch seam

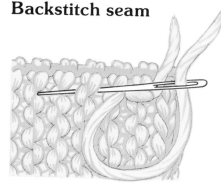

1 Thread a tapestry needle with matching yarn and begin at the right-hand end of the seam, securing the end of the yarn with a double stitch. Make a stitch by pushing the needle through both layers and bringing it back again to the front of the seam.

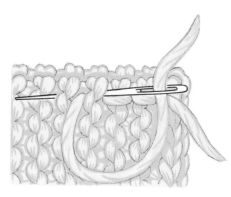

2 Insert the needle back into the fabric as shown and bring it to the front again. Continue in this way to the end of the seam.

Basic Skills

Holding the yarn and the needles

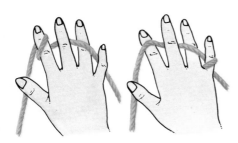

1 The working yarn can be held in either the left or the right hand. Threading the yarn between the fingers helps control both the speed and evenness of the knitting. The two methods shown are right-hand methods, in which the yarn is looped either around the index finger or around the little finger.

2 There are several ways of holding the needles. Most people experiment until they find a method that suits them and is both comfortable and efficient. The method shown is popular since it provides a firm, but not rigid, hold in which the needles can be easily used. The needle in the left hand is referred to as the left-hand needle, the needle held in the right hand as the right-hand needle.

14

Casting on (Cable method)

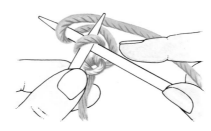

1 The cable method produces a firm, elastic edge suitable for most purposes. Make a slip loop and place it on the left-hand needle. Insert the right-hand needle through the front of the loop as shown. Take the yarn under and over the point of the right-hand needle.

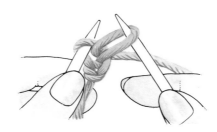

2 Draw the yarn through the loop on the left-hand needle, thus making a new loop on the right-hand needle. Transfer the loop on the right hand needle to the left-hand needle.

3 Insert the right-hand needle between the loops on the left-hand needle. Take the yarn under and over the point of the right-hand needle.

4 Draw the yarn between the loops on the left-hand needle. Place the new loop on the left-hand needle. Repeat stages 3 and 4 until the required number of stitches have been cast on.

Casting on (Knitting on method)

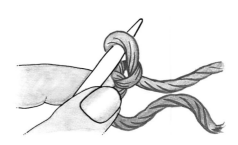

1 This produces a looser, more elastic edge than the cable method. Make a slip loop and place it on the left-hand needle.

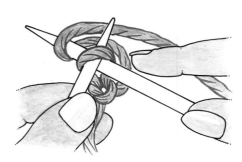

2 Insert the right-hand needle through the loop from front to back. Take the yarn under and over the point of the right-hand needle.

Single casting on

3 Draw a loop through and place it on the left-hand needle. Tighten the loop.

1 This is a lightweight edge ideal for children's and baby clothes and for casting on when making buttonholes. Place a slip loop on the right-hand needle and wind the yarn from the ball around the left thumb as shown above.

4 In a variation of this technique (sometimes called the Continental method) the stitches are cast onto two needles held together and the yarn wound around the thumb and third finger as shown. This edge is looser and more elastic.

5 A further variation produces a decorative knotted edge. Cast on two stitches singly. Lift the second stitch over the first. Cast on two more stitches. Slip second stitch over the first. Continue until required number of stitches have been cast on.

4 Insert the right-hand needle through the new loop on the left-hand needle. Take the yarn under and over the point of the right-hand needle and draw the loop through. Place the new loop on the left-hand needle. Continue in this way until all the stitches have been cast on.

2 Take the needle up through the loop on the thumb and take it onto the needle.

Invisible casting on

This method produces an edge that can be picked up and knitted in the opposite direction. Place a slip loop on two needles held together. Hold a length of contrasting yarn under the needles. With the yarn from the ball, make loops on the needles, taking them in front of the contrasting yarn and behind it alternately as shown. When the required stitches have been cast on, remove one needle. Knit the first row through the front of the loops. Remove the contrasting yarn and pick up loops to knit in the opposite direction.

5 The edge can be made slightly firmer by knitting the first row through the back of the loops.

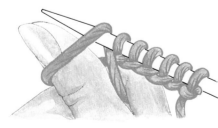

3 Continue making loops on the right-hand needle until the required stitches have been cast on.

The knit stitch (K)

1 Take the needle holding the stitches in your left hand. With the yarn at the back of the work, insert the right-hand needle through the front of the first stitch.

2 Take the yarn under and over the point of the right-hand needle.

3 Draw the yarn on the right-hand needle through the stitch on the left-hand needle.

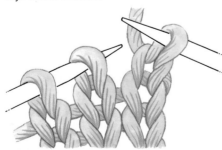

4 Slip the left-hand stitch off the needle, so completing the knit stitch. Knitting every row forms a garter stitch (g st) fabric.

16

The purl stitch (P)

1 Hold the needle with the cast-on stitches in your left hand. With the yarn at the front of the work, insert the right-hand needle through the front of the first stitch from right to left.

2 Take the yarn over and under the point of the right-hand needle.

3 Draw the yarn on the right-hand needle through the stitch on the left-hand needle. Slip the left-hand stitch off the needle, so completing the purl stitch.

Joining in new yarn

Ideally the new yarn should be joined in at the beginning of a row. It takes a length of yarn roughly four times the width of the knitting to complete a row. If the yarn is too short, let it hang at the edge of the work. Take a new ball and start the new row. Knot and darn both ends in at the wrong side when finishing.

Splicing yarn

Occasionally new yarn must be joined in the middle of a row: for example, to avoid excessive waste of expensive yarn or when knitting a scarf where yarn joins at the edge would show. In such cases the best method is to splice the ends of the old and new balls Unravel both ends for about 3in. Twist the ends together to make a single thread. Work the next stitches very carefully.

Binding off knitwise

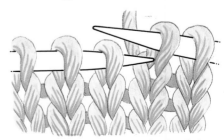

1 With the yarn at the back of the work, knit the first two stitches on the left-hand needle as usual.

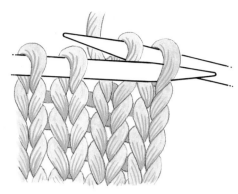

2 With the tip of the left-hand needle lift the first stitch knitted over the second stitch knitted and off the needle. One stitch has been bound off.

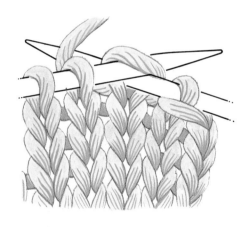

3 Work the next stitch on the left-hand needle as usual. Lift the second stitch knitted over it and off the needle. Two stitches have been bound off.

4 Repeat step 3 across the row. Break off the yarn, thread it through the last stitch and tighten.

Binding off purlwise

1 Occasionally it is necessary to bind off on purl rows. Purl the first two stitches on the left-hand needle.

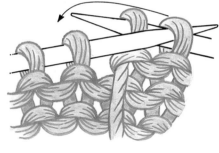

2 Lift the first stitch on the right-hand needle over the second stitch on the right-hand needle and off the needle.

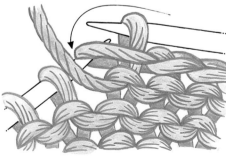

3 Purl the next stitch on the left-hand needle. Lift the first stitch on the right-hand needle over the second stitch on the right-hand needle and off the needle. Continue in this way until all the stitches have been bound off.

Binding off in ribbing

1 Ribbed edgings are usually bound off in ribbing, producing a more elastic edge. On a single rib, knit the first stitch on the left-hand needle and purl the second stitch. Lift the knit stitch over the purl stitch and off the needle.

2 Knit the next stitch on the left-hand needle. Lift the purl stitch over the knit stitch and off the needle.

3 Purl the next stitch on the left-hand needle. Lift the knit stitch over the purl stitch and off the needle. Continue in this way until all the stitches have been bound off.

Holding stitches

1 *Inserting pockets or working neckbands and neck edges usually requires that a number of stitches be held without being bound off until later in the pattern. If the number of stitches is very small, they can be held on a safety pin.*

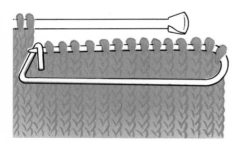

2 *More than ten stitches should be held on a special stitch holder with the end closed to secure them.*

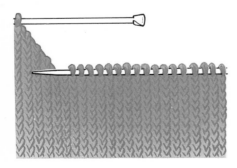

3 *Large numbers of stitches — for example, on the front of a V-necked sweater, can be held on a spare needle.*

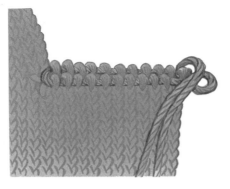

4 *In intricate patterns where a spare needle or stitch holder would be awkward to handle (for example, on gloves) the stitches can be held on a piece of spare yarn.*

Picking up stitches

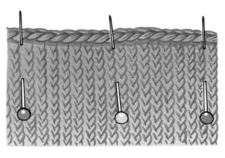

1 *Stitches often need to be picked up around neck edges and armholes so that a neckband and armhole band can be knitted. To insure they are picked up evenly, divide the edge into equal sections and mark them with pins.*

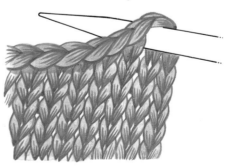

2 *Divide the number of sections into the number of stitches specified in the pattern and start picking up an equal number of stitches per section. Insert the tip of the needle into a row end on vertical edges or a stitch on horizontal edges.*

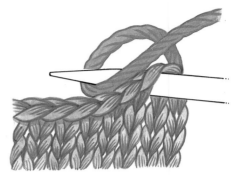

3 *With the yarn at the back of the work, take it under and over the point of the needle, and draw a loop through.*

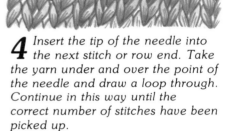

4 *Insert the tip of the needle into the next stitch or row end. Take the yarn under and over the point of the needle and draw a loop through. Continue in this way until the correct number of stitches have been picked up.*

Picking up a dropped stitch run

Dropping stitches, even several rows down, is not necessarily a disaster. If the stitch is a simple one like stockinette stitch the stitch can be picked up easily with a crochet hook. With the right side of work facing, insert the hook from the front into the dropped stitch, then under the horizontal thread just above it. Pull the thread through the dropped stitch. Continue upward until all the threads have been picked up.

Increasing and Decreasing

Simple increasing
Increase one stitch (inc 1)

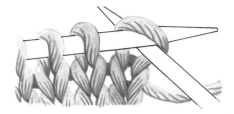

1 This method is used most often to make increases at the beginnings and ends of rows. Insert the right-hand needle knitwise into the front of the stitch on the left-hand needle.

2 Knit the stitch on the left-hand needle as usual but without slipping it off the needle.

3 Insert the right-hand needle into the back of the same stitch knitwise. Take the yarn under and over the point of the right-hand needle.

4 Draw the loop through, discarding the stitch on the left-hand needle, thus making two stitches out of one. This method is also called "knitting into the front and back of the same stitch."

Make one knitwise

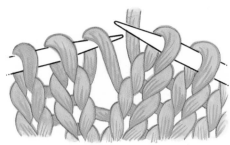

1 With the left-hand needle pick up the loop between the stitch just worked and the next stitch on the left-hand needle from front to back.

2 Knit as usual into the back of the raised loop on the left-hand needle. This makes an almost invisible increase.

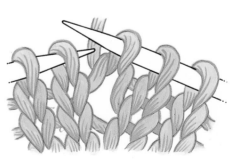

3 A visible hole, which can be used for decorative purposes, is formed by knitting the raised loop through the front rather than the back.

Make one purlwise

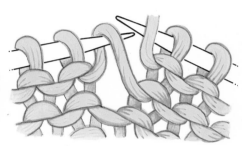

1 On purl rows, with the left-hand needle pick up the loop between the stitch just worked and the next stitch on the left-hand needle, from front to back.

2 Purl into the back of the raised loop on the left-hand needle. This makes an almost invisible increase.

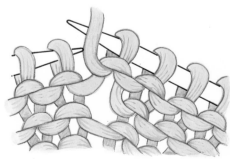

3 This method can also be varied to make a visible hole in the fabric by purling the raised loop through the front rather than the back.

19

Lifted increase (knitwise)

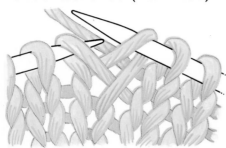

1 This is one of the least visible forms of increasing. Insert the right-hand needle into the stitch below the next stitch on the left-hand needle from front to back.

2 Lift the stitch and knit it in the usual way by taking the yarn under and over the point of the right-hand needle and drawing it through the stitch.

3 Knit the stitch above the lifted stitch as usual. This method is often referred to as "knit one below."

Lifted increase (purlwise)

1 On purl rows, insert the right-hand needle into the stitch below
20

the next stitch on the left-hand needle from back to front. Lift and purl it.

2 Insert the needle into the stitch above the lifted stitch and purl it as usual. This method is often referred to as "purl one below."

Double increasing

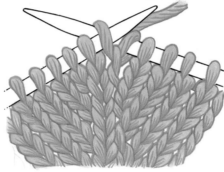

1 Double increases are made by adding one stitch on each side of a center stitch. Work to the center stitch. Pick up the loop between the last stitch knitted and the next stitch and knit into the back of it.

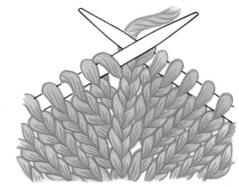

2 Knit the next stitch as usual. Pick up the loop between the last stitch knitted and the next stitch and knit into the back of it. Repeat this procedure on all subsequent right-side (knit) rows. All the wrong-side rows are purled.

Decorative, or "yarn over" increases

Between two knit stitches: after the first knit stitch the yarn is at the back of the work. Bring the yarn forward and over the right-hand needle. Knit the next stitch as usual.

Between two purl stitches: after the first purl stitch the yarn is at the front of the work. Take the yarn over then under the right-hand needle. Purl the next stitch as usual.

Between a knit and a purl stitch: after the knit stitch take the yarn under, over, then under the right-hand needle. Purl the next stitch as usual.

Between a purl and a knit stitch: after the purl stitch the yarn is at the front of the work. Take yarn over the right-hand needle. Knit the next stitch as usual.

Decreasing
Knit two together (K2 tog)

1 Insert the right-hand needle knitwise into the second, then the first stitch on the left-hand needle. Take the yarn under and over the point of the right hand needle.

2 Draw the yarn through the first and second stitches on the left-hand needle, discarding both stitches at the same time, making one stitch.

Purl two stitches together (P2 tog)

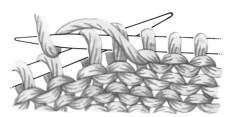

1 Insert the right-hand needle purlwise into the first, then the second stitch on the left-hand needle. Take the yarn over and under the point of the right-hand needle.

2 Draw the yarn through the first and second stitches on left-hand needle, making one stitch out of two.

Slip one, knit one, pass slipped stitch over
(sl 1, K1, psso)

1 Insert the right-hand needle into the next stitch on the left-hand needle as if to knit it. Slip the stitch onto the right-hand needle.

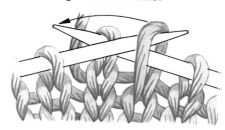

2 Knit the next stitch on the left-hand needle as usual. With the point of the left-hand needle, lift up the slipped stitch and pass it over the stitch just knitted and off the needle.

Double decreasing

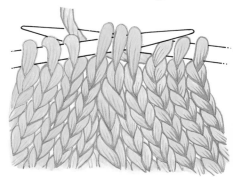

1 Double decreases are made by losing one stitch on each side of a center stitch. Work to within one stitch of the center stitch. Knit the next three stitches together through the back of the loops. Repeat this on all right-side (knit) rows. All the wrong-side rows are purled. The decrease overlaps to the left.

2 To overlap the stitches to the right, work as for step one, but knit the three stitches through the front of the loops.

Mitered double decrease

1 Work to within one stitch of the center stitch. Slip the next stitch onto the right-hand needle without knitting it. Knit the next two stitches together.

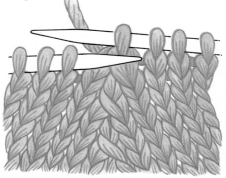

2 Pass the slipped stitch over the first stitch on the right-hand needle, completing the decrease. Repeat this procedure on all subsequent right-side (knit) rows. All the wrong-side rows are purled.

21

Working into the Back of the Loop

Stitches are usually knitted or purled through the front of the loops. For some stitch patterns, however, they must be worked through the back of the loops thus twisting or crossing them. This technique is characteristic of early Arabic knitting and is similar to the cross-knit looping of early Peruvian textiles. Sometimes the entire fabric is composed of twisted knit and purl stitches. They can also be used singly to emphasize the lines of a textured pattern, as twisted stitches are more prominent than ordinary stitches.

Twisting purlwise

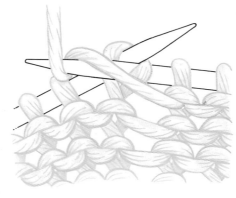

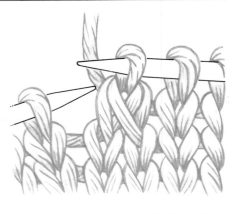

1 Insert the right-hand needle through the back of the next stitch on the left-hand needle. Take the yarn over and under the point of the right-hand needle.

2 Draw a loop through both stitches and drop them off the left-hand needle at the same time to complete the decrease.

Twisted decreasing (purlwise)

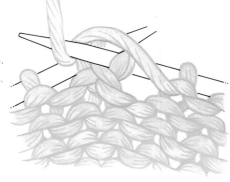

1 Insert the right-hand needle through the backs of the next two stitches on the left-hand needle as shown. Take the yarn over and under the point of the right-hand needle.

Twisting knitwise

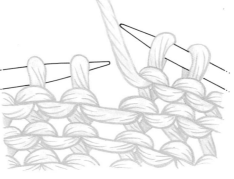

1 Insert the right-hand needle through the back of the next stitch on the left-hand needle as shown. Take the yarn under and over the point of the right-hand needle.

2 Draw a loop through the stitch and drop the stitch off the left-hand needle to complete it.

Twisted decreasing (knitwise)

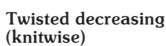

2 Draw a loop through the stitch and drop the stitch off the left-hand needle to complete it.

1 Insert the right-hand needle through the backs of the next two stitches on the left-hand needle. Take the yarn under and over the point of the right-hand needle.

2 Draw a loop through both stitches and drop them off the left-hand needle, so completing the decrease.

Slipping Stitches

Stitches are "slipped", that is, passed from one needle to another without being worked – for a variety of reasons. They can be slipped knitwise or purlwise and with the yarn at the front or back. Stitches may be slipped singly, or several stitches may be slipped at a time.

Slipping purlwise

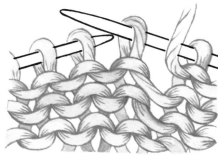

1 Stitches are slipped purlwise when they form part of a decrease on a purl row or of any fancy pattern that requires the same stitch to be worked on the next or subsequent rows – for example, mosaic stitches and slipstitch textured patterns. Insert the right-hand needle into the next stitch on the left-hand needle as if to purl it, but pass it to the right-hand needle without purling it.

2 To slip more than one stitch purlwise, simply insert the right-hand needle into the required number of stitches as if to purl them and transfer them onto the right-hand needle without purling them.

Yarn front, or forward

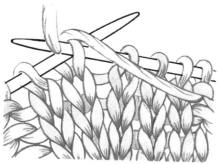

1 The front of the work refers to the side facing the knitter, regardless

of whether it is the right or wrong side of the fabric. When slipping after purl stitches the yarn is already forward. Slip the required number of stitches and knit or purl the next stitch as instructed.

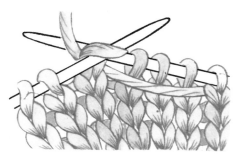

2 After knit stitches bring the yarn to the front between the needles. Slip the required number of stitches and purl or knit the next stitch as instructed in the pattern.

Yarn back

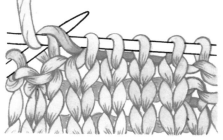

1 The back of the work refers to the side facing away from the knitter, regardless of whether it is the right or wrong side of the fabric. When slipping after knit stitches the yarn is already at the back. Slip the required number of stitches and knit or purl the next stitch as instructed.

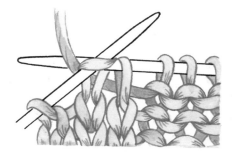

2 After purl stitches take the yarn back between the needles, slip the required number of stitches and knit or purl the next stitch.

Slipping knitwise

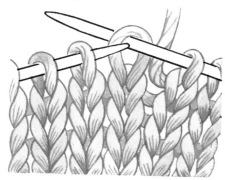

1 Stitches are always slipped knitwise when they form part of a slipstitch decrease on a knit row. Insert the right-hand needle into the front of the next stitch on the left-hand needle as if to knit it, but transfer the stitch onto the right-hand needle without knitting it. Work the next stitch as usual.

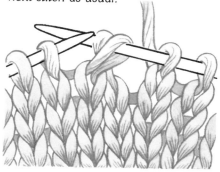

2 On some double decreases two stitches must be slipped at once. In such cases insert the right-hand needle into the fronts of the next two stitches on the left-hand needle as if to knit them together and transfer them to the left-hand needle without knitting them.

Working with Color

Knitting with several different colored yarns is not easy but the results are so spectacular that it's worthwhile making the effort to learn the technique.

Using a bobbin

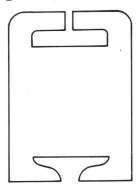

1 When working single motifs in plain knitting, wind the different colors on a plastic bobbin. (You can, instead, make bobbins from stiff cardboard, using this shape.)

2 Wind the yarn around the bobbin until it is full, passing the working end through the thinner notch.

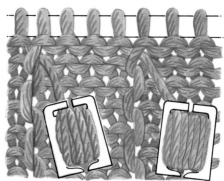

3 When in use the bobbins hang down on the wrong side of the work, keeping the colors separate and preventing the different yarns from tangling.

Weaving yarns

1 Hold the yarn in use in your right hand and the yarn not in use in your left hand. Knit the first stitch as usual. On the next and every other stitch insert the right-hand needle knitwise. Take the yarn in the left hand over the right-hand needle, then knit with the yarn in the right hand as usual.

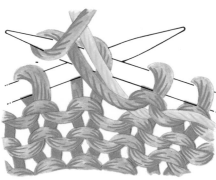

2 On purl rows, work in exactly the same way. Bring the yarn not in use over the top of the right-hand needle on every other stitch, but do the weaving at the front of the work and purl the stitches. This method is used where the yarn is carried over more than five stitches.

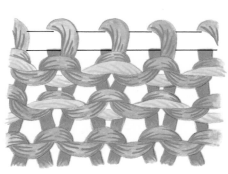

3 Weaving yarns prevents untidy long strands on the wrong side of the work.

Stranding yarns

1 On right-side rows, knit the appropriate number of stitches with the first color. Drop the yarn. Pick up the second color and knit the appropriate number of stitches with that. Pick up the first color again and carry it loosely across the back of the work before knitting the next stitches.

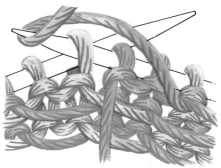

2 On wrong-side rows, work in exactly the same way as for right-side rows but purl the stitches and carry the yarn loosely across the front of the work. This method is used where the yarn is carried over no more than three or four stitches.

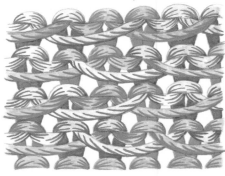

3 The wrong side of the work will be neat, provided the yarns are carried evenly and at the same tension as the knitting. If the yarns are carried too tightly the right side of the work will pucker.

Using a Cable Needle

The use of a cable needle is the basis of many knitting techniques including cable stitch patterns, Aran, and traveling stiches. Cable needles are short double-pointed needles. They are used to move stitches from one position to another in the same row and so change the order in which they are worked. On knit rows, cabling to the front twists the stitches to the left on the right side of the work; cabling to the back twists them to the right on the right side. On purl rows cabling front twists the stitches to the right and cabling back to the left.

3 *Holding the cable needle in your left hand, knit off the 2 stitches on the cable needle.*

Cable 4 back

1 *Slip the next 2 stitches onto the cable needle and leave it at the back of the work.*

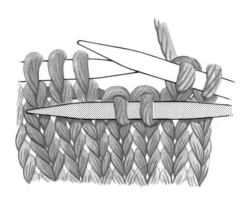

2 *Knit the next 2 stitches on the left-hand needle in the usual way.*

Cable 4 front

1 *Slip the next 2 stitches onto the cable needle and leave it at the front of the work.*

2 *Knit the next 2 stitches on the left-hand needle in the usual way.*

3 *Holding the cable needle in your left hand, knit off the 2 stitches on the cable needle.*

Cable 4 front purlwise

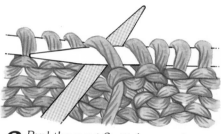

1 *Slip the next 2 stitches onto the cable needle and leave it at the front of the work.*

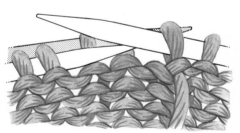

2 *Purl the next 2 stitches on the left-hand needle in the usual way, then purl the 2 stitches on the cable needle.*

Cable 4 back purlwise

1 *Slip the next 2 stitches onto the cable needle and leave it at the back of the work.*

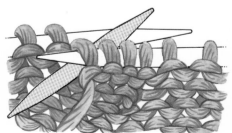

2 *Purl the next 2 stitches on the left-hand needle in the usual way, then purl the 2 stitches on the cable needle.*

25

Making Eyelets

Eyelets are small holes arranged decoratively on a knitted background. They are formed in many different ways, but the basic principle is the same: each eyelet is composed of a decorative increase and a compensating decrease.

Chain eyelet

1 This is the most popular single eyelet method. Work to the position of the eyelet. Bring the yarn forward between the needles and take it over the needle to knit the next 2 stitches together.

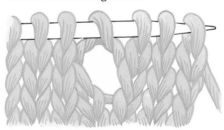

2 Purl the next row including the yarn taken over the needle.

Open eyelet

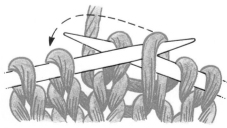

1 This is rounder and more clearly defined than the chain eyelet. Work to the eyelet position. Bring the yarn forward between the needles. Slip the next stitch knitwise. Take the yarn over the needle to knit the following stitch. Pass the slipped stitch over the knit stitch.

26

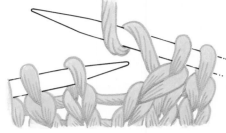

2 Purl the next row including the yarn taken over the needle.

Double eyelet

1 This makes a large round eyelet. Work to the eyelet position. Knit the next two stitches together. Bring the yarn forward.

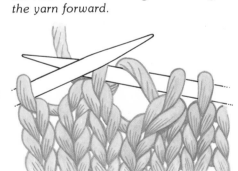

2 Slip the next stitch knitwise. Take the yarn over the needle to knit the following stitch. Pass the slipped stitch over the knit stitch.

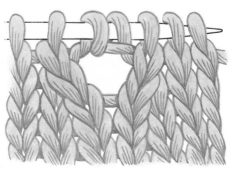

3 On the next row, purl every stitch but purl and knit into the yarn taken over the needle.

Picot eyelet

1 Work to the eyelet position. Knit the next 2 stitches together. Take the yarn twice over the needle.

2 Slip the next stitch knitwise. Knit the following stitch. Pass the slipped stitch over the knit stitch.

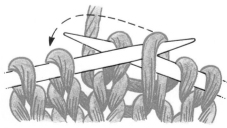

3 On the next row, purl every stitch but purl the first loop taken over the needle and knit the second.

Picot hem

Eyelets are used to make picot hems. Work a row of chain eyelets along the fold line of the hem as close together as possible. When the garment is completed, fold the hem along the picot row and slipstitch the edge in place.

Making Bobbles

Bobbles are made in various ways depending on whether they are large or small, and knit or purl, but the basic principle remains the same: several increases are made into one stitch; these stitches are worked on in various ways to form a small piece of knitting attached to the main work by one stitch, then decreased until only one stitch is left. The bobble "sits" on top of the background fabric.

4 *Turn the work. Slip one stitch, knit two stitches together. Pass the slipped stitch over the decrease to complete the bobble.*

Small knit bobble

1 *To make a knit bobble, knit into the next stitch without slipping it off the needle, bring the yarn over the needle, knit again into the same stitch and slip it off the needle.*

Large knit bobble

1 *Work to the bobble position. Knit into the next stitch without slipping it off the needle, bring the yarn over the needle, knit again into the same stitch, yarn over, knit again into the same stitch and slip it off the left-hand needle.*

Large purl bobble

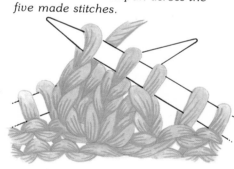

1 *Work as for step one of the large knit bobble. Turn the work and knit across the five made stitches. Turn the work and purl across the five made stitches.*

2 *Turn the work. Purl the three "made" stitches. Turn the work and knit the three made stitches. Turn the work, purl two stitches together, purl one stitch. Turn the work, slip one stitch, knit one stitch, pass the slipped stitch over the knit stitch to complete the bobble.*

Small purl bobble

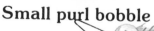

2 *Turn the work. Purl across the five "made" stitches. Turn the work and knit across the five stitches.*

2 *Turn the work and knit two stitches together, knit one stitch, knit two stitches together across the five stitches.*

1 *Work to the bobble position. Knit into the next stitch without slipping it off the needle, bring the yarn over the needle, knit again into the same stitch and slip it off the needle. Turn the work. Knit the three "made" stitches.*

3 *Turn the work and purl two stitches together, purl one stitch, purl two stitches together across the five stitches.*

3 *Turn the work. Slip one stitch, purl two stitches together. Pass the slipped stitch over the decrease to complete the bobble.*

2 *Turn the work. Purl the three made stitches. Turn the work, knit two stitches together, knit one stitch. Turn the work, slip one stitch, purl one, pass the slipped stitch over the purl stitch and off the needle.*

Duplicate Stitch

Duplicate stitch (also called Swiss darning) is one of the most popular and versatile ways of decorating knitted garments. As the name "Swiss darning" suggests, it was originally a means of reinforcing worn areas of a garment and was worked in the same yarn and color as the original knitting. Now it is usually worked in contrasting colors to add motifs to plain stockinette stitch fabrics. The object is to cover the stitches entirely with the new yarn, which must be the same weight as that used for the background.

Horizontal lines

1 Thread a tapestry needle with the chosen yarn and begin at the lower right-hand corner of the motif to be worked. Bring the yarn through from back to front of the base of the first stitch to be covered. Insert the needle from right to left behind the base of the stitch above.

2 Pull the yarn through. Insert the needle through the base of the stitch from front to back, then through the base of the stitch to the left.

3 Pull the yarn through, thus covering the first stitch. Continue

28

in this way across the row, covering each stitch in turn and working from right to left.

4 Work the next row of stitches above the first, working from left to right, as shown.

Vertical lines

1 Beginning at the bottom of the line, bring the yarn through from back to front at the base of the first stitch. Insert the needle from right to left behind the base of the next stitch above. Pull the yarn through, then insert the needle vertically behind the head of the stitch below as shown.

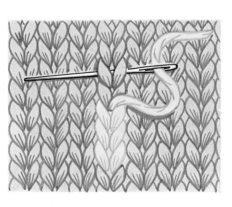

2 Pull the yarn through, thus covering the first stitch. Continue in this way, working from the bottom of the line to the top.

Working from charts

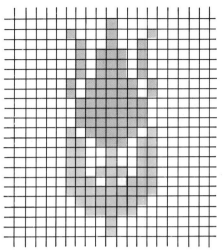

1 Duplicate stitch is usually worked from charts similar to those used for Fair Isle and jacquard patterns. Each square on the chart represents one stitch on the knitted fabric. Since knitted stitches are rectangular rather than square, the motif on the knitted fabric will appear somewhat more flattened than it does on the chart.

2 Use each color separately, working as far as possible from right to left, then from left to right, to keep the back of the work neat and smooth. Keep an even tension on the yarn, taking particular care not to pull it too tightly. Finish off the ends at the back of the work by threading them through two or three stitches before cutting off the surplus.

Beading

Beads can be sewn onto a completed garment, but it is neater and, in the long run, easier and quicker to knit them in as you go along. In order to prevent the beads from slipping to the back of the work they must be placed securely in position. There are various methods – the choice depending on the size and shape of bead and on whether they are used as accents or to provide a densely beaded fabric (called purse beading). Except in purse beading, beads are placed on the right-side (knit) rows only.

Threading beads

1 Fold a 12in length of sewing thread in half. Thread both ends together through the eye of a sharp-pointed sewing needle.

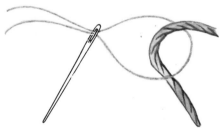

2 Thread the end of the knitting yarn through the loop in the thread.

3 Insert the point of the needle into the bead and pass it down over the needle and thread and onto the yarn. Thread the beads in reverse order to the way they are worked before beginning to knit.

Placing small beads

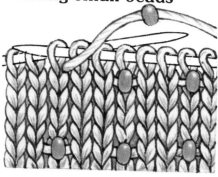

1 This method places the bead in front of the stitch on the right side of the work. Knit to the bead position. Pass the yarn forward to the right side of the work. Slip the next stitch.

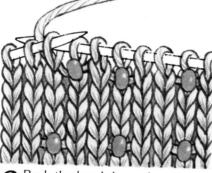

2 Push the bead down the yarn as close as possible to the last stitch knitted. Take the yarn back. Knit the next stitch on the left-hand needle. This method is also suitable for placing horizontal beads. More than one stitch can be slipped if necessary.

Placing large beads

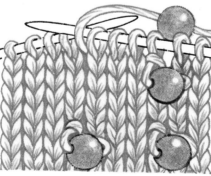

1 This method places the beads between the stitches on the right side of the work. Knit as usual to the bead position. Pass the yarn forward to the right side of the work.

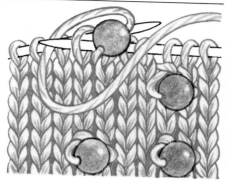

2 Slip the bead as close as possible to the last stitch knitted. Purl the next stitch, then knit as usual.

Purse beading

1 In purse beading the beads sit on top of the knitted stitches, completely covering them. On knit rows, knit the first stitch through the back of the loop. Knit the next stitch through the back of the loop, pushing the bead through the stitch to the front of the work as the yarn is pulled through. Beads are placed on every stitch except the first and last.

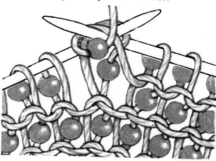

2 On purl rows, purl the first stitch through the back of the loop. Purl the next stitch through the back of the loop, pushing the bead through the stitch to the back of the work as the yarn is pulled through. Beads are placed on every stitch in the row except the first and the last one. All the knit rows and all the purl rows are beaded.

Left-handed Skills

Many left-handed people learn to knit in a "right-handed" way. This has advantages, since the instructions in most publications (including this one) are written for right-handed people. However, there are ways of handling the needles and making the stitches that are much more natural for a left-handed person. One alternative is to hold the yarn with the left hand – the so-called Continental method. This distributes the work more evenly between the two hands. Knitting instructions can be followed exactly as they are written.

Another method is to reverse the right-hand method throughout. If you decide to learn this method, you may find it helpful to hold a mirror up to the illustrations on pages 14–16. The movements are exactly the same as for the right-hand method, but reversed, so that the work proceeds from left to right.

Casting on and binding off

1 Make a slip loop as usual and place it on one of the needles. Hold this needle in your right hand.

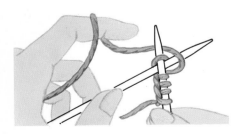

2 Hold the other needle in your left hand and insert it into the slip loop. Take the yarn under and over the left-hand needle. Draw a loop through and place it on the right-

30

hand needle. Now insert the left-hand needle between the two loops and take the yarn under and over it.

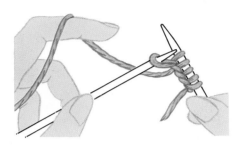

3 Draw a loop through between the stitches and place it on the right-hand needle. Continue in this way until the required number of stitches have been cast on.

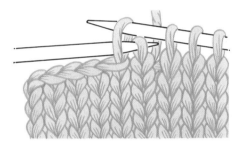

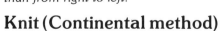
4 Binding off is worked as in the right-handed method (pages 16–17) except that if you are using the reversed method, the stitches are bound off from left to right rather than from right to left.

Knit (Continental method)

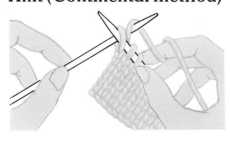

1 Wind the yarn over the fingers of the left hand as shown. This hand also holds the needle with the previously-worked stitches. Insert the working (right-hand) needle through the first stitch on the left-hand needle, at the same time pivoting the left hand to bring the yarn around the needle.

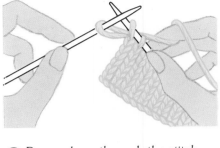

2 Draw a loop through the stitch. Drop the original stitch off the left-hand needle, thus completing a new stitch. Continue in this way across the row. The work thus progresses from right to left, exactly as if the yarn were held by the right hand.

Purl (Continental method)

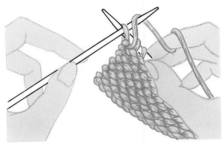

1 Hold the needle with the stitches in your left hand, looping the yarn around the left forefinger. Insert the right-hand needle through the first stitch on the left-hand needle and hook it under the yarn.

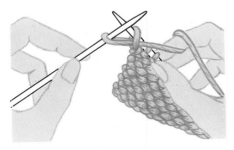

2 Draw a loop through the stitch. Drop the original stitch off the left-hand needle, thus completing a new stitch. Continue in this way across the row, working from right to left.

Cabling

If you are using the reverse method, you work from left to right. This has the effect of reversing the twist on cable patterns.

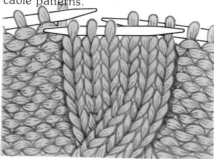

1 *For right-to-left knitters, cabling forward (holding the cable needle with the stitches at the front of the work) produces a twist to the left. For reverse knitters, it produces a twist to the right.*

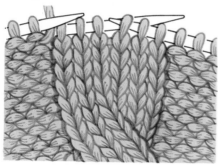

2 *Cabling back (holding the needle at the back of the work) produces a twist to the left for reverse knitters. When following a pattern these knitters should cable back when the pattern says cable forward, and forward when it says cable back.*

Decreasing

1 *The direction of decreases is reversed for reverse knitters. For example, knitting two stitches*

together through the front of the loops produces a decrease that slants to the left rather than the right.

2 *The slipstitch decrease (slip one, knit one, pass slipped stitch over) produces a decrease that slants to the right rather than the left. When reading a pattern in which decreases are paired (for instance in raglan shaping), read "K2 tog" for "sl 1, K1, psso" and vice versa.*

Decorative increasing

1 *Eyelets and lace stitches are worked similarly for reverse knitters as for right-to-left knitters." "Yarn overs" create new stitches between existing stitches. Between a knit and a purl stitch hook the needle around the yarn as shown before purling.*

2 *Between two purl stitches hook the left-hand needle around yarn as shown.*

3 *Between two knit stitches bring the yarn forward between the needles before inserting the left-hand needle to knit the next stitch.*

4 *Between purl and knit stitches simply take the yarn over the needle from its position at the front of the work to knit the next stitch.*

Following patterns using the reverse method

Most patterns are written for people who knit from right to left. However, these can be used by reverse-method knitters provided they follow a few basic guidelines. All references to left-hand and right-hand needle should be reversed. When reading charts you should read knit rows from left to right and purl rows from right to left. Be especially careful when reading shaping instructions. In right-handed knitting the shaping of right-hand edges is carried out at the beginnings of right-side rows and/or the ends of wrong-side rows, while the shaping of left-hand edges is carried out at the ends of right-side rows and/or the beginnings of wrong-side rows. The situation is reversed for reverse-method knitters.

Circular Knitting

Circular knitting is carried out using a set of four or more double-pointed needles or a circular needle. It produces a tubular, seamless fabric, ideal for items such as socks and gloves. Many traditional types of sweater such as Aran, Fair Isle and especially Guernsey were also worked in the round. Since circular knitting is worked with the right side facing on every round, the construction of stitch patterns is different from that which obtains in flat knitting. Stockinette stitch, for example, is worked by knitting every round, and garter stitch by alternately knitting and purling rounds. Circular needles can also be used for flat knitting when the number of stitches is too great for ordinary needles.

Casting onto four needles

1 Using any of the usual methods, cast the required number of stitches onto one of the needles.

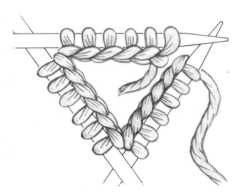

2 Distribute these stitches among three of the set of four needles. Form the needles into a triangle, making sure that the stitches are not twisted as you do so.

32

3 Place a marker loop to mark the beginning of rounds. Join the stitches into a round by using the fourth needle and the working yarn from last stitch on third needle to knit first stitch on first needle.

4 Continue knitting off the stitches on the first needle, then use the first needle to knit off the stitches on the second needle, and so on until the round is completed. Slip the marker loop at the beginning of each round. Alternatively use the end of yarn left after casting on as a marker.

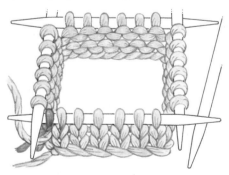

5 When using a set of five needles, cast on the stitches onto four needles and use the fifth needle to work off the stitches. The same principle holds for working with larger sets of needles — cast onto one less than the total number of needles and use the extra needle as the actual working needle.

Using a circular needle

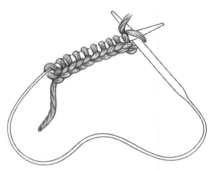

1 Circular needles come in lengths varying from 16 to 36in. They can only be used where the number of cast-on stitches is sufficient to reach from one point to the other. Use one point to cast stitches onto the other point in the usual way.

2 When the stitches have been cast on, join them into a round by transferring the left-hand point to the right hand and vice versa, then knit the first cast-on stitch using the working yarn from the right-hand point.

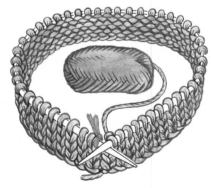

3 Continue using the right-hand point to knit off the stitches until the round is completed. Mark the beginning of rounds using a marker loop or the cast-on end of yarn.

Textured Patterns

Knitting is one of the few textile crafts in which it is possible to produce an extraordinarily wide range of textured fabrics. With even the simplest, most basic stitches, knit and purl, you can make different textures, including the smoothness of stockinette stitch, vertical ribbed stitches, basketweave (page 56) and horizontal ridges (page 37). Then there is a whole range of embossed stitches like that used in the loganberry sweater on page 34 and in the leaf-stitch sweater on page 46, where the embossing is used to create a raised leaf motif on plain background.

With twisted stitches (page 40) and cabling techniques the possibilities for spectacularly textured effects become almost limitless, with fabrics taking on a beautiful, three-dimensional effect. The dress on page 49 and the tweedy coat on page 58 are exceptionally fine examples.

Loganberry Sweater

This tight-fitting thirties-style sweater is knitted in a pretty
openwork embossed stitch. The shaped side seams and
V-shaped ribbing on the yoke add to the period flavor.

Sizes

To fit 32–34[36–38]in bust
Length 22½[23½]in
Sleeve seam 19¼in

Note Instructions for the larger size are in brackets []: where there is one set of figures it applies to both sizes.

Gauge

30 sts and 29 rows to 4in over patt on size 5 needles.

Materials

450[600]g double knitting yarn (see page 9) or 19[25]oz knitting worsted 1 pair each sizes 3 and 5 knitting needles

Back

**Using smaller needles, cast on 100[112] sts. Work in K1. P1 rib for 3in, ending with a RS row.
Next row Rib 9[7], *work twice into next st, rib 9[11], rep from * ending last rep rib 10[8]. 109[121] sts.
Change to larger needles and commence loganberry patt.
1st row (RS) P3, *K1, P5, rep from * to last 4 sts, K1, P3.

2nd row K3 tog, *yo, (K1, yo, K1) all into next st, yo, K2 tog tbl, K3 tog, sl the 2nd st on RH needle over the last st, rep from * to last 4 sts, yo, (K1, yo, K1) all into next st, yo, K3 tog tbl.
3rd row K1, *P5, K1, rep from * to end.
4th row P1, *K5, P1, rep from * to end.
5th row As 3rd row.
6th row Work twice into first st, *yo, K2 tog tbl, K3 tog, sl the 2nd st on RH needle over the last st, yo, (K1, yo, K1) all into next st, rep from * to last 6 sts, yo, K2 tog tbl, K3 tog, sl the 2nd st on RH needle over the last st, yo, inc into last st.
7th row As first row.
8th row K3, *P1, K5, rep from * to last 4 sts, P1, K3.
These 8 rows form the patt. Rep these 8 rows 2[3] more times.
Cont in patt, inc 1 st at each end of the 4th and 8th patt rows until there are 133[145] sts, ending with an 8th patt row. Work even.
Work the first–8th patt rows twice more, then work first–6th rows once.

Begin yoke

Next row P3, (K1, P5) 10[11] times, (K1, P1) 3 times, (K1, P5) 10[11] times, K1, P3.
Next row K3, (P1, K5) 10[11] times, (P1, K1) 3 times, (P1, K5) 10[11] times, P1, K3.
These 2 rows establish the yoke. Keeping loganberry patt correct, cont as foll:
Next row Patt 63[69], (K1, P1) 3 times, K1, patt 63[69].
Next row Patt 63[69], (P1, K1) 3 times, P1, patt 63[69].
Next row Patt 60[66], (K1, P1) 6 times, K1, patt 60[66].
Next row Patt 60[66], (P1, K1) 6 times, P1, patt 60[66].
Rep the last 2 rows once.
Next row Patt 57[63], (K1, P1) 9 times, K1, patt 57[63].
Next row Patt 57[63], (P1, K1) 9 times, P1, patt 57[63].
Rep the last 2 rows once.
Next row Patt 54[60], (K1, P1) 12 times, K1, patt 54[60].
Next row Patt 54[60], (P1, K1) 12 times, P1, patt 54[60].
Rep the last 2 rows once. **
Cont in this way, working 3 sts less in

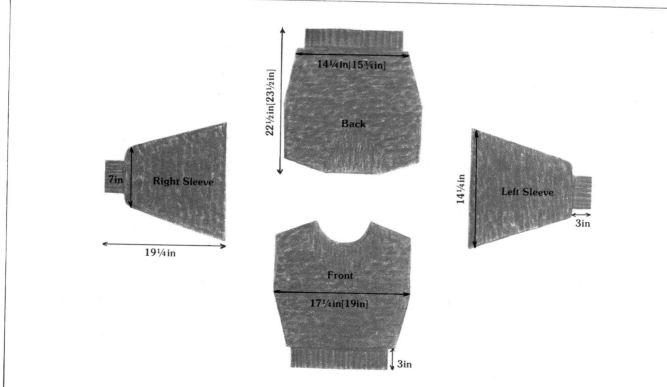

35

patt at each side of ribbing on the next and every foll 4th row until the row Patt 30[36], (K1, P1) 36 times, K1, patt 30[36] has been worked. Work 3 rows.

Shape shoulders

Still inc ribbing sts as before, bind off 9 sts at beg of next 2 rows, 6 sts at beg of foll 2 rows, 9 sts at beg of next 2 rows and 9[10] sts at beg of foll 2 rows.

Now bind off 8[9] sts at beg of next 2 rows and 8[10] sts at beg of foll 2 rows.

Leave the rem 35[39] sts on a spare needle.

Front

Work as for back from ** to **.

Cont in this way, working 3 sts less in patt at each side of rib on the next and every foll 4th row until the row Patt 36[42], (K1, P1) 30 times, K1, patt 36[42] has been worked.

Divide for neck

Next row Patt 36[42], (P1, K1) 12 times, P1, bind off 11, (P1, K1) 12 times, P1, patt 36[42].

Still inc ribbing sts as before,

complete left side of neck first.

*** Next row Work to lasts 2 sts, work 2 tog.

Next row Bind off 2[3] sts, work to end.

Rep last 2 rows once.

Dec 1 st at neck edge on next 5 rows, ending at armhole edge.

Shape shoulder

Bind off 9 sts at beg of next row and 6 sts at beg of every other row once.

Bind off 9 sts at beg of next row and 9[10] sts at beg of foll row.

Bind off 8[9] sts at beg of next row.

Work 1 row.

Bind off rem 8[10] sts.

With RS of work facing, rejoin yarn to sts for right side of neck.

Work 1 row.

Then work as for first side from *** to end.

Sleeves

Using smaller needles cast on 42 sts.

Work in K1, P1 rib for 3in, ending with a RS row.

Next row Rib 3, *work twice into next st, rib 2, rep from *to end. 55 sts.

Change to larger needles and cont in

loganberry patt as for back, inc 1 st at each end of every 4th and 8th patt row until there are 109 sts. Work even in patt until the patt has been worked 15 times. Bind off.

To finish

Join left shoulder.

Neck border

With RS of work facing, using smaller needles, work in K1, P1 rib across sts on back neck, pick up and K 49 sts from front neck. 84[88] sts.

Work in K1, P1 rib for 2½in.

Bind off loosely in rib.

Join right shoulder and neck border.

Set in sleeves. Join side and underarm seams. Press if appropriate for yarn used.

Special technique – binding off in mid-row

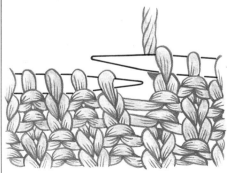

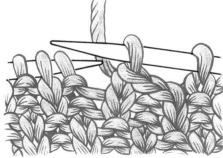

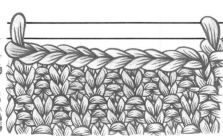

1 The neck shaping on the basic sweater involves binding off stitches in the middle of a row. Work the pattern as instructed to the bind-off position.

2 Then bind off the next stitch as follows. Knit the next two stitches. Lift the 2nd stitch on the right-hand needle over the first stitch and off the needle. Knit the next stitch. Lift the 2nd stitch on the right-hand needle over the first stitch and off the needle.

3 Continue in this way until the required number of stitches (in this case 11) have been bound off. Then work in pattern to the end of the row. The stitch used in binding off is counted as the first pattern stitch on the left-hand side on the neck.

T-shape Dress and Pullover

This simple sporty dress and
pullover are both so easy to knit.
Made from basic rectangular shapes in stockinette stitch
with garter stitch ridges and borders,
they are ideal garments for beginners.

Sizes
To fit 32[34:36:38]in bust
Sweater length 28[28:30:30]in
Dress length 36[36:38:38]in
Sleeve seam 14in
Note Instructions for larger sizes are in brackets []; where there is only one set of figures it applies to all sizes.

Gauge
22 sts and 30 rows to 4in over st st on size 5 needles.

Materials
Pullover
600[600:700:700]g double knitting yarn (see page 9) or 25 [25:29:29]oz knitting worsted
Dress
700[800:900:900]g double knitting yarn (see page 9) or 29 [33:37:37]oz knitting worsted
1 pair each sizes 3 and 5 knitting needles

Pullover
Back
Using smaller needles, cast on 108 [114:120:126] sts.

Next row (WS) K.
Next row K.
Cont in garter st (every row K). Work 45[45:39:39] rows.
Change to larger needles.
*Beg with a K row work 15 rows in st st.
Next row (WS) K.
Next row K.
Next row K.*
Rep from * to * 7[7:8:8] more times.
Work 15 rows st st, ending with a K row.
Change to smaller needles.
Work 35 rows garter st.
Bind off.

Front
Work as for back.

Sleeves
Using smaller needles, cast on 82 [88:94:100] sts.
Work 23 rows in garter st.
Change to larger needles.
Work as for back from * to * 3 times.
Work 15 rows st st, ending with a K row.
Change to smaller needles.

Work 35 rows garter st.
Bind off.

To finish
Press lightly if appropriate for yarn used, omitting garter st borders.
Using a backstitch seam, join

Special technique – setting sleeves in flat

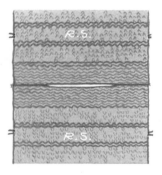

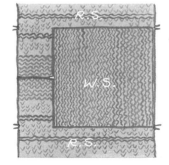

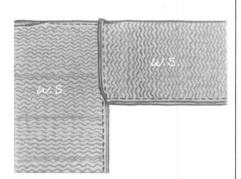

1 Join the shoulder seam. Place a marker on the front and back of the garment at the distance from the shoulder seam given in the pattern.

2 With right sides together, place the center of the bound-off edge of the sleeve at the shoulder seam.

3 Join the seam between the markers. Join the side and sleeve seams.

shoulder seams leaving the center 10in free for neck opening. Mark down 7½[8:8¾:9]in from shoulder on back and front. Placing the center of bound-off edge of sleeve at shoulder seam, set in sleeves between markers. Join sleeve and side seams leaving garter st border at hem free to form slits.

Dress
Back
Using smaller needles, cast on 108 [114:120:126] sts.
Next row (WS) K.
Next row K.
Cont in garter st (every row K). Work 51[51:49:49] rows.
Change to larger needles.
Work as for back of pullover from * to * 11[11:12:12] times. Work 15 rows in st st, ending with a K row.
Change to smaller needles.
Work 35 rows in garter st.
Bind off.

Front
Work as for back.

Sleeves
Work as for pullover.

To finish
Complete as for pullover, but join garter stitch border to hem omitting slits.

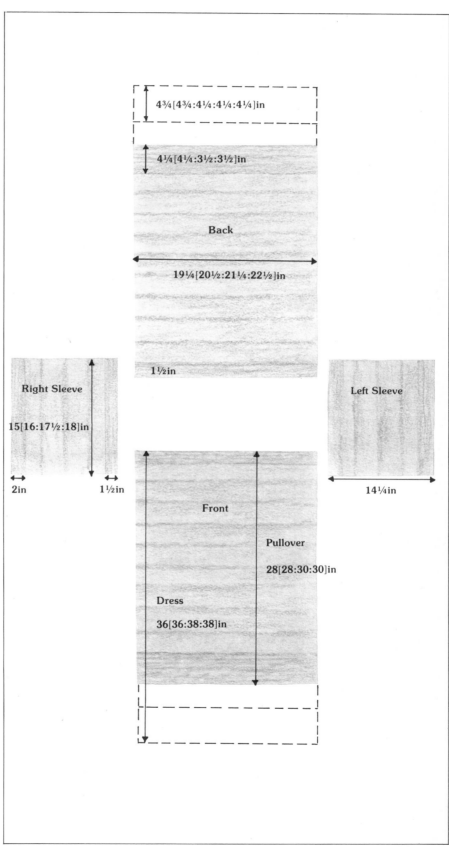

4¾[4¾:4¼:4¼:4¼]in

4¼[4¼:3½:3½]in

Back

19¼[20½:21¼:22½]in

1½in

Right Sleeve

15[16:17½:18]in

2in   1½in

Left Sleeve

14¼in

Front

Pullover

28[28:30:30]in

Dress

36[36:38:38]in

Country Casuals

A crunchy textured twisted fern stitch is worked all over
this loose easy-to-wear jerkin and echoed in panels on a
matching turtleneck pullover and legwarmers.

Sizes
To fit 38[40:42]in chest
Pullover length 26½[27:28]in
Pullover sleeve seam 22½[23¼:24]in
Jerkin length 31[32:32¾]in
Legwarmers length 24in
Note Instructions for the larger sizes are in brackets []; where there is only one set of figures it applies to all three sizes.

Gauge
20 sts and 24 rows to 4in over reverse st st on size 6 needles
24 sts and 28 rows to 4in over twisted-stitch patt on size 6 needles

Materials
Pullover
38[40:42]oz knitting worsted
Jerkin
40[42:44]oz knitting worsted
Legwarmers
15 oz knitting worsted
1 pair each sizes 4 and 5 knitting needles

Pullover
Back
** Using smaller needles, cast on 100[106:112] sts. Work in twisted rib as foll:
1st row *K1 tbl, P1, rep from * to end.
This row forms twisted rib. Cont in rib for 3in.**
Change to larger needles.
Next row (WS) K.
Next row P.
These 2 rows form reverse st st. Rep these 2 rows until work measures 16¼[16¼:17]in, ending with a K row.

Shape armholes
Bind off 3 sts at beg of next 2 rows. 94[100:106] sts.
Work even until work measures 9[9½:10]in from beg of armhole shaping, ending with a K row.
Change to twisted rib.
Work a further 1¼in.
Shape shoulders
Bind off 28[30:32] sts in rib at beg of next 2 rows. Bind off in rib rem 38[40:42] sts.

Front
Work as for back from ** to **, inc

6 sts evenly across last row. 106[112:118] sts.
Change to larger needles and beg working in reverse st st with twisted stitch panels as foll:
1st, 3rd, 5th, 7th and 9th rows (WS) K9[11:13], *P1, (K2, P5, K2, P1) twice*, K46[48:50], rep from * to * again, K to end.
2nd, 4th, 6th, 8th and 10th rows P9[11:13], *K1 tbl, (P2, K2 tog but do not sl sts off LH needle, K first st again, then sl both sts from needle, – called RT –, K1, K tbl 2nd st on LH needle but do not sl sts off needle, K2 tog tbl first and 2nd sts and sl both sts from needle – called LT –, P2, K1 tbl) twice*, P46[48:50], rep from * to * again, P to end.
11th, 13th, 15th, 17th and 19th rows K9[11:13], *P3, (K2, P1, K2, P5) twice ending last rep P3*, K46[48:50], rep from * to * again, K to end.
12th, 14th, 16th, 18th and 20th rows P9[11:13], *K1, (LT, P2, K1, tbl, P2, RT, K1) twice,* P46[48:50], rep from * to * again, P to end.
These 20 rows form the patt. Cont in patt until work measures 16¼[16¼:17]in, ending with a WS row.
Shape armholes
Bind off 3 sts at beg of next 2 rows. 100[106:112] sts.
Work even until work measures 6¼[6¾:7]in from beg of armholes, ending with a WS row.
Shape neck
Next row Patt 39[41:43] sts and turn, leave rem sts on a spare needle. Dec 1 st at neck edge of next and every other row until 31[33:35] sts rem. Work even until work measures 9[9½:10]in from beg of armholes, ending with a WS row.
Change to twisted rib.
Next row K1 tbl, *P1, K1 tbl, rep from * to end.
Next row P1, *K1 tbl, P1, rep from * to end.
Rep last 2 rows for 1¼in, ending at armhole edge.
Shape shoulder
Bind off rem sts in rib. With RS of work facing, return to sts on spare needle, bind of center 22[24:26] sts, patt to end.
Complete to match first side of neck, reversing shapings.

Sleeves
Using smaller needles, cast on 50[52:54] sts. Work 3in twisted rib as for back.
Change to larger needles. Beg with a P row cont in reverse st st, inc 1 st at each end of every foll 4th row until there are 104[108:112] sts.
Work even until work measures 22[22¾:23¾]in ending with a K row. Change to twisted rib as for back. Work a further 1¼in.
Bind off in rib.

To finish
Join right shoulder seam.
Turtleneck collar
With RS of work facing, using larger needles, pick up and K 18 sts down left side of neck, pick up and K 22[24:26] sts from center front, pick up and K 18 sts up right side of neck and 38[40:42] sts across back neck. 96[100:104] sts. Work in twisted rib as for back for 8in. Bind off in rib. Join left shoulder and collar, reversing seam to roll onto RS. Set in sleeves flat joining bound-off sts at underarms to final rows on sleeve. Join side and sleeve seams.

Jerkin
Back
Using larger needles, cast on 131[141:151] sts. Work twisted rib as foll:
1st row (RS) K1 tbl, * P1, K1 tbl, rep from * to end.
2nd row P1, * K1 tbl, P1, rep from * to end.
Rep last 2 rows for 2in ending with a RS row. Beg twisted-stitch patt.
1st, 3rd, 5th, 7th and 9th rows (WS) P1, (K2, P5, K2, P1) to end.
2nd, 4th, 6th, 8th and 10th rows K1 tbl, (P2, RT, K1, LT, P2, K1 tbl) to end.
11th, 13th, 15th, 17th and 19th rows P3, (K2, P1, K2, P5) to last 8 sts, K2, P1, K2, P3.
12th, 14th, 16th, 18th and 20th rows K1, (LT, P2, K1 tbl, P2, RT, K1) to end.
These 20 rows form the patt.
Cont in patt until work measures 20[20½:21]in from cast-on edge, ending with a WS row.
Shape armholes
Bind off 5 sts at beg of next 2 rows. 121[131:141] sts.

Work even until work measures 9¾[10¼:10½]in from beg of armholes, ending with a WS row. Change to twisted rib as for back. Work 1¼in, ending with a WS row.

Shape shoulders

Bind off in rib 40[44:48] sts at beg of next 2 rows. Bind off rem sts in rib.

Pocket linings (make 2)

Using larger needles, cast on 26 sts. Work 6in st st, ending with a P row. Leave sts on a holder.

Right front

Using larger needles, cast on 75[79:85] sts. Work 2in twisted rib as for back. Inc 1 st at end of last row on 2nd size only. 75[80:85] sts. Beg twisted patt with rib border as foll:

1st, 3rd, 5th, 7th and 9th rows (WS) P1, (K2, P5, K2, P1) to last 14[19:14] sts, K0[5:0], rib to end.

2nd, 4th, 6th, 8th and 10th rows Rib 14, P0[5:0], K1 tbl, (P2, RT, K1, LT, P2, K1 tbl) to end.

11th, 13th, 15th, 17th and 19th rows P3, (K2, P1, K2, P5) to last 22 [27:22] sts, K2, P1, K2, P3, K0[5:0], rib to end.

12th, 14th, 16th, 18th and 20th rows Rib 14, P0[5:0], K1, (LT, P2, K1 tbl, P2, RT, K1) to end. These 20 rows form twisted-stitch patt. *** Cont in patt, taking 1 more st into rib at inner border edge on the 8th and every foll 10th row, *at the same time*, place pocket when work measures 8in from cast-on edge, ending at side edge, as foll:

Next row Patt 15, bind off 26 sts, patt across sts of pocket lining, patt to end. Cont as set, taking sts into ribbing as before until work measures 20[20½:21]in ending at side edge.

Shape armhole

Bind off 5 sts at beg of next row. 70[75:80] sts.

Work even until there are 30[31:32] sts in rib and 40[44:48] sts in patt. Cont as set until work measures 9¾[10¼:10½]in from beg of armhole shaping, ending with a WS row. Cont in twisted rib only. Work 1¼in, ending at armhole edge. ***

Shape shoulder

Bind off these sts in rib.

Left front

Using larger needles, cast on
42

75[79:85] sts. Work 2in twisted rib as for back. Inc 1 st at beg of last row on 2nd size only. Beg twisted-stitch patt with rib border as foll:

1st, 3rd, 5th, 7th and 9th rows (WS) Rib 14, K0[5:0], P1, (K2, P5, K2, P1) to end.

2nd, 4th, 6th, 8th and 10th rows K1 tbl, (P2, RT, K1, LT, P2, K1 tbl) to last 14[19:14] sts, P0[5:0], rib to end.

11th, 13th, 15th, 17th and 19th rows Rib 14, K0[5:0], P3, (K2, P1, K2, P5) to last 8 sts, K2, P1, K2, P3.

12th, 14th, 16th, 18th and 20th rows, K1, (LT, P2, K1 tbl, P2, RT, K1) to last 14[19:14] sts, P0[5:0], rib to end. These 20 rows form the patt. Complete to match right front working from *** to ***.

Shape shoulder

Bind off in rib 40[44:48] sts, rib to end. Cont in rib on rem sts for a further 7[7½:8]in. Bind off in rib.

To finish

Join shoulder seams and sew collar to back of neck. Join collar edges.

Armbands

With RS of work facing, using larger needles, pick up and K 157[167:173] sts around armhole edge. Work 2in twisted rib as for back. Bind off. Fold rib in half onto WS and catch down.

Pocket edgings

With RS facing, using larger needles, pick up and K 26 sts along pocket edge.

Work 1¼in twisted rib. Bind off in rib. Sew down pocket linings and edges.

Legwarmers

Using smaller needles, cast on 71 sts. Work 4in twisted rib as for jerkin back. Change to larger needles.

1st row K25, work from * to * as for first row of pullover front, K25.

2nd row P25, work from * to * as for 2nd row of pullover front, P25. Cont working patt panel as for pullover front, until work measures 20in, ending with WS row. Change to smaller needles, work 4in in twisted rib as for jerkin back. Bind off in rib. Join side seam.

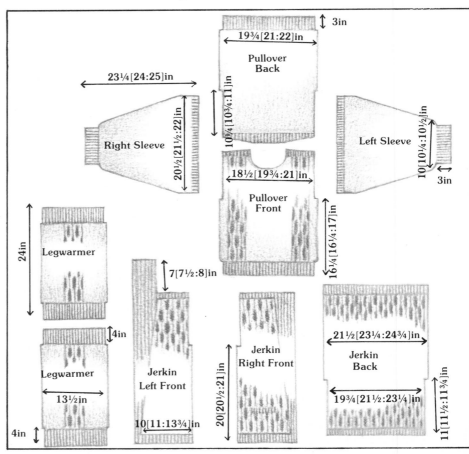

Two-tone Suit

Two different slipstitch patterns are used for the top of this elegant two-piece suit — one for the main fabric and a two-color slipstitch rib for the waistband/cuffs. The gently flared skirt is knitted in simple stockinette stitch.

Sizes
Sweater
To fit 34[36:38]in bust
Length 23[24:24½]in
Sleeve seam 17in
Skirt
To fit 36[38:40]in hips
Length 24[24½:25]in

Note Instructions for larger sizes are in brackets []; where there is only one set of figures it applies to all sizes.

Gauge
Sweater
27½ sts and 42 rows to 4in over patt on size 6 needles
Skirt
23 sts and 30 rows to 4in over st st on size 4 needles

Materials
Sweater
500[500:550]g double knitting yarn (see page 9) or 21[21:23]oz knitting worsted in main color (A)
75[125:125]g or 3[5:5]oz, respectively, in contrasting color (B)
Size 3 circular needle
1 pair each sizes 3 and 6 needles
3 buttons
Skirt
400[450:500]g double knitting yarn or 17[19:21]oz knitting worsted in contrasting color (B)
Size 3 circular needle (length 16in)
Size 4 circular needle (length 16in)
Length of elastic for waistband

Sweater
Back
**Using smaller circular needle and B, cast on 128[136:144] sts. Work in rows in 2-color rib patt as foll:
1st row (RS) With B, *ybk, sl 2 P-wise, yfwd, P2, rep from * to end, do not turn.
Join in A to beg of first row.
2nd row (RS) With A, *K2, sl 2 P-wise, rep from * to end, turn.
3rd row (WS) With B, *K2, yfwd, sl 2 P-wise, ybk, rep from * to end, do not turn.
4th row (WS) With A, *sl 2 P-wise, P2, rep from * to end, turn work.
These 4 rows form the 2-color rib patt.
Rep these 4 rows for 3in, ending with a 2nd row.
Cont in A only.
44

Next row (WS) P to end, inc 1 st at each end of row. 130[138:146] sts. Change to larger needles and beg patt. Work backward and forward in rows.
1st row (RS) *K2, yfwd, sl 2 P-wise, ybk, rep from * to last 2 sts, K2.
2nd row P1, *ybk, sl 2 P-wise, yfwd, P2, rep from * to last st, P1.
3rd row *Yfwd, sl 2 P-wise, ybk, K2, rep from * to last 2 sts, yfwd, sl 2 P-wise.
4th row P3, *ybk, sl 2 P-wise, yfwd, P2, rep from * to last 3 sts, ybk, sl 2 P-wise, yfwd, P1.
5th-12th rows Rep first–4th rows twice more.
13th row *Yfwd, sl 2 P-wise, ybk, K2, rep from * to last 2 sts, yfwd, sl 2 P-wise.
14th row P1, *ybk, sl 2 P-wise, yfwd, P2, rep from * to last st, P1.
15th row *K2, yfwd, sl 2 P-wise, ybk, rep from * to last 2 sts, K2.
16th row P3, ybk, sl 2 P-wise, yfwd, P2, rep from * to last 3 sts, ybk, sl 2 P-wise, yfwd, P1.
17th-24th rows Rep 13th-16th rows twice more.
These 24 rows form the patt. Cont in patt until work measures approx 15in from cast-on edge, ending with a 24th patt row.
Shape armholes
Keeping patt correct, bind off 6[6:7] sts at beg of next 2 rows. Dec 1 st at each end of the next 7 rows. Work 1 row. Dec 1 st at each end of the next and every other row until 98[106:110] sts rem.**
Work even until work measures 8[9:9½]in from beg of armholes, ending with a WS row.
Shape shoulders
Bind off 7[8:8] sts at beg of next 6 rows and 6[6:7] sts at beg of foll 2 rows. Bind off rem 44[46:48] sts.

Front
Work as for back from ** to **.
Work even until work measures 2[2¾:3]in from beg of armhole shaping, ending with a RS row.
Divide for front opening
Next row Patt 51[55:57] and leave these sts on a spare needle, patt to end.
Complete left side of neck first.
Next row Patt 47[51:53], cast on 4 sts for button band. 51[55:57] sts.

Cont in patt until 23 rows less than back to shoulder shaping have been worked, ending with a RS row.
Shape neck
Keeping patt correct, bind off 12 [13:14] sts at beg of next row.
Dec 1 st at neck edge on next 5 rows. Work 1 row.
Dec 1 st at neck edge on next and every other row 5 times.
Work 3 rows.
Dec 1 st at neck edge on next row. 27[30:31] sts.
Work 1 row.
Shape shoulder
Bind off 7[8:8] sts at beg of next and every other row twice. Work 1 row. Bind off rem 6[6:7] sts.
Mark the positions of 3 buttons on button band, the first to come ¾in above base of opening with the other 2 at 1½in intervals.
With RS of work facing, join in yarn to sts on spare needle, patt to end. Complete to match first side of neck, reversing shapings and making buttonholes opposite markers as foll:
1st buttonhole row (RS) Patt 2, cast off 2 sts, patt to end.
2nd buttonhole row Patt to end, casting on 2 sts over those bound off in previous row.

Sleeves
Using smaller circular needle and B, cast on 52[56:60] sts.
Work in 2-color rib patt as for back for 2½in, ending with a 2nd row.
Cont in A.
Next row (WS) P5[3:4], make 1 by picking up the loop between last st worked and next st on LH needle and working into the back of it – called M1, (P2[3:2], M1, P3, M1) 8[8:10] times, P3, M1, P4[2:3]. 70[74:82] sts.
Change to larger needles and beg with a 13th row beg patt as for back. Inc and work into patt 1 st at each end of the 7th and every foll 8th row until there are 106[110:116] sts.
Work even until work measures approx 17in, ending with a 24th patt row.

Shape top
Keeping patt correct, bind off 6[6:7] sts at beg of next 2 rows. Dec 1 st at each end of the next and every foll 4th row until 84[88:92] sts rem.

Dec 1 st at each end of every other row until 44 sts rem, ending with a WS row.
Bind off 2 sts at beg of next 2 rows and 3 sts at beg of foll 2 rows. Bind off 4 sts at beg of next 2 rows and 5 sts at beg of foll 2 rows.
Bind off rem 16 sts.

Collar

Using smaller circular needle and B, cast on 110[114:122] sts.
Work in rows in 2-color rib as foll:
1st row (RS) With B, P2, *ybk, sl 2 P-wise, yfwd, P2, rep from * to end, do not turn.
Join in A to beg of first row.
2nd row (RS) With A, sl 2 P-wise, *K2, sl 2 P-wise, rep from * to end, turn.
3rd row (WS) With B, K2, *yfwd, sl 2 P-wise, ybk, K2, rep from * to end, do not turn.
4th row (WS) With A, sl 2 P-wise, *P2, sl 2 P-wise, rep from * to end, turn.
These 4 rows form the 2-color rib patt.
Rep these 4 rows until work measures approx 2½in from cast-on edge, ending with a 4th patt row.

With A only, bind off K-wise.
Front borders (alike)
With RS of work facing, using smaller needles and A, pick up and K 27 sts along front opening edge.
Bind off very loosely.

Skirt

Using smaller circular needle and B, cast on 160[172:184] sts. Mark beg of round. Work in rounds of K2, P2 rib for 1¼in for waistband.
Change to larger circular needle.
Work 7 rounds st st (every round K).
Beg shaping
Next round K9[10:11], (M1, K1, M1, K19[20:22], M1, K1, M1, K19[21:22]) 3 times, M1, K1, M1, K19[20:22], M1, K1, M1, K10[11:11]. 176[188:200] sts.
Work 8 rounds st st.
Next round K10[11:12], (M1, K1, M1, K21[22:24], M1, K1, M1, K21[23:24]) 3 times, M1, K1, M1, K21[22:24], M1, K1, M1, K11[12:12]. 192[204:216] sts.
Work 8 rounds st st.
Next round K11[12:13], (M1, K1, M1, K23[24:26], M1, K1, M1, K23[25:26]) 3 times, M1, K1, M1, K23[24:26], M1, K1, M1,

K12[13:13]. Work 10 rounds st st. 208[220:232] sts.
Cont in this way, inc on next and 2 foll 11th rounds. 256[268:280] sts. Work 14 rounds st st.
Now cont to inc as before on the next and every foll 15th round until there are 320[332:344] sts. Work even until work measures 24[24½:25]in from waistband, (length may be adjusted here).
Next row (to form hemline) P.
Work 6 rounds st st.
Bind off.

To finish

Press or block if appropriate for yarn used.
Sweater
Join shoulders. Place collar ⅜in from front border edges and sew to neck. Join side and sleeve seams. Set in sleeves. Sew base of button band under buttonhole band. Sew on buttons.
Skirt
Cut elastic to fit waist. Join in a ring and sew to rib waistband using herringbone stitch.
Fold lower edge to WS at hem-line and slipstitch down.

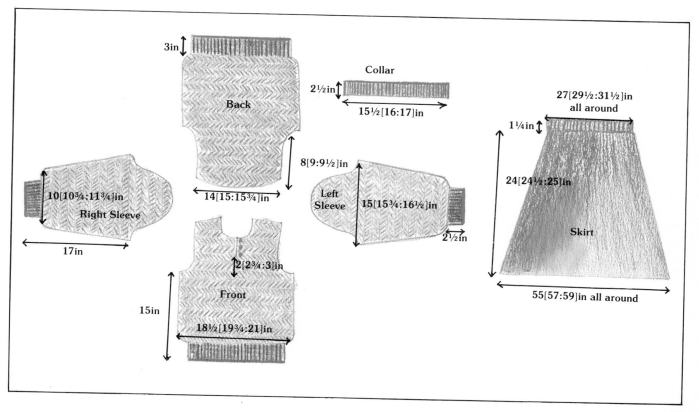

Leaf-stitch Sweater

The leaves are falling all over this beautiful cowl-necked sweater – just right for long country walks on misty autumnal mornings

Sizes
To fit 34[36:38]in bust
Length 26½in
Sleeve seam 17½in

Note Instructions for larger sizes are in brackets []; where there is only one set of figures it applies to all sizes.

Gauge
22 sts and 30 rows to 4in over st st on size 5 needles

Materials
600[650:650]g double knitting yarn (see page 9) or 25[27:27]oz knitting worsted
1 pair each sizes 3 and 5 knitting needles

Back
** Using smaller needles, cast on 94 [100:106] sts. Work in K1, P1 rib for 4in, ending with a RS row.
Next row Rib 7[10:5], pick up the loop lying between st just worked and next st on LH needle and work into the back of it − called M1 −, (rib 5[5:6], M1) 16 times, rib to end. 111[117:123] sts.
Change to larger needles and beg patt.
1st row (RS) P11[8:11], *P2, K1 tbl, P9, rep from * to last 4[1:4] sts, P to end.
2nd row K4[1:4], *K9, P1 tbl, K2, rep from * to last 11[8:11] sts, K to end.
3rd–6th rows Rep first and 2nd rows twice.
7th row P11[8:11], *P2, (K1, yo, K1, yo, K1) all into next st, P9, rep from * to last 4[1:4] sts, P to end.
8th row K4[1:4], *K9, P5, K2, rep from * to last 11[8:11] sts, K to end.
9th row P11[8:11], *P2, K into front and back of next st − called inc 1 F −, K3, K into back and front of next st − called inc 1 B −, P9, rep from * to last 4[1:4] sts, P to end.
10th row K4[1:4], *K9, P7, K2, rep from * to last 11[8:11] sts, K to end.
11th row P11[8:11], *P2, inc 1 F, K5, inc 1 B, P9, rep from * to last 4[1:4] sts, P to end.
12th row K4[1:4], *K9, P9, K2, rep from * to last 11[8:11] sts, K to end.
13th row P7[4:7], K1 tbl, P3, *P2, sl 1, K1, psso, K5, K2 tog, P5, K1 tbl,

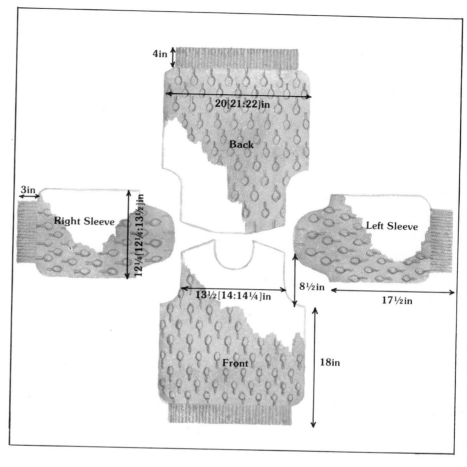

P3, rep from * to last 4[1:4] sts, P to end.
14th row K4[1:4], *K3, P1 tbl, K5, P2 tog, P3, P2 tog tbl, K2, rep from * to last 11[8:11] sts, K3, P1 tbl, K to end.
15th row P7[4:7], K1 tbl, P3, *P2, sl 1, K1, psso, K1, K2 tog, P5, K1 tbl, P3, rep from * to last 4[1:4] sts, P to end.
16th row K4[1:4], *K3, P1 tbl, K5, P3 tog, K2, rep from * to last 11[8:11] sts, K3, P1 tbl, K to end.
17th row P7[4:7], K1 tbl, P3, *P8, K1 tbl, P3, rep from * to last 4[1:4] sts, P to end.
18th row K4[1:4], *K3, P1 tbl, K8, rep from * to last 11[8:11] sts, K3, P1 tbl, K to end.
19th–22nd rows Rep 17th–18th rows twice.
23rd row P7[4:7], (K1, yo, K1, yo, K1) all into next st, P3, *P8, (K1, yo, K1, yo, K1) all into next st, P3, rep from * to last 4[1:4] sts, P to end.
24th row K4[1:4], *K3, P5, K8, rep

from * to last 15[12:15] sts, K3, P5, K7[4:7].
25th row P7[4:7], inc 1 F, K3, inc 1 B, P3, *P8, inc 1 F, K3, inc 1 B, P3, rep from * to last 4[1:4] sts, P to end.
26th row K4[1:4], *K3, P7, K8, rep from * to last 17[14:17] sts, K3, P7, K to end.
27th row P7[4:7], inc 1 F, K5, inc 1 B, P3, *P8, inc 1 F, K5, inc 1 B, P3, rep from * to last 4[1:4] sts, P to end.
28th row K4[1:4], *K3, P9, K8, rep from * to last 19[16:19] sts, K3, P9, K to end.
29th row P7[4:7], sl 1, K1, psso, K5, K2 tog, P3, *P2, K1 tbl, P5, sl 1, K1, psso, K5, K2 tog, P3, rep from * to last 4[1:4] sts, P to end.
30th row K4[1:4], *K3, P2 tog, P3, P2 tog tbl, K5, P1 tbl, K2, rep from * to last 17[14:17] sts, K3, P2 tog, P3, P2 tog tbl, K to end.
31st row P7[4:7], sl 1, K1, psso, K1, K2 tog, P3, *P2, K1 tbl, P5, sl 1,

K1, psso, K1, K2 tog, P3, rep from * to last 4[1:4] sts, P to end.
32nd row K4[1:4], *K3, P3 tog, K5, P1 tbl, K2, rep from * to last 13[10:13] sts, K3, P3 tog, K to end.
These 32 rows form the patt.
Cont in patt until work measures approx 18in, ending with a 12th patt row.

Shape armholes
Keeping patt correct, bind off 4 sts at beg of next 2 rows. Dec 1 st at each end of the next 7[7:11] rows, then dec 1 st at each end of the next and every other row until 75[77:79] sts rem. ** Work even until work measures approx 26½in, ending with a 12th patt row.

Shape shoulders
Keeping patt correct, bind off 6 sts at beg of next 4 rows, and 6[6:5] sts at beg of next 2 rows. Leave rem 45 [51:55] sts on a spare needle.

Front
Work as for back from ** to **.
Work until work measures 23in, ending with a 16th patt row.

Shape neck
Next row Patt 26[27:26], P2 tog, turn leaving rem sts on spare needle. Complete left side of neck first. Dec 1 st at neck edge on every other row until 18[18:17] sts rem.
Work even until work matches back to shoulder shaping, ending with a WS row.

Shape shoulder
Bind off 6 sts at beg of next and every other row once.
Work 1 row. Bind off rem 6[6:5] sts. With RS facing, return to sts on spare needle, sl center 19[19:23] sts onto a stitch holder, join yarn to rem sts, P2 tog, patt to end. Complete to match first side, reversing shapings.

Sleeves
Using smaller needles, cast on 40[44:46] sts.
Work in K1, P1 rib for 3in, ending with a RS row.
Next row Rib 6[10:9], M1, (rib 1, M1) 28[24:28] times, rib to end. 69[69:75] sts.

Change to larger needles and cont in patt as for 2nd[2nd:first] size on back until work measures approx 17½in, ending with a 12th patt row.

Shape top
Bind off 4 sts at beg of next 2 rows. Dec 1 st at each end of next and every foll 4th row until 57[57:63] sts rem. Work 1 row.
Dec 1 st at each end of next and every other row until 35 sts rem. Work 1 row. Bind off.

To finish
Join right shoulder seam.
Collar
With RS of work facing, using larger needles, pick up and K 24 sts down left side of neck, K19[19:23] sts from center front, pick up and K 24 sts up right side of neck and K across 45[51:55] sts across back neck. 112[118:126] sts. Beg with a P row, cont in reverse st st until border measures 7in, ending with a K row. Bind off. Join left shoulder and neck border. Join side and sleeve seams. Set in sleeves.

Special technique – working a cluster

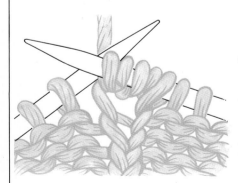

1 The leaf motif on the sweater is formed from a cluster worked on the 7th–16th rows. On the 7th row work to the cluster position and make five stitches from one. Purl these stitches on wrong-side rows.

2 Increase one stitch on each side of the cluster on the 9th and 11th rows. Continue to purl the cluster stitches on wrong-side rows.

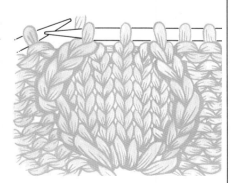

3 Now decrease one stitch on each side of the cluster stitches on every row until three cluster stitches remain. Purl these three stitches together, completing the cluster. Clusters are worked the same way on the 23rd–32nd rows.

Multi-textured Dress

Interlaced cables woven through with contrasting threads add an original touch to an attractive Aran-style sweater dress that's both warm and stylish.

Sizes
To fit 32[34:36]in bust
Length 35½[36:36½]in
Sleeve seam 17¾[18:18½]in

Note Instructions for the larger sizes are in brackets []; where there is only one set of figures it applies to all three sizes.

Gauge
20 sts and 24 rows to 4in over seed st on size 6 needles
28 sts and 24 rows to 4in over central cable panel on size 6 needles

Materials
53[57:60]oz of knitting worsted in main color (A)
3oz in each of two contrasting colors (B) and (C)
1 pair each sizes 5 and 6 knitting needles

Size 5 circular needle 16in long
Cable needle

Special note When weaving contrasting yarns on patchwork panels, use separate balls of yarn for each panel, carrying yarn up WS of work when not in use. See also Special Technique.

Patchwork cable panel patt
(worked over 19 sts)
1st row (RS) P2, K2, (K1 weaving B on RS thus, bring contrasting yarn B to RS, K1A, take B to WS – called K1wB –, P1) 3 times, K1wB, K4, P4.
2nd row K4, P4, (K1, P1 weaving B on RS thus, take contrasting yarn B to RS, P1A, bring B to WS – called P1wB –), 3 times, K1, P2, K2.
3rd row P2, sl next 2 sts onto cable needle and hold at front of work, P1,

then K2 from cable needle – called Tw3F – (P1, K1wB) 3 times, sl next 2 sts onto cable needle and hold at front of work, K2, then K2 from cable needle – called C4F –, P4.
4th row K4, P4, (K1, P1wB), 3 times, P2, K3.
5th row P3, Tw3F, K1wB, P1, K1wB, sl next 2 sts onto cable needle and hold at back of work, K2, then P2 from cable needle – called Tw4B –, sl next 2 sts onto cable needle and hold at front of work, K1, then K2 from cable needle – called C3F –, P3.
6th row K3, P2, P1 tbl weaving C on RS thus, take contrasting yarn C to RS, P1A tbl, bring C to WS – called P1 tblwC –, K1, P1 tblwC, P2, K1, P1wB, K1, P2, K4.
7th row P4, Tw3F, Tw4B, K1 tbl weaving C on RS thus, bring contrasting yarn C to RS, K1 tbl, take

---

Special technique – knitting in weaving threads

1 The woven-look effect on the patchwork cable is achieved by weaving in contrasting yarns as you knit. On right-side rows secure the end of the weaving thread at the back of the work, bring it to the front, then work the next stitch in the main color. Take the weaving thread to the back.

2 On wrong-side rows the weaving thread begins at the front of the work. Take it through to the back (the right side of the work), work the next stitch in the main color, then bring the weaving thread back to the front. The contrasting yarns are thus woven from back to front of the work but never actually knitted.

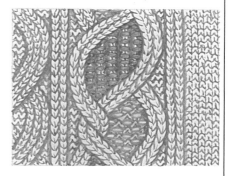

3 The weaving threads are arranged in two different ways in the basic pattern. On one section of the cable the threads on the right side are staggered above each other. On the other section they lie directly above each other.

C to WS – called K1 tblwC –, P1, K1 tblwC) Tw3F, P2.
8th row K2, P2, (K1, P1 tblwC) 3 times, P4, K5.
9th row P5, Tw4B, (K1 tblwC, P1) 3 times, K2, P2.
10th row K2, P2, (K1, P1 tblwC) 4 times, P2, K5.
11th row P3, Tw4B, (K1 tblwC, P1) 3 times, K1 tblwC, sl next st onto cable needle and hold at back of work, K2, then P1 from cable needle – called Tw3B –, P2.
12th row K3, P2, (P1 tblwC, K1) 4 times, P1 tblwC, P2, K3.
13th row P2, Tw3B, (K1 tblwC, P1) 3 times, K1 tblwC, Tw4B, P3.
14th row K5, P2, (P1 tblwC, K1) 4 times, P2, K2.
15th row P2, K2, (P1, K1 tblwC) 3 times, sl next 2 sts onto cable needle and hold at back of work, K2, then K2 from cable needle – called C4B –, P5.
16th row K5, P4, (P1 tblwC, K1) 3 times, P2, K2.
17th row P2, Tw3F, K1 tblwC, P1, K1 tblwC, Tw4B, C3F, P4.
18th row K4, P2, K1, P1wB, K1, P2, P1 tblwC, K1, P1 tblwC, P2, K3.
19th row P3, Tw3F, Tw4B, K1wB, P1, K1wB, Tw3F, P3.
20th row K3, P2, (P1wB, K1) 3 times, P4, K4.
21st row P4, C4F, (K1wB, P1) 3 times, C3F, P2.
22nd row K2, P2, (K1, P1wB) 3 times, K1, P4, K4.
23rd row P4, K4, (K1wB, P1) 3 times, K1wB, K2, P2.
24th row K2, P2, (K1, P1wB) 3 times, K1, P4, K4.
25th row P4, C4F, (K1wB, P1) 3 times, Tw3B, P2.
26th row K3, P2, (P1wB, K1) 3 times, P4, K4.
27th row P3, sl next st onto cable needle and hold at back of work, K2, then K1 from cable needle – called Cr3B, –, sl next 2 sts onto cable needle and hold at front of work, P2, then K2 from cable needle – called Tw4F –, K1wB, P1, K1wB, Tw3B, P3.
28th row K4, P2, K1, P1wB, K1, P2, P1 tblwC, K1, P1 tblwC, P2, K3.
29th row P2, Tw3B, K1 tblwC, P1, K1 tblwC, Tw4F, Tw3B, P4.
30th row K5, P4, (P1 tblwC, K1) 3 times, P2, K2.

31st row P2, K2, (P1, K1 tblwC) 3 times, Tw4F, P5.
32nd row K5, P2, (P1 tblwC, K1) 4 times, P2, K2.
33rd row P2, Tw3F, (K1 tblwC, P1) 3 times, K1 tblwC, Tw4F, P3.
34th row K3, P2, (P1 tblwC, K1) 4 times, P1 tblwC, P2, K3.
35th row P3, Tw4F, (K1 tblwC, P1) 3 times, K1 tblwC, Tw3F, P2.
36th row K2, P2, (K1, P1 tblwC) 4 times, P2, K5.
37th row P5, C4F, (K1 tblwC, P1) 3 times, K2, P2.
38th row K2, P2, (K1, P1 tblwC) 3 times, P4, K5.
39th row P4, Cr3B, Tw4F, K1 tblwC, P1, K1 tblwC, Tw3B, P2.
40th row K3, P2, P1 tblwC, K1, P1 tblwC, P2, K1, P1wB, K1, P2, K4.
41st row P3, Tw3B, K1wB, P1, K1wB, Tw4F, Tw3B, P3.
42nd row K4, P4, (K1, P1wB) 3 times, P2, K3.
43rd row P2, Cr3B, (P1, K1wB) 3 times, C4F, P4.
44th row K4, P4, (K1, P1wB) 3 times, K1, P2, K2.
These 44 rows form patchwork cable panel patt, referred to throughout as "cable 19".

Central cable panel patt (worked over 31 sts)
1st row (RS) K2, P1, K3, (P4, K6) twice, P3, K2.
2nd and every other row K the P sts and P the K sts of previous row.
3rd row K2, P1, K3, (P4, sl next 3 sts onto cable needle and hold at front of work, K3, then K3 from cable needle) twice, P3, K2.
5th row K2, P1, (sl next 3 sts onto cable needle and hold at front of work, P2, then K3 from cable needle – called C5F –, sl next 2 sts onto cable needle and hold at back of work, K3, then P2 from cable needle – called C5B –,) twice, C5F, P1, K2.
7th row K2, P3, (sl next 3 sts onto cable needle and hold at back of work, K3, then K3 from cable needle, P4) twice, K3, P1, K2.
9th row K2, P1, (C5B, C5F) twice, C5B, P1, K2.
10th row As 2nd row.
These 10 rows form the central cable panel patt, referred to throughout as "cable 31".

Back
** Using smaller needles and A, cast on 114[118:122] sts. Work in twisted K1, P1 rib as foll:
1st row (RS) *K1 tbl, P1, rep from*.
2nd row *K1, P1 tbl, rep from*.
Rep the last 2 rows until work measures 1¼in, ending with a WS row.
Next row Rib 29[30:31], (work twice into next st – called inc 1 –, rib 27[28:29]) twice, inc 1, rib to end. 117[121:125] sts.
Next row K.
Change to larger needles and beg patt.
1st row (RS) (K1, P1) 11[12:13] times, K2, work first row of cable 19, first row of cable 31, first row of cable 19, K2, (P1, K1) 11[12:13] times.
2nd row (K1, P1) 11[12:13] times, P2, work 2nd row of cable 19, 2nd row of cable 31, 2nd row of cable 19, P2, (P1, K1) 11[12:13] times.
These 2 rows establish the patt of cable panels between st st borders and seed st edge sts.
Keeping patt correct, inc and work into seed st 1 st at each end of 18th and every foll 20th row until there are 125[131:137] sts. Cont in patt until work measures 25½[26:26½]in, ending with a WS row.
Shape armholes
Next row Patt 26[29:32] sts and sl onto a st holder, patt 73, turn, sl last 26[29:32] sts onto a st holder. **
Cont in patt until work measures 35½[36:36½]in, ending with a RS row.
Next row P3, K to last 3 sts, P3.
Leave these sts on a spare needle.

Front
Work as for back from ** to **.
Cont in patt until work measures 5 rows less than back.
Shape neck
Next row (WS) P2, K2 tog, turn.
Next row P1, K2, turn.
Next row P1, P2 tog, turn.
Next row K2, turn.
Next row P2 tog, K 65 sts at center, K2 tog, P2, turn.
Next row K2, P1, turn.
Next row P2 tog, P1, turn.
Next row K2, turn.
Next row P2 tog.
Break off yarn, leave rem 67 sts on a spare needle.

Left sleeve

*** Using smaller needles and A, cast on 50[52:54] sts. Work 1¼in twisted K1, P1 rib as for back, ending with a WS row.

Next row Rib 3[2:14], *inc 1, rib 1[1:0], rep from * to last 3[2:14] sts, inc 1, rib to end. 73[77:81] sts.

Next row K.

Change to larger needles and beg patt.

1st size only

1st row K2, cable 19, cable 31, cable 19, K2.

2nd row P2, cable 19, cable 31, cable 19, P2.

These 2 rows establish the patt.

2nd and 3rd sizes only

1st row (K1, P1)[1:2] times, K2, cable 19, cable 31, cable 19, K2 (P1, K1)[1:2] times.

2nd row (K1, P1)[1:2] times, P2, cable 19, cable 31, cable 19, P2, (P1, K1)[1:2] times.

These 2 rows establish the patt.

All sizes

Keeping patt correct, inc and work into seed st, 1 st at each end of the 2nd[4th:4th] and every foll 4th row until there are 121 sts.***

Work even until work measures 17¾[18:18½]in, ending with a RS row.

Shape pocket lining

Next row Cast on 20 sts, P20, patt to end.

Next row Patt to last 20 sts, K20.

Rep the last 2 rows until work measures 5⅛[5⅝:6¼]in from beg of pocket lining, ending with a RS row.

Next row K.

Bind off loosely.

Right sleeve

Work as for left sleeve from *** to ***. Work even until work measures 17¾[18:18½]in, ending with a WS row.

Shape pocket lining

Next row Cast on 20 sts, K20, patt to end.

Next row Patt to last 20 sts, P20.

Complete to match left sleeve.

To finish

Join side seams.

Left pocket border

Using smaller needles and A, with WS of work facing, K across the 26[29:32] sts left on stitch holder at left front armhole, then K across the 26[29:32] sts on stitch holder at left back armhole. 52[58:64] sts. Work 8 rows twisted K1, P1 rib as for back, beg with a 2nd row.

Bind off in rib.

Right pocket border

Work as for left pocket border but K across sts on holder at right back armhole, then across sts on holder at right front armhole. 52[58:64] sts. Complete as for left pocket border. Join underarm seams to pocket lining. Fold pocket borders to RS and catch down sides.

Set in sleeves. Catch down pocket linings to WS.

Collar

Using circular needle, with RS of work facing, pick up and K 4 sts from left side of neck, K across 67 sts at center front, pick up and K 4 sts up right side of neck, K across 73 sts on back neck. 148 sts.

Work in rounds.

1st round *P1 tbl, K1, rep from * to end.

Rep this round until work measures 11in.

Bind off in rib.

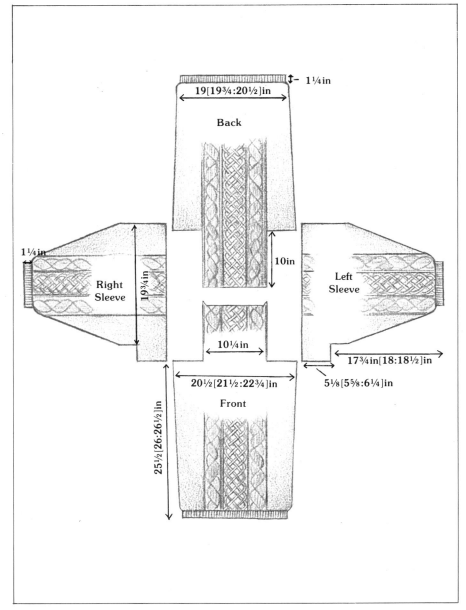

Woven-look Sweater

This military-style sweater in an interesting woven-look
stitch pattern has practical shoulder buttoning and would
look good on any active youngster.

Sizes
To fit 24−27[28−31]in chest
Length 19[21]in
Sleeve seam 13[15¼]in

Note Instructions for larger size are in brackets []; where there is only one set of figures it applies to both sizes.

Gauge
28 sts and 36 rows to 4in over st st on size 3 needles

Materials
300[350]g four-ply yarn (see page 9) or 14[16]oz sport-weight yarn in main color (A)
125g or 6oz, respectively in contrasting color (B)
1 pair each sizes 2 and 3 knitting needles
6 buttons

Back
Using larger needles and A, cast on 64[72] sts loosely. Form base triangles by working turning rows.
1st row (WS) P2, turn.
2nd row K2.
3rd row P3, turn.
4th row K3.
5th row P4, turn.
6th row K4.
7th row P5, turn.
8th row K5.
9th row P6, turn.
10th row K6.
11th row P7, turn.
12th row K7.
13th row P8, do not turn.
First triangle completed. Leave these 8 sts on right-hand needle and rep last 13 rows 7[8] more times, so forming 8[9] triangles.
Cut off A.
*Join in B and work across first 8 sts for selvage triangle.
1st row K2, turn.
2nd row P2.
3rd row Inc in first st by working into front and back of st, sl 1, K1, psso, turn.
4th row P3.
5th row Inc in first st, K1, sl 1, K1, psso, turn.
6th row P4.
7th row Inc in first st, K2, sl 1, K1, psso, turn.
8th row P5.

9th row Inc in first st, K3, sl 1, K1, psso, turn.
10th row P6.
11th row Inc in first st, K4, sl 1, K1, psso, turn.
12th row P7.
13th row Inc in first st, K5, sl 1, K1, psso, do not turn. Selvage triangle completed. Leave these 8 sts on right-hand needle. Work first rectangle.
**1st row Pick up and K 8 sts along side of base triangle, turn.
2nd row P8.
3rd row K7, sl 1, K1, psso, turn — two sections joined.
Rep 2nd and 3rd rows until all 8 sts from base triangle have been dec, ending with a 3rd row.**
Rep from ** to ** 6[7] more times.
Work selvage triangle.
1st row Pick up and K 8 sts along side of last triangle worked, turn.
2nd row P2 tog, P6, turn.
3rd and every other row K.
4th row P2 tog, P5, turn.
6th row P2 tog, P4, turn.
8th row P2 tog, P3, turn.
10th row P2 tog, P2, turn.
12th row P2 tog, P1, turn.
14th row P2 tog. Cut off B.
Join in A and work rectangles.
1st row Pick up and P 7 sts along side of triangle just worked. 8 sts.
2nd row K8.
3rd row P7, P2 tog, turn.
Rep 2nd and 3rd rows until all 8 sts from next rectangle have been dec, ending with a 3rd row.
Do not turn after last row.
Leave these 8 sts on right-hand needle.
*** Pick up and P 8 sts along side of next rectangle.
Rep 2nd and 3rd rows until all 8 sts from next rectangle have been dec, ending with a 3rd row.
Do not turn after last row.***
Rep from *** to *** 6[7] more times. Cut off A.*
Rep from * to * until work measures approx 11½[13]in, ending with a row of rectangles and two selvage triangles worked in B. Cut off B.
Join in A and work a row of triangles to complete patt.
1st row Pick up and P 8 sts along side of last triangle worked, turn.
9 sts.
2nd row K9.

3rd row P2 tog, P6, P2 tog, turn.
4th row K8.
5th row P2 tog, P5, P2 tog, turn.
6th row K7.
7th row P2 tog, P4, P2 tog, turn.
8th row K6.
9th row P2 tog, P3, P2 tog, turn.
10th row K5.
11th row P2 tog, P2, P2 tog, turn.
12th row K4.
13th row P2 tog, P1, P2 tog, turn.
14th row K3.
15th row (P2 tog) twice, turn.
16th row K2.
17th row P3 tog, do not turn.
Rep first − 17th rows until 8[9] triangles have been worked and 1 st rem. Do not cut off yarn, turn.
Beg yoke
With RS facing, using larger needles and A, pick up and K 98[110] sts across top of triangles just worked. 99[111] sts. Beg with a P row, work 4[4½]in st st, ending with a K row.
Shape shoulders
1st row P to last 8[9] sts, turn.
2nd row Sl 1, K to last 8[9] sts, turn.
3rd row Sl 1, P to last 16[18] sts, turn.
4th row Sl 1, K to last 16[18] sts, turn.
5th row Sl 1, P to last 24[26] sts, turn.
6th row Sl 1, K to last 24[26] sts, turn.
7th row Sl 1, P to last 31[34] sts, turn.
8th row Sl 1, K to last 31[34] sts, turn.
9th row P across all 99[111] sts.
Cut off A.

Back neck border
Sl 31[34] sts from each side onto a holder.
With RS facing, using smaller needles and A, K across center 37[43] sts inc 2 sts evenly across row. 39[45] sts.
Next row P1, *K1, P1, rep from * to end.
Next row K1, *P1, K1, rep from * to end.
Rep the last 2 rows 3 more times. Bind off in rib.

Front
Work as for back until 11[13] rows less have been worked to beg of shoulder shaping, ending with a P row.

Divide for neck

Next row K37[42], K2 tog, turn and leave rem sts on a spare needle. Complete left side of neck first. Dec 1 st at neck edge on next 6[8] rows. Work 1 row.
Dec 1 st at neck edge on next row. 31[34] sts.
Work 2 rows.

Shape shoulder

1st row (WS) P23[25], turn.
2nd and every other row S1, 1, K to end.
3rd row P15[16], turn.
5th row P7[8], turn.
6th row K.
Leave all 31[34] sts on a holder. With RS facing place center 21[23] sts from spare needle on a holder, join A to next st, K2 tog, K to end. 38[43] sts.
Work to match first side, reversing shaping.

Sleeves

Using smaller needles and A, cast on 46[50] sts.
Work 2½in in K1, P1 rib.
Next row (WS) Rib 1[5], pick up and K the loop between last st worked and next st on left-hand needle — called M1 —, (rib 4[3], M1) 11[13] times, rib 1[6]. 58[64] sts.
Change to larger needles and beg with a K row, work in st st inc 1 st each end of every foll 5th row until there are 90[102] sts.
Work even until work measures 13[15¼]in, ending with a P row.
Bind off.

To finish

Press sleeves and yoke only on WS if appropriate for yarn used.
Front neck border
With RS facing, using smaller needles and A, pick up and K 14[16] sts down left side of neck, K the sts from holder, then pick up and K 14[16] sts up right side of neck. 49[55] sts.
Work 8 rows in K1, P1 rib, as for back neck border.
Bind off in rib.
Shoulder borders
Right back
With RS facing, using smaller needles and A, K31[34] sts from shoulder inc 2 sts evenly across, then pick up and

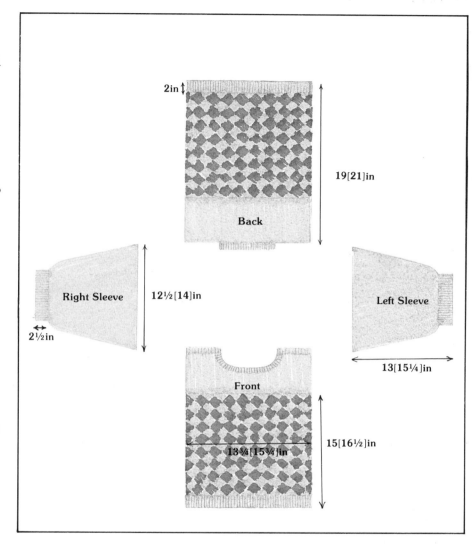

2in

19[21]in

Back

12½[14]in

Right Sleeve

2½in

Left Sleeve

13[15¼]in

Front

15[16½]in

13¾[15¾]in

K 6 sts evenly from side of the back neck border. 39[42] sts.
Work 8 rows in K1, P1 rib as for back neck border.
Bind off in rib.

Left back
Start at top of back neck border and work as for right back border.
Left front
As RS facing, using smaller needles and A, K31[34] sts from shoulder inc 2[3] sts evenly, then pick up and K 6 sts up side of front neck border. 39[43] sts.
Work 3 rows K1, P1 rib as for back neck border.
1st buttonhole row (Rib 10[11], bind off 2) 3 times, rib 3[4].
2nd buttonhole row Rib to end, casting on 2 sts over those bound off

in previous row.
Work 3 rows in rib.
Bind off in rib.

Right front
Work as for left front, starting at top neck border and working first buttonhole row as foll:
Buttonhole row Rib 3[4], (bind off 2, rib 10[11] sts) 3 times.

Waistbands (back and front alike)
With RS facing, using smaller needles and A, pick up and K 96[102] sts evenly along lower edge.
Work 2in K1, P1 rib. Bind off in rib.
Lap front over back to depth of ribbing. Place markets 6¼[7]in down from shoulders on back and front. Sew in sleeves between markers, then join side and sleeve seams. Sew on buttons.

Basketweave Sweater

Casual and sporty, but elegant enough for town wear, a
classic V-necked sweater is given textural interest with a
basketweave pattern

Sizes
To fit 38[40:42]in chest
Length 25[25:27]in
Sleeve seam 20½in

Note Instructions for larger sizes are in brackets []; where only one set of figures it applies to all sizes.

Gauge
12 sts and 20 rows to 4in over patt using size 10 needles.

Materials
34[37:41]oz bulky yarn
1 pair each sizes 8 and 10 knitting needles

Back
Using smaller needles, cast on 62[65:68] sts.
Work in K2, P2 rib as foll:
Next row K2[1:0], *P2, K2, rep from * to end of row.
Next row *P2, K2, rep from * to last 2[1:0] sts, P2[1:0].
Rep last 2 rows until work measures 3in.
Change to larger needles and work in patt as foll:
**1st, 3rd, 5th and 7th rows K1, *K3, P3, rep from * to last 1[4:1] sts, K1[4:1].
2nd and every other row K1, P to last st, K1.
9th, 11th, 13th and 15th rows K1, *P3, K3, rep from * to last 1[4:1] sts, K1[(P3, K1):K1].
16th row As 2nd row.**
These 16 rows form patt.
Rep from ** to ** 6 times. Work first 0[0:8] rows of patt once more.
Shape shoulders
Keeping patt correct, bind off 11[11:12] sts at beg of next 4 rows.
Leave rem 18[21:20] sts on stitch holder for neckband.

Front
Work as for back until work measures 18in from beg, ending with WS row.
Divide for neck
Work in patt for 31[32:34] sts, turn, leaving rem sts on a spare needle.
Next row P2 tog, P to last st, K1.
Keeping patt correct, dec 1 st at neck edge on every foll 4th row until 22[22:24] sts rem.

Work even in patt until front matches back to beg of shoulder shaping, ending with a WS row.
Shape shoulders
Bind off 11[11:12] sts at beg of next row. Work 1 row. Bind off.
Rejoin yarn to center front.
Next row Dec 0[1:0] sts, work in patt to end of row.
Next row K1, P to last 2 sts, P2 tog. Complete to match first side, reversing all shaping.

Sleeves (alike)
Using smaller needles, cast on 32 sts and work in K2, P2 rib until work measures 3in.
Change to larger needles and work in patt as for first size of back.
Keeping patt correct, inc 1 st at each end of every foll 6th row until there are 56 sts, ending with a WS row.
Work even in patt for 17 rows.
Bind off loosely P-wise.

To finish
Join right shoulder seam.

Neckband
With RS facing, using smaller needles pick up and K 52[53:58] sts along right front edge, K the 18[21:20] sts on stitch holder for back. 70[74:78] sts.
Next row P2, *K2, P2, rep from *.
Next row K2, *P2, K2, rep from *.
Rep these 2 rows for 2in.
Bind off loosely in rib.
With RS facing, using smaller needles, pick up and K 52[52:56] sts along left front neck edge. Work in K2, P2 rib for 2in.
Bind off loosely in rib.
Join left shoulder seam and neckband seam. Slipstitch neckband into position at center front, lapping left neckband over right. Sew in sleeves. Join sleeve and side seams.

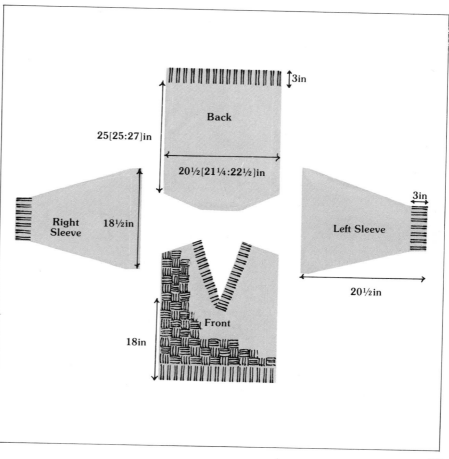

Tweedy Coat and Hat

Treat yourself to a warm winter in a beautiful tweedy coat
encrusted with richly textured stitch patterns. Complete the
picture with a snug ribbed hat to match.

Sizes
To fit 32[34:36]in bust
Length 38½[39:39½]in
Sleeve seam 17½in

Note Instructions for larger sizes are in brackets []; where there is only one set of figures it applies to all sizes.

Gauge
15 sts and 20 rows to 4in over st st on size 10 needles

Materials
Coat
60[62:64]oz bulky yarn
Hat
7oz bulky yarn
1 pair each sizes 8 and 10 knitting needles
Size 8 circular needle
Cable needle
11 buttons

Back
Using smaller needles, cast on 66[70:74] sts.
Work in K2, P2 rib as foll:
1st row K2, *P2, K2, rep from * to end.
2nd row P2, *K2, P2, rep from * to end.
Rep the last 2 rows for 3in, ending with a first row.
Next row Rib 8[10:10] pick up loop between last st worked and next st on LH needle and work into the back of it – called M1 –, (rib 2, M1) 25[25:27] times, rib to end.
92[96:102] sts.
Change to larger needles.
Beg patt.
1st row (RS) P4[6:2], K1 tbl, *P4, sl next 2 sts onto cable needle and leave at front of work, K2, then K2 from cable needle – called C4F –, P4, sl next st onto cable needle and hold at front of work, K1 tbl, then K1 tbl from cable needle – called C2Ftbl –, rep from * to last 17[19:15] sts, P4, C4F, P4, K1 tbl, P4[6:2].
2nd and every other row K the P sts and P the K sts of previous row.
3rd row P4[6:2], * sl next st onto cable needle and hold at front of work, P1, then K1 tbl from cable needle – called Tw2F –, P2, sl next st onto cable needle and hold at back of work, K2, then P1 from cable

needle – called Tw3B –, sl next 2 sts onto a cable needle and hold at front of work, P1, then K2 from cable needle, – called Tw3F –, P2, sl next st onto cable needle and hold at back of work, K1 tbl then P1 from cable needle, – called Tw2B –, rep from * to last 4[6:2] sts, P to end.
5th row P4[6:2], *P1, Tw2F, Tw3B, P2, Tw3F, Tw2B, P1, rep from * to last 4[6:2] sts, P to end.
7th row P4[6:2], *P2, sl next st onto cable needle and hold at back of work, K2, then K1 tbl from cable needle – called Cr3B –, P4, sl next 2 sts onto cable needle and hold at front of work, K1 tbl, then K2 from cable needle – called Cr3F –, P2, rep from * to last 4[6:2] sts, P to end.
9th row P4[6:2], *P1, Tw3B, Tw2F, P2, Tw2B, Tw3F, P1, rep from * to last 4[6:2] sts, P to end.
11th row P4[6:2], *Tw3B, P2, Tw2F, Tw2B, P2, Tw3F, rep from * to last 4[6:2] sts, P to end.
13th row P4[6:2], K2, *P4, sl next st onto cable needle and hold at back of work, K1 tbl, then K1 tbl from cable needle – called C2Btbl –, P4, sl next 2 sts onto cable needle and hold at back of work, K2, then K2 from cable needle – called C4B –, rep from * to last 16[18:14] sts, P4, C2Btbl, P4, K2, P to end.
15th row P4[6:2], *Tw3F, P2, Tw2B, Tw2F, P2, Tw3B, rep from * to last 4[6:2] sts, P to end.
17th row P4[6:2], P1, Tw3F, Tw2B, P2, Tw2F, Tw3B, P1, rep from * to last 4[6:2] sts, P to end.
19th row P4[6:2], *P2, Cr3F, P4, Cr2B, P2, rep from * to last 4[6:2] sts, P to end.
21st row P4[6:2], *P1, Tw2B, Tw3F, P2, Tw3B, Tw2F, P1, rep from * to last 4[6:2] sts, P to end.
23rd row P4[6:2], *Tw2B, P2, Tw3F, Tw3B, P2, Tw2F, rep from * to last 4[6:2] sts, P to end.
24th row As 2nd row.
These 24 rows form the patt. Rep these 24 rows 4 more times.
Now cont in bobble patt as foll:
1st row (RS) P4[6:2], K1 tbl, *P5, K2, rep from * to last 10[12:8] sts, P5, K1 tbl, P4[6:2].
2nd and every other row K4[6:2], P1, *K5, P2, rep from * to last

10[12:8] sts, K5, P1, K4[6:2].
3rd row P4[6:2], K1 tbl, *P5, (K1, P1) twice into next st, P4, turn, K4, turn, P2 tog, P2 tog tbl, turn, sl 1, K1, psso – called make bobble (MB) –, K1, P5, K2, rep from * to last 17[19:15] sts, P5, MB, K1, P5, K1 tbl, P4[6:2].

5th row P4[6:2], K1 tbl, *P4, MB, K1, MB, P5, K2, rep from * to last 17[19:15] sts, P4, MB, K1, MB, P5, K1 tbl, P4[6:2].
7th row P4[6:2], K1 tbl, *P3, MB, P1, MB, K1, MB, P4, K2, rep from * to last 17[19:15] sts, P3, MB, P1, MB, K1, MB, P4, K1 tbl, P4[6:2].
9th row As first row.
11th row P4[6:2], K1 tbl, *P5, K2, P5, MB, K1, rep from * to last 17[19:15] sts, P5, K2, P5, K1 tbl, P4[6:2].
13th row P4[6:2], K1 tbl, *P5, K2, P4, MB, K1, MB, rep from * to last 17[19:15] sts, P5, K2, P5, K1 tbl, P4[6:2].
15th row P4[6:2], K1 tbl, P1, *P4, K2, P3, MB, P1, MB, K1, MB, rep from * to last 16[18:14] sts, P4, K2, P5, K1 tbl, P4[6:2].
16th row As 2nd row.
These 16 rows form bobble patt.
Shape armholes
Keeping patt correct, bind off 3 sts at beg of next 2 rows.
Dec 1 st at each end of next 7[7:5] rows and then on every other row until 62[62:76] sts rem.
Work even until work measures 38½[39:39½]in, ending with a WS row.

Shape shoulders

Keeping patt correct, bind off 8[8:11] sts at beg of next 2 rows and 8[7:10] sts at beg of foll 2 rows. Bind off rem 30[32:34] sts.

Left front

** Using smaller needles cast on 34[34:38] sts. Work 3in K2, P2 rib as for back, ending with a first row.
Next row Rib 5[3:1], M1, (rib 2[2:3], M1), 12[14:12] times, rib to end. 47[49:51] sts.**
Change to larger needles and beg patt.
1st row (RS) P4[6:2], K1 tbl, *P4, C4F, P4, C2Ftbl, rep from * to last 14[14:20] sts, P4, C4F, P4, K1 tbl, P1[1:7].

2nd and every other row K the P sts and P the K sts of previous row.
3rd row P4[6:2], *Tw2F, P2, Tw3B, Tw3F, P2, Tw2B, rep from * to last 1[1:7] sts, P1[1:7].
5th row P4[6:2], *P1, Tw2F, Tw3B, P2, Tw3F, Tw2B, P1, rep from * to last 1[1:7] sts, P1[1:7].
7th row P4[6:2], *P2, Cr3B, P4, Cr3F, P2, rep from * to last 1[1:7] sts, P1[1:7].
9th row P4[6:2], *P1, Tw3B, Tw2F, P2, Tw2B, Tw3F, P1, rep from * to last 1[1:7] sts, P1[1:7].
11th row P4[6:2], *Tw3B, P2, Tw2F, Tw2B, P2, Tw3F, rep from * to last 1[1:7] sts, P1[1:7].
13th row P4[6:2], K2, *P4, C2Btbl, P4, C4B, rep from * to last 13[13:19] sts, P4, C2Btbl, P4, K2, P to end.

15th row P4[6:2], *Tw3F, P2, Tw2B, Tw2F, P2, Tw3B, rep from * to last 1[1:7] sts, P1[1:7].
17th row P4[6:2], *P1, Tw3F, Tw2B, P2, Tw2F, Tw3B, P1, rep from * to last 1[1:7] sts, P1[1:7].
19th row P4[6:2], *P2, Cr3F, P4, Cr3B, P2, rep from * to last 1[1:7] sts, P1[1:7].
21st row P4[6:2], *P1, Tw2B, Tw3F, P2, Tw3B, Tw2F, P1, rep from * to last 1[1:7] sts, P1[1:7].
23rd row P4[6:2], *Tw2B, P2, Tw3F, Tw3B, P2, Tw2F, rep from * to last 1[1:7] sts, P1[1:7].
24th row As 2nd row.
These 24 rows form the patt. Rep these 24 rows 4 more times.
Now cont in bobble patt as foll:
1st row (RS) P4[6:2], K1 tbl, *P5, K2, rep from * to last 7[7:13] sts, P5, K1 tbl, P1[1:7].
2nd and every other row K1[1:7], P1, K5, *P2, K5, rep from * to last 5[7:3] sts, P1, K4[6:2].
3rd row P4[6:2], K1 tbl, *P5, MB, K1, P5, K2, rep from * to last 14[14:20] sts, P5, MB, K1, P5, K1 tbl, P1[1:7].
5th row P4[6:2], K1 tbl, *P4, MB, K1, MB, P5, K2, rep from * to last 14[14:20] sts, P4, MB, K1, MB, P5, K1 tbl, P1[1:7].
7th row P4[6:2], K1 tbl, *P3, MB, P1, MB, K1, MB, P4, K2, rep from * to last 14[14:20] sts, P3, MB, P1, MB, K1, MB, P4, K1 tbl, P1[1:7].
9th row As first row.
11th row P4[6:2], K1 tbl, *P5, K2, P5, MB, K1, rep from * to last 14[14:20] sts, P5, K2, P5, K1 tbl, P1[1:7].
13th row P4[6:2], K1 tbl, *P5, K2, P4, MB, K1, MB, rep from * to last 14[14:20] sts, P5, K2, P5, K1 tbl, P1[1:7].
15th row P4[6:2], K1 tbl, P1, *P4, K2, P3, MB, P1, MB, K1, MB, rep from * to last 13[13:19] sts, P4, K2, P5, K1 tbl, P1[1:7].
16th row As 2nd row.
These 16 rows form bobble patt.
Shape armhole and neck
Next row Bind off 3 sts, patt to last 2 sts, P2 tog.
Patt 1 row.
Dec 1 st at neck edge on next and every other row, *at the same time*, dec 1 st at armhole edge on next

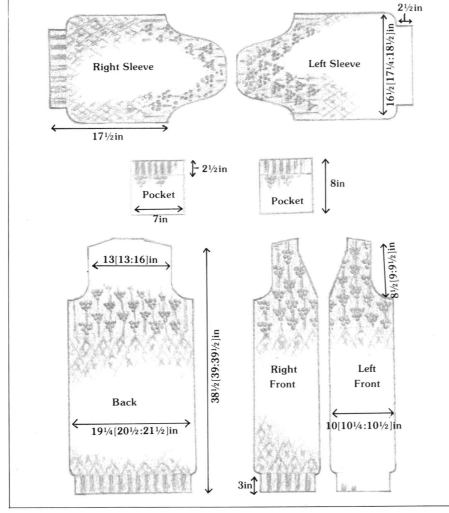

Right Sleeve

Left Sleeve

2½in

16½[17¼:18½]in

17½in

2½in

Pocket

7in

8in

Pocket

13[13:16]in

38½[39:39½]in

8½[9:9½]in

Back

19¼[20½:21½]in

Right Front

Left Front

10[10¼:10½]in

3in

7[7:5] rows, then on every other row until 22[20:29] sts rem.
Keeping armhole edge straight cont to dec at neck edge as before until 16[15:21] sts rem. Work even until work matches back to shoulder shaping, ending at armhole edge.

Shape shoulder
Bind off 8[8:11] sts at beg of next row.
Work 1 row.
Bind off rem 8[7:10] sts.

Right front
Work as for left front from ** to **.
Change to larger needles.
Beg patt.
1st row (RS) P1[1:7], K1 tbl, *P4, C4F, P4, C2Ftbl, rep from * to last 17[19:15] sts, P4, C4F, P4, K1 tbl, P4[6:2].
2nd and every other row K the P sts and P the K sts of previous row.
3rd row P1[1:7], *Tw2F, P2, Tw3B, Tw3F, P2, Tw2B, rep from * to last 4[6:2] sts, P4[6:2].
5th row P1[1:7], *P, Tw2F, Tw3B, P2, Tw3F, Tw2B, P1, rep from * to last 4[6:2] sts, P4[6:2].
7th row P1[1:7], *P2, Cr3B, P4, Cr3F, P2, rep from * to last 4[6:2] sts, P4[6:2].
9th row P1[1:7], *P1, Tw3B, Tw2F, P2, Tw2B, Tw3F, P1, rep from * to

last 4[6:2] sts, P4[6:2].
11th row P1[1:7], *Tw3B, P2, Tw2F, Tw2B, P2, Tw3F, rep from * to last 4[6:2] sts, P4[6:2].
13th row P1[1:7], K2, *P4, C2Btbl, P4, C4B, rep from * to last 16[18:14] sts, P4, C2Btbl, P4, K2, P to end.
15th row P1[1:7], *Tw3F, P2, Tw2B, Tw2F, P2, Tw3B, rep from * to last 4[6:2] sts, P4[6:2].
17th row P1[1:7], * P1, Tw3F, Tw2B, P2, Tw2F, Tw3B, P1, rep from * to last 4[6:2] sts, P4[6:2].
19th row P1[1:7], *P2, Cr3F, P4, Cr3B, P2, rep from * to last 4[6:2] sts, P4[6:2].
21st row P1[1:7], *P1, Tw2B, Tw3F, P2, Tw3B, Tw2F, P1, rep from * to last 4[6:2] sts, P4[6:2].
23rd row P1[1:7], *Tw2B, P2, Tw3F, Tw3B, P2, Tw2F, rep from * to last 4[6:2] sts, P4[6:2].
24th row As 2nd row.
These 24 rows form the patt. Rep these 24 rows 4 more times.
Now cont in bobble patt as foll:
1st row (RS) P1[1:7], K1 tbl, *P5, K2, rep from * to last 10[12:8] sts, P5, K1 tbl, P4[6:2].
2nd and every other row K4[6:2], P1, K5, *P2, K5, rep from * to last 2[2:8] sts, P1, K1[1:7].
3rd row P1[1:7], K1 tbl, *P5, MB,

K1, P5, K2, rep from * to last 17[19:15] sts, P5, MB, K1, P5, K1 tbl, P4[6:2].
5th row P1[1:7], K1 tbl, *P4, MB, K1, MB, P5, K2, rep from * to last 17[19:15] sts, P4, MB, K1, MB, P5, K1 tbl, P4[6:2].
7th row P1[1:7], K1 tbl, *P3, MB, P1, MB, K1, MB, P4, K2, rep from * to last 17[19:15] sts, P3, MB, P1, MB, K1, MB, P4, K1 tbl, P4[6:2].
9th row As first row.
11th row P1[1:7], K1 tbl, *P5, K2, P5, MB, K1, rep from * to last 17[19:15] sts, P5, K2, P5, K1 tbl, P4[6:2].
13th row P1[1:7], K1 tbl, *P5, K2, P4, MB, K1, MB, rep from * to last 17[19:15] sts, P5, K2, P5, K1 tbl, P4[6:2].
15th row P1[1:7], K1 tbl, P1, *P4, K2, P3, MB, P1, MB, K1, MB, rep from * to last 16[18:14] sts, P4, K2, P5, K1 tbl, P4[6:2].
16th row As 2nd row.
These 16 rows form the bobble patt. Complete to match left front, reversing all shapings.

Sleeves
Using smaller needles, cast on 30[34:34] sts. Work 2½in K2, P2 rib as for back, ending with a first row.
Next row Rib 1, *M1, rib 1, rep from

Special technique – sewing on a patch pocket

 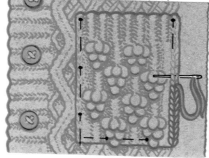 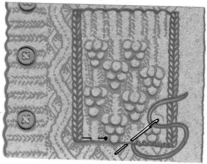

1 Patch pockets can be sewn on with decorative embroidery stitches such as cross stitch or blanket stitch, or as on the coat, almost invisibly. Position the pocket on the coat, matching the pocket pattern to that on the coat, then pin it in place.

2 Thread a tapestry needle with matching yarn and, working through both layers, work a vertical line of duplicate stitch (see page 28) through the edge stitches of the pocket on both sides.

3 Join the bottom edge of the pocket to the coat with neat overcasting. (On plain stockinette stitch pockets this join can also be made with duplicate stitch.)

* to end. 59[67:67] sts.
Next row K3[6:4], M1, *K3[4:3], M1, rep from * to last 2[5:3] sts, K to end. 78[82:88] sts.
Change to larger needles and beg patt as for back beg with a 13th patt row. Work 13th–24th rows once, then work first–24th rows again. Now work first–16th rows of bobble patt as for back.

Shape top
Keeping continuity of patt, bind off 3 sts at beg of next 2 rows. Dec 1 st at each end of next and every other row until 30[36:44] sts rem. Work 1 row.

2nd and 3rd sizes only
Dec 1 st at each end of every row until 30 sts rem. Work 1 row.

All sizes
Bind off.

Pockets (make 2)
Using larger needles, cast on 37 sts and work in patt as foll:
1st row (RS) K2, *P5, K2, rep from * to end.
2nd and every other row P2, *K5, P2, rep from * to end.
3rd row K2, (P5, MB, K1, P5, K2) twice, P5, K2.
5th row K2, (P4, MB, K1, MB, P5, K2) twice, P5, K2.

7th row K2, (P3, MB, P1, MB, K1, MB, P4, K2) twice, P5, K2.
9th row As first row.
11th row K2, (P5, K2, P5, MB, K1) twice, P5, K2.
13th row K2, (P5, K2, P4, MB, K1, MB) twice, P5, K2.
15th row K2, P1, (P4, K2, P3, MB, P1, MB, K1, MB) twice, P4, K2.
16th row As 2nd row.
Rep these 16 rows once more, dec 3 sts evenly across last row.
Change to smaller needles and work 2½in K2, P2 rib as for back.
Bind off in rib.

To finish
Join shoulders.

Button band
With RS of work facing, using circular needle, pick up and K 9[11:12] sts from center back neck to shoulder seam, 35[37:40] sts from shoulder seam to beg of neck shaping, then 114 sts from beg of neck shaping to cast-on edge. 158[162:166] sts.
Work in rows. Beg with a 2nd row work 15 rows K2, P2 rib as for back. Bind off in rib.

Buttonhole band
With RS of work facing, using smaller needles, pick up and K 114 sts from

cast-on edge to beg of neck shaping, 35[37:40] sts from beg of neck shaping to shoulder, and 9[11:12] sts from shoulder to center back neck. 158[162:166] sts.
Beg with a 2nd row work 7 rows K2, P2 rib as for back.
1st buttonhole row Rib 6, bind off 2 sts, *rib 8 (including st used in binding off), bind off 2, rep from * 9 more times, rib to end.
2nd buttonhole row Rib to end, casting on 2 sts over those bound off in previous row.
Rib a further 6 rows. Bind off in rib.
Join center back neck seam of bands. Join side and sleeve seams. Set in sleeves, easing fullness at top.
Sew on pockets. (See Special Technique.)
Sew on buttons.

Hat
Using smaller needles, cast on 74 sts.
1st row K2, *P2, K2, rep from *.
2nd row P2, *K2, P2, rep from *.
Rep last 2 rows for 8in, ending with a first row.
Next row Rib 19, (M1, rib 18) twice, M1, rib 19. 77 sts.
Change to larger needles.
Beg patt.
1st row (RS) K1, *P3, K1, rep from * to end.
2nd row P1, *K3, P1, rep from *.
Rep these 2 rows until work measures 14in, ending with a WS row.

Shape crown
1st row K1, *P2 tog, P1, K1, rep from * to end. 58 sts.
2nd row P1, *K2, P1, rep from *.
3rd row K1, *P2, K1, rep from *.
4th row As 2nd row.
5th row K1, *P2 tog, K1, rep from * to end. 39 sts.
6th row P1, *K1, P1, rep from *.
7th row K1, *P1, K1, rep from *.
8th row As 6th row.
9th row K1, *K2 tog, rep from * to end. 20 sts.
10th row (P2 tog) 10 times. 10 sts.
Break yarn, thread through rem sts, draw up, and fasten off.

To finish
Join seam, reversing K2, P2 ribbing section to roll back. Roll brim onto RS and sew in place.

Lacy Patterns

Knitting is such a versatile craft: it can produce the thick crunchy textures of cable patterns but also the fine delicacy of lace. Lace knitting is often thought to be impossibly difficult, and it is true that there are some lace stitch patterns that demand a high degree of skill. However, there are many others that are well within the capabilities of most average knitters. Lace knitting is based largely on a technique known as "decorative increasing" (see page 20) and on basic eyelet formations (page 26). It's worthwhile persevering with these skills since the results are so impressive.

The patterns in the following pages include several lacy garments that are quite easy and would make sensible starting points for newcomers to this type of knitting. The openwork sweater on page 70 and the striped lace top on page 77 come into this category. The exquisite lace collar on page 80, on the other hand, should be attempted only by experienced knitters.

Frilly Bedjacket

This extravagantly pretty bedjacket is knitted in a lacy chevron pattern and bordered with a deep lace edging. The harmonizing ribbon ties are further decorated with tiny beads and sequins.

Sizes
To fit 34–36 [38–40]in bust
Length 25½in including edging
Sleeve seam 18½in including edging

Note Instructions for the larger size are in brackets []; where there is only one set of figures it applies to both sizes.

Gauge
24 sts and 34 rows to 4in over st st on size 2 needles

Materials
16[18]oz fingering yarn
1 pair size 2 knitting needles
4½yd narrow satin ribbon
Beads or sequins to trim ribbon ties

Back
Using knitting needles, cast on 137[154] sts.
**Beg patt.
1st row (WS) P.
2nd row K1, *(yo, sl 1, K1, psso, K4, K2 tog) twice, yo, K1, rep from * to end.
3rd row P8, *K1, P15, rep from * to last 9 sts, K1, P8.
4th row K1, *yo, sl 1, K1, psso, K3, K2 tog, yo, P1, yo, sl 1, K1, psso, K3, K2 tog, yo, K1, rep from * to end.
5th row P7, *K3, P13, rep from * to last 10 sts, K3, P7.
6th row K1, *yo, sl 1, K1, psso, K2, K2 tog, yo, P3, yo, sl 1, K1, psso, K2, K2 tog, yo, K1, rep from * to end.
7th row P6, *K5, P11, rep from * to last 11 sts, K5, P6.
8th row K1, *yo, sl 1, K1, psso, K1, K2 tog, yo, K1, yo, P3 tog, yo, K1, yo, sl 1, K1, psso, K1, K2 tog, yo, K1, rep from * to end.
9th row P8, *K into front and back of next st, P15, rep from * to last 9 sts, K into front and back of next st, P8.
10th row K1, *yo, sl 1, K1, psso, K2 tog, yo, K8, yo, sl 1, K1, psso, K2 tog, yo, K1, rep from * to end.
11th row P.
12th row K1, *yo, sl 1, K2 tog, psso, yo, K10, yo, K3 tog, yo, K1, rep from * to end.
These 12 rows form the patt. Rep them 15 more times.
Bind off**.

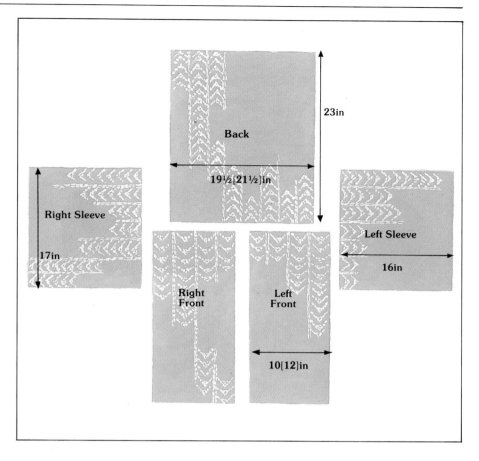

Left and right front (alike)
Using knitting needles, cast on 69[86] sts. Work as for back from ** to **.

Sleeves
Using knitting needles, cast on 120 sts. Cont in patt as for back. Rep the 12 patt rows 11 times.
Bind off loosely.

Sleeve edging (make 2)
***Using knitting needles, cast on 11 sts. K one row. Beg patt.
1st row K3, yo, K2 tog, K1, sl 1, K1, psso, cast on 4 sts, K2 tog, K1. 13 sts.
2nd row K10, yo, K2 tog, K1.
3rd row K3, yo, K2 tog, sl 1, K1, psso, (yo, K1) 4 times, yo, K2 tog. 16 sts.
4th row K13, yo, K2 tog, K1.
5th row K3, yo, K2 tog, sl 1, K1, psso, (yo, K1) twice, yo, sl 1, K2 tog, psso, (yo, K1) twice, yo, K2 tog. 18 sts.
6th row K15, yo, K2 tog, K1.
7th row K3, yo, K2 tog, K11, K2 tog. 17 sts.

8th row Bind off 6 sts, K7, yo, K2 tog, K1. 11 sts.
These 8 rows form the patt. ***Rep the last 8 rows until edging fits edge of sleeve. Bind off.

Front and hem edging (one piece)
Work as for sleeve edging from *** to ***.
Rep the last 8 rows until work measures 103in. Bind off.

To finish
Press. Join shoulder seams, matching patt and making a 3in tuck, 1 patt rep wide, on front shoulder.
Mark 8½in down from shoulders on back and front. Set in sleeves between markers. Join side and sleeve seams. Sew on sleeve edging. Beg at center back hem edge, sew on front and hem edging, gathering slightly at corners and across back neck.
Thread ribbon through lace patt at wrists and waistline. Decorate ribbon ends with beads or sequins.

Party Dress and Pinafore

This gorgeous party dress, straight from the pages of a
fairy tale, will delight any little girl. The dress is trimmed
with two layers of bell-like ruffles. The matching over-
pinafore is knitted in a delicate eyelet pattern with lacy
edging around the hem and yoke.

Sizes
Dress
To fit 23[24:25]in chest
Length 18[19¼:20]in
Sleeve seam 2½in
Pinafore
To fit 23–25in chest
Length 18in

Note Instructions for larger sizes are in brackets []; where there is only one set of figures it applies to all sizes.

Gauge
Dress
28 sts and 32 rows to 4in over st st on size 2 needles
Pinafore
32 sts and 40 rows to 4in over st st on size 1 needles

Materials
Dress
13[13:15]oz size 5 silky cotton yarn, such as Pingouin Fil d'Ecosse No. 5
1 pair each sizes 1 and 2 knitting needles
3 buttons
Ribbon (optional)

Pinafore
13oz size 5 silky cotton yarn
1 pair size 1 knitting needles
2 buttons
Ribbon (optional)

Dress
Back
Using larger needles cast on 160[168:176] sts.
Next row *K1 tbl, P1, rep from * to end.
Rep the last row until work measures ⅜in.
Beg patt.
1st row P4, * cast on 10 sts onto RH needle, P8, rep from * ending last rep P4.
2nd row K4, *P10, K8, rep from * ending last rep K4.
3rd row P4, *K10, P8, rep from * ending last rep P4.
4th row As 2nd row.
5th row As 3rd row.
6th row As 2nd row.
7th row P4, *sl 1, K1, psso, K6, K2 tog, P8, rep from * ending last rep P4.
8th row K4, *P8, K8, rep from *

ending last rep K4.
9th row P4, *sl 1, K1, psso, K4, K2 tog, P8, rep from * ending last rep P4.
10th row K4, *P6, K8, rep from * ending last rep K4.
11th row P4, * sl 1, K1, psso, K2, K2 tog, P8, rep from * ending last rep P4.
12th row K4, *P4, K8, rep from * ending last rep K4.
13th row P4, *sl 1, K1, psso, K2 tog, P8, rep from * ending last rep P4.
14th row K4, *P2, K8, rep from * ending last rep K4.
15th row P4, *K2 tog, P8, rep from * ending last rep P4.
16th row K4, *P1, K8, rep from * ending last rep K4.
17th row P3, *K2 tog, P7, rep from * ending last rep P4.
18th row K to end.
These 18 rows form the patt. Work a further 18 rows.
Change to st st. Beg with a K row work a further 1½[2:2½]in, ending with a P row.
This point marks "hipline" – skirt length may be adjusted here.
Next row K2[0:1], *K1, K2 tog, rep from * to last 2[0:1] sts, K2[0:1]. 108[112:118] sts.
Next row P.
Next row K10[1:4], *K2[3:3], K2 tog, rep from * to last 10[1:4] sts, K10[1:4]. 86[90:96] sts.
Beg with a P row cont in st st until work measures 14[15¼:16]in from the beg, ending with a P row. Length to armhole may be adjusted here.
Shape armholes
Bind off 6[8:11] sts at beg of next 2 rows and 2 sts at beg of foll 4 rows. 66 sts.**
Cont in st st until work measures 18[19¼:20]in, ending with a P row.
Shape shoulders
Bind off 4 sts at beg of next 4 rows and 10 sts at beg of foll 2 rows.
Bind off the rem sts.

Front
Work as for back to **. Cont in st st until work measures 16[17¼:18]in, ending with a P row.
Shape neck
Next row K22, bind off 22 sts, K to end.

Work right side of neck first.
Next row P to last 2 sts, P2 tog.
Next row K2 tog, K to end.
Rep the last 2 rows once more. 18 sts. Beg with a P row cont in st st until work matches back to shoulder shaping, ending at armhole edge.
Shape shoulder
Bind off 4 sts at beg of the next and every other row once. Work 1 row. Bind off rem sts. Return to sts on left side of neck. With WS facing, rejoin yarn to next st.
Next row P2 tog, P to end.
Next row K to last 2 sts, K2 tog.
Rep the last 2 rows once more. Complete to match first side of neck, reversing shaping.

Sleeves
Using smaller needles cast on 60 sts.
Next row *K1 tbl, P1, rep from *.
Rep the last row until work measures 1¼in.
Change to larger needles.
Next row *K twice into next st, rep from * to end. 120 sts.
Beg with a P row, cont in st st until work measures 2½in, ending with a P row. Sleeve length may be adjusted here.
Shape sleeve top
Bind off 8 sts at beg of next 2 rows and 2 sts at beg of foll 4 rows. 96 sts.
Dec 1 st at each end of every row until 48 sts rem. Bind off 6 sts at beg of next 4 rows.
Bind off the rem 24 sts.

Detachable collar
Using larger needles cast on 18 sts.
Next row (WS) K6, P7, K5.
Beg patt.
1st row Sl 1, K2, yo, K2 tog, K2, K2 tog, yo, K5, yo, K2 tog, (yo, K1) twice.
2nd row K6, yo, K2 tog, P7, K2, yo, K2 tog, K1.
3rd row Sl 1, K2, yo, K2 tog, K1, (K2 tog, yo) twice, K4, yo, K2 tog, (yo, K1) twice, K2.
4th row K8, yo, K2 tog, P7, K2, yo, K2 tog, K1.
5th row Sl 1, K2, yo, K2 tog, (K2 tog, yo) 3 times, K3, yo, K2 tog, (yo, K1) twice, K4.
6th row K10, yo, K2 tog, P7, K2, yo, K2 tog, K1.
7th row Sl 1, K2, yo, K2 tog, K1,

(K2 tog, yo) twice, K4, yo, K2 tog, (yo, K1) twice, K6.
8th row Bind off 8 sts, K4 including st used in binding off, yo, K2 tog, P7, K2, yo, K2 tog, K1.
These 8 rows form the patt.
Rep these 8 rows 14 more times.
* * * Cont in garter st (every row K). Bind off 4 sts at beg of next 2 rows. Dec 1 st at each end of the next and every other row until 2 sts rem.
Next row K2 tog and fasten off.
With RS of work facing, pick up and K 10 sts from cast-on edge.
Work from * * * to end.

To finish
Join right shoulder seam.

Neckband
With RS of work facing, using smaller needles pick up and K 84 sts evenly around neck edge.
Work in rib as for back for ⅜in, ending with a WS row. Bind off in rib. Press lightly if appropriate for yarn used, taking care not to flatten patt. Join side seams, matching patt.

Sew together ⅜in at armhole edge of left shoulder seam. Join sleeve seams, set in sleeves gathering sleeve cap to fit. Sew buttons to front shoulder and make button loops to correspond.
Pin collar to a curve to fit neck edge and press firmly. Either thread ribbon through eyelet holes on collar or make a braided cord.

Pinafore
Back
Using smaller needles cast on 336 sts.
Beg with a K row work 5 rows in st st.
Next row * P2 tog, rep from * to end. 168 sts.
Beg patt.
1st row K.
2nd and every other row P.
3rd row *K6, yo, K2 tog, rep from * to end.
5th row K.
7th row K2, * yo, K2 tog, K6, rep from * ending last rep K4.
8th row P.
These 8 rows form the patt. Cont in patt until work measures 9in, ending

with an 8th patt row. Pinafore length may be adjusted here.
Next row (RS) *K2 tog, rep from * to end. 84 sts.
Next row P. * *
Next row *K1 tbl, P1, rep from * to end.
Rep the last row 5 more times.
Bind off in rib.

Front
Work as for back to * *.
1st row (K1, tbl, P1) 10 times, K7, (yo, K2 tog, K6) 4 times, yo, K2 tog, K3, (P1, K1 tbl) 10 times.
2nd row (P1, K1 tbl) 10 times, P44, (K1 tbl, P1) 10 times.
3rd row (K1 tbl, P1) 10 times, K44, (P1, K1 tbl) 10 times.
4th row As 2nd row.
5th row (K1 tbl, P1) 10 times, K3, (yo, K2 tog, K6) 5 times, K1, (P1, K1 tbl) 10 times.
6th row As 2nd row.
7th row Bind off 20 sts in rib, K to last 20 sts, (P1, K1 tbl) 10 times.
8th row Bind off 20 sts in rib, P to end. 44 sts.

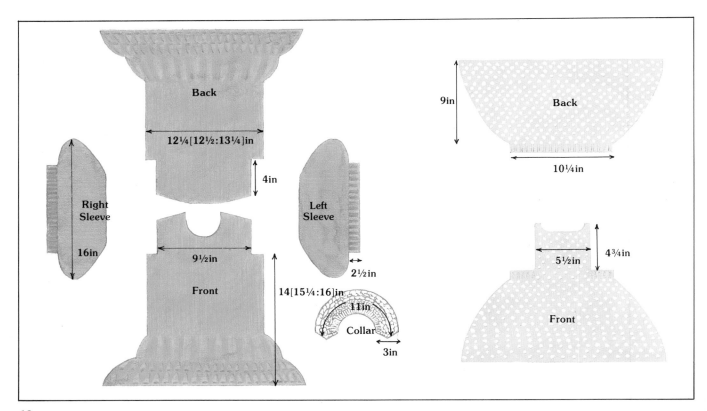

Cont in patt.
1st row (RS) K1, *K6, yo, K2 tog, rep from * to last 3 sts, K3.
2nd and every other row P.
3rd row K.
5th row K3, yo, K2 tog, *K6, yo, K2 tog, rep from * to last 7 sts, K7.
7th row K.
8th row P.
These 8 rows form the patt. Rep these 8 rows 4 more times, ending with an 8th patt row. Length of pinafore may be adjusted here.
Shape neck
Next row K8, bind off 28 sts, K to end. Complete right side of neck first.
Next row P to last 2 sts, P2 tog.
Next row K2 tog, K to end.
Rep the last 2 rows twice.
Bind off rem 2 sts.
Return to sts at left side of neck. With WS of work facing, rejoin yarn to next st.
Next row P2 tog, P to end.
Next row K to last 2 sts, K2 tog.
Rep the last 2 rows twice.
Bind off rem 2 sts.

Hem edging (Make 2 pieces)
The pieces are worked sideways.

Using smaller needles cast on 18 sts.
Next row (WS) K6, P7, K5.
Beg patt.
1st row Sl 1, K2, yo, K2 tog, K2, K2 tog, yo, K5, yo, K2 tog, (yo, K1) twice.
2nd row K6, yo, K2 tog, P7, K2, yo, K2 tog, K1.
3rd row Sl 1, K2, yo, K2 tog, K1, K2 tog, yo) twice, K4, yo, K2 tog, (yo, K1) twice, K2.
4th row K8, yo, K2 tog, P7, K2, yo, K2 tog, K1.
5th row Sl 1, K2, yo, K2 tog, (K2 tog, yo) 3 times, K3, yo, K2 tog, (yo, K1) twice, K4.
6th row K10, yo, K2 tog, P7, K2, yo, K2 tog, K1.
7th row Sl 1, K2, yo, K2 tog, K1, (K2 tog, yo) twice, K4, yo, K2 tog, (yo, K1) twice, K6.
8th row Bind off 8 sts, K3, yo, K2 tog, P7, K2, yo, K2 tog, K1.
These 8 rows form the patt.
Rep first–8th rows 41 more times.
Bind off.

Yoke edging (make 2 pieces)
Work as for hem edging for 16in ending with an 8th patt row. Bind off.

Neckband and straps
Using smaller needles cast on 8 sts.
Next row *K1 tbl, P1, rep from * to end.
Rep last row until work measures ³⁄₈in.
1st buttonhole row Rib 3, bind off 2, rib to end.
2nd buttonhole row Rib, casting on over those sts bound off in previous row.
Cont in rib until work measures 19½in from the beg, ending with a WS row. Length may be adjusted here.
Now work the 2 buttonhole rows again.
Work a further ³⁄₈in in rib.
Bind off in rib.

To finish
Press as appropriate for yarn used.
Join hem edging pieces and sew to hem. Sew neckband to yoke. Sew edging to yoke and band, gathering slightly.
Cut ribbon into 4, or make 4 simple braided cords and sew to pinafore at underarms.
Sew buttons to waistband at center back.

Special technique – making buttonholes

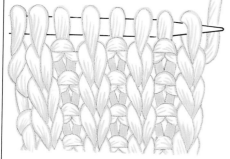

1 The back straps of the pinafore are fastened with a small buttonhole on the end of each one, buttoning two buttons on the back waistband. Work in twisted rib to the buttonhole row.

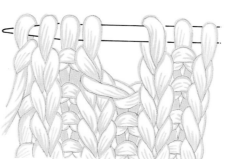

2 On the next row work to the buttonhole position. Bind off 2 stitches (more stitches can be bound off for a larger buttonhole). Work to the next buttonhole position or to end of row.

3 On the next row work to the buttonhole position. Cast onto the right-hand needle the same number of stitches as were bound off on the previous row. Work to next buttonhole position or end of row.

Openwork Sweater

This lovely sweater is knitted in a cool cotton yarn. Its
fresh, crisp look is accentuated by a geometric arrangement
of faggot stitch motifs crossed by garter stitch ridges.

Sizes
To fit 32[34:36:38]in bust
Length 22 [22½:23:23½]in
Sleeve seam 17in
Note Instructions for larger sizes are in brackets []; where there is only one set of figures it applies to all sizes.

Gauge
22 sts and 30 rows to 4in over st st on size 5 needles

Materials
26[28:28:30]oz of a thick cotton yarn such as Neveda Double Cotton
1 pair each sizes 3 and 5 knitting needles

Back
Using smaller needles, cast on 86 [94:98:106] sts. Work in K2, P2 rib as foll:
1st row (RS) *K2, P2, rep from * to last 2 sts, K2.
2nd row *P2, K2, rep from * to last 2 sts, P2. Rep the last 2 rows for 2½in, ending with a WS row.
Next row Rib 8[9:13:10], pick up loop between needles and work into the back of it − called M1 −, (rib 14 [15:24:17], M1) 5[6:3:5] times, rib 8 [10:13:11]. 92[100:102:112] sts. Change to larger needles and beg patt.
1st row (WS) P.
2nd row P.
3rd row K.
4th row K2 [2:3:0], *K1, (yo, K2 tog tbl) 3 times, K1, rep from * to last 2[2:3:0] sts, K2[2:3:0].
5th, 7th, 9th and 11th rows P.
6th row K2[2:3:0], *K2, (yo, K2 tog tbl) twice, K2, rep from * to last 2 [2:3:0] sts, K2[2:3:0].
8th row K2[2:3:0], *K3, yo, K2 tog tbl, K3, rep from * to last 2[2:3:0] sts, K2[2:3:0].
10th row As 6th row.
12th row As 4th row.
Rep the last 12 rows working K2 tog, yo instead of yo, K2 tog tbl.
The last 24 rows form the patt. Cont in patt until work measures 14½ [14½:15:15]in, ending with a WS row.

Shape armholes
Bind off 11 sts at beg of next 2 rows. 70[78:80:90] sts.
Work even until work measures 22[22½:23:23½]in from beg, ending with a WS row.

Shape shoulders
Bind off 7[7:7:9] sts at beg of next 2 rows and 6[8:8:9] sts at beg of foll 4 rows. Leave rem 32[32:34:36] sts on a spare needle.

Front
Work as for back until work measures 36[40:42:46] rows less than back to shoulder shaping, ending with a WS row.

Divide for neck
Next row Patt 19[23:23:27], turn, leaving rem sts on a spare needle. Complete left side of neck first.

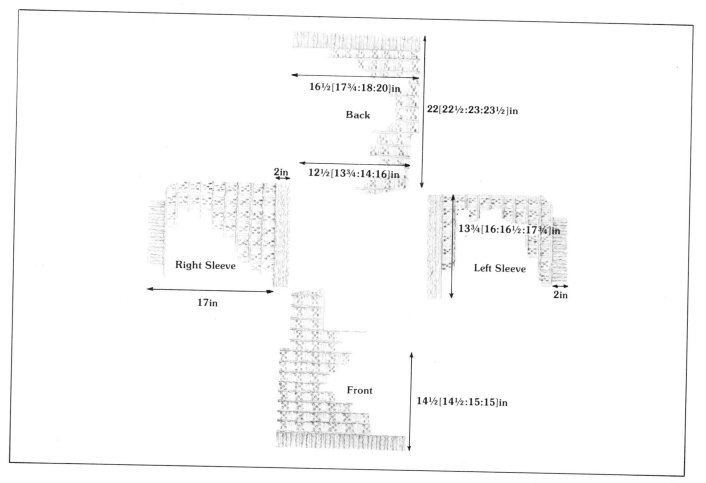

16½[17¾:18:20]in

Back

22[22½:23:23½]in

2in 12½[13¾:14:16]in

Right Sleeve

17in

13¾[16:16½:17¾]in

Left Sleeve

2in

Front

14½[14½:15:15]in

Work even until work matches back to shoulder shaping, ending at armhole edge.

Shape shoulder
Bind off 7[7:7:9] sts at beg of next row and 6[8:8:9] sts at beg of every other row once.
Patt 1 row. Bind off rem 6[8:8:9] sts.
With RS of work facing, return to sts on spare needle, sl center 32 [32:34:36] sts onto a stitch holder, rejoin yarn to next st, patt to end.
Complete to match first side of neck reversing shaping.

Sleeves
Using smaller needles, cast on 38 [42:42:46] sts and work in K2, P2 rib as for back, for 2in, ending with a WS row.
Next row (Work 3 times into next st) 2[3:4:4] times, *work twice into next st, rep from * to last 2[3:4:4] sts, (work 3 times into next st) 2[3:4:4] times. 80[90:92:100] sts.
Change to larger needles.
Beg patt.
1st row (WS) P.
2nd row P.

3rd row K.
4th row K0[1:2:2] *K1, (yo, K2 tog tbl) 3 times, K1, rep from * to last 0[1:2:2] sts, K0[1:2:2].
5th, 7th 9th and 11th rows P.
6th row K0[1:2:2], *K2, (yo, K2 tog tbl) twice, K2, rep from * to last 0[1:2:2] sts, K0[1:2:2].
8th row K0[1:2:2], *K3, yo, K2 tog tbl, K3, rep from * to last 0[1:2:2] sts, K0[1:2:2].
10th row As 6th row.
12th row As 4th row.
Rep the last 12 rows working K2 tog, yo instead of yo, K2 tog tbl.
The last 24 rows form the patt. Cont in patt until work measures approx 17in from beg, ending with a 12th patt row.
Change to smaller needles and cont in garter st (every row K) for 2in, ending with an RS row.
Bind off loosely.

To finish
Darn in yarn ends neatly.
Omitting garter st borders, press lightly on WS if appropriate for yarn used.
Using a backstitch seam join right

shoulder seam.

Neck border
With RS of work facing, using smaller needles, pick up and K 20[21:21:22] sts down left side of neck, pick up and K 1 st from corner (mark this st with a contrasting thread), K across the 32[32:34:36] sts from front neck, pick up and K 1 st from corner (mark this st with a contrasting thread), pick up and K 20[21:21:22] sts up right side of neck, K across 32[32:34:36] sts from back neck. 106[108:112:118] sts.
Next row (K to within 2sts of marker, K2 tog, K1, K2 tog) twice, K to end.
Next row K.
Rep the last 2 rows until 90 [92:96:102] sts rem, ending with a RS row.
Bind off loosely, dec on this row as before.
Join left shoulder and neck border. Place center of bound-off edge of sleeve at shoulder seam and set in sleeve, joining garter st section of sleeve to bound-off sts at underarm. Join side and sleeve seams.

Special technique – garter-stitch mitered corners

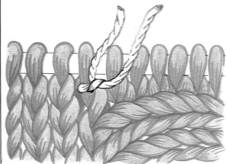

1 The corners of the square neckband on the sweater are mitered. Pick up and knit the stitches around the neck edge as instructed in the pattern, marking the corner stitch with a contrasting thread.

2 On the next row knit to within two stitches of the corner stitch, then knit two together, knit one, knit two together. Work the next corner stitch in the same way.

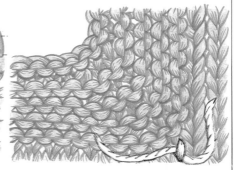

3 Knit the next row. Repeat the last two rows until the neckband is the required depth. Bind off loosely, decreasing at the corners as before.

Mohair Shawl

This long, luxurious shawl will add a sparkle to any party.
Wrap it loosely around your neck and shoulders, leaving
the pompoms to hang freely and you will see how naturally
the folds of the shawl will fall.

Shawl
85in from end to end

Gauge
8 sts and 7 rows to 4in over mesh
patt worked on size 13 needles.

Materials
11oz mohair with glitter in main color
(A)
1oz in 3 contrasting colors (for
pompons)
1 pair size 13 knitting needles
Artificial flowers (for decoration)

Shawl
Using knitting needles and A, cast on
3 sts.
Next row K.
Next row K.
Cont in garter st (every row K), inc 1
st at beg of next and every other row
until there are 12 sts.
Next row K.
1st row K into front and back of first
st – called inc 1 –, K4, yo, K2 tog,
K5.
2nd row K5, P to last 5 sts, K5.
3rd row Inc 1, K4, yo, K2 tog, K6.
**4th, 6th, 8th, 10th, 12th and 14th
rows** As 2nd row.
5th row Inc 1, K4, (yo, K2 tog)
twice, K5.
7th row Inc 1, K4, (yo, K2 tog)
twice, K6.
9th row Inc 1, K4, (yo, K2 tog) 3
times, K5.
11th row Inc 1, K4, * yo, K2 tog,
rep from * to last 6 sts, K6.
13th row Inc 1, K4 * yo, K2 tog, rep
from * to last 5 sts, K5.
Rep 11th–14th rows until there are
79 sts on needle.
Next row K2 tog, K4, * yo, K2 tog,
rep from * to last 5 sts, K5.
Next row As 2nd row.
Next row K2 tog, K4 * yo, K2 tog,
rep from * to last 6 sts, K6.
Next row As 2nd row.
Rep last 4 rows until there are 13 sts
on needle.

Next row K2 tog, K4, yo, K2 tog,
K5.
Next row K5, P2, K5.
Cont in g st, dec 1 st at beg of next
and every other row until 3 sts rem.
K one row. Bind off.

To finish
Make six pompoms in a variety of
colors. Attach them to the corners
of the shawl with braided cords of
varying lengths. Wind artificial flowers
into the pompoms.

Bobble Lace Sweater

An openwork chevron stitch pattern dotted with tiny bobbles creates a delightfully pretty top in a light, cool cotton yarn. It can be knitted with long or short sleeves.

Sizes

To fit 34[36]in bust
Length 21[21½]in
Short sleeve seam 6in
Long sleeve seam 17½in

Gauge

28 sts and 32 rows to 4in over patt on size 3 needles

Materials

Short sleeve version
15oz size 5 silky cotton yarn, such as Pingouin Fil d'Ecosse No. 5
Long sleeve version
16oz size 5 silky cotton yarn
1 pair each sizes 2 and 3 knitting needles
Size B crochet hook
2 small buttons

Back

Using smaller needles cast on 100[120] sts, working into the back of every st for a firm edge.
Work 33 rows K2, P2 rib.
Next row Rib 10, *work into the front and back of next st, rib 3[4], rep from * to last 10 sts, work into the front and back of next st, rib to end. 121[141] sts.
Change to larger needles and patt.
1st row K1, *yo, sl 1, K1, psso, K15, K2 tog, yo, K1, rep from * to end.
2nd row P2, *yo, P2 tog, P13, P2 tog tbl, yo, P3, rep from * to last 19 sts, yo, P2 tog, P13, P2 tog, yo, P2.
3rd row K3, *yo, sl 1, K1, psso, K11 K2 tog, yo, K5, rep from * to last 18 sts, yo, sl 1, K1, psso, K11, K2 tog, yo, K3.
4th row P4, *yo, P2 tog, P9, P2 tog tbl, yo, P7, rep from * to last 17 sts, yo, P2 tog, P9, P2 tog, yo, P4.
5th row K5, *yo, sl 1, K1, psso, K3, (K1, P1, K1, P1, K1) all into next st, turn, K5, turn, bind off 4 – called make bobble (MB), K3, K2 tog, yo, K9, rep from * to last 16 sts, yo, sl 1, K1, psso, K3, MB, K3, K2 tog, yo, K5.
6th row P6, *yo, P2 tog, P5, P2 tog tbl, yo, P11, rep from * to last 15 sts, yo, P2 tog, P5, P2 tog, yo, P6.
7th row K7, *yo, sl 1, K1, psso, K3,

K2 tog, yo, K6, MB, K6, rep from * to last 14 sts, yo, sl 1, K1, psso, K3, K2 tog, yo, K7.
8th row P8, *yo, P2 tog, P1, P2 tog tbl, yo, P15, rep from * to last 13 sts, yo, P2 tog, P1, P2 tog, yo, P8.
9th row K9, *yo, sl 1, K2 tog, psso, yo, K17, rep from * to last 12 sts, yo, sl 1, K2 tog, psso, yo, K9.
10th row P to end.
These 10 rows form the patt. Cont in patt until work measures 14in from the beg, ending with a WS row.
Shape armholes
Keeping patt correct bind off 6[8] sts at beg of the next 2 rows and 5 sts at beg of foll 2[4] rows. 99[105] sts.**
Work even until work measures 7[7½]in from beg of armhole shaping, ending with a WS row.
Shape shoulders
Bind off 10[11] sts at beg of next 6 rows.
Bind off rem 39 sts.

Front

Work as for back to **.
Work even until work measures

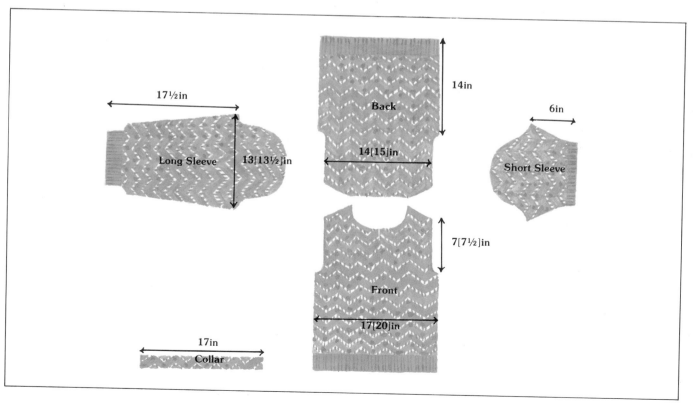

4[4½]in from beg of armhole shaping, ending with a WS row.

Divide for neck

Next row Patt 49[52], turn and leave rem sts on a spare needle. Complete left side of neck first.

Work even until work measures 5½[6]in from the beg of armhole shaping, ending at neck edge.

Bind off 5 sts at beg of next and every other row once.

Dec 1 st at neck edge on every row until 30[33] sts rem.

Work even until work matches back exactly to beg of shoulder shaping, ending with a WS row.

Shape shoulder

Bind off 10[11] sts at beg of next and every other row once.

Work 1 row. Bind off.

Return to sts on spare needle. With RS facing, join yarn to next st, cast off 1 st and patt to end.

Complete to match first side, reversing shaping.

Short sleeves

Using smaller needles cast on 80 sts.

Work 10 rows K2, P2 rib, inc 1 st at end of last row. 81 sts.

Change to larger needles and patt as for back, inc and work into st st 1 st at each end of the 3rd and every foll 4th row until there are 91[95] sts. Work even until work measures 6in from beg, ending with a WS row.

Shape top

Bind off 2 sts at beg of every row until 21 sts rem.

Bind off.

Long sleeves

Using smaller needles cast on 64 sts. Work 31 rows K2, P2 rib.

Next row Rib 8, *work into front and back of next st, rib 2, rep from * to last 8 sts, work into front and back of next st, rib to end. 81 sts.

Change to larger needles and patt as for back, inc and work into st st 1 st at each end of every foll 10th row until there are 91[95] sts. Work even until work measures 17½in beg, ending with a WS row.

Shape top

Bind of 2 sts at beg of every row until

21 sts rem.

Bind off.

Collar

Using larger needles cast on 121 sts. Cont in patt as for back until work measures 2in, ending with a WS row. Bind off.

To finish

Do not press. Darn in yarn ends neatly. Join shoulder seams. Set in sleeves. Join side and sleeve seams. Slipstitch the cast-on edge of collar to neck edge.

Collar edging

Join yarn to collar at neck edge. Using the crochet hook, work edging as foll: * 1sc in next st, skip next st, 3dc in next st, skip next st, rep from * around collar, then work 1 row of sc around neck opening. Sl st in each sc down first side of opening, then work two 2-ch button loops on other side of opening.

Sew buttons in place on the front opening.

Special technique – working the bobble

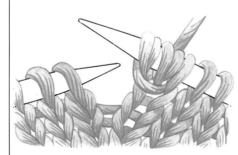

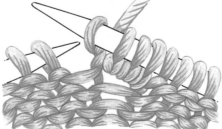

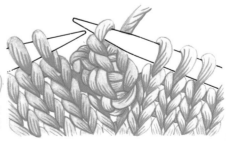

1 All bobbles are made by increasing several times into one stitch. In this case knit, purl, knit, purl, then knit again all into one stitch, making five stitches out of one.

2 Turn the work and hold the RH needle in the left hand and the LH needle in the right hand. Knit the five stitches made from one stitch.

3 Turn the work again. Bind off four of the five stitches. The bobble is now complete. Continue working in pattern to the next bobble.

Striped Lace Top

This pretty pastel-striped sweater, perfect for summer, can be worn on or off the shoulder, and it is made in a marvelously practical thick cotton yarn. The lacy pattern looks impressive but is very easy to work.

Sizes
To fit 34[36:38]in bust
Length 21½[22:22]in
Note Instructions for larger sizes are in brackets []; where there is only one set of figures it applies to all three sizes.

Gauge
20 sts and 28 rows to 4in over st st on size 5 needles

Materials
13[16:20]oz thick cotton yarn such as Scheepjeswol Mayflower Cotton Helårsgarn in main color (A)
5[8:8]oz thick cotton yarn in constrasing color (B)
8[8:12]oz in contrasting color (C)
8[12:12]oz in contrasting color (D)
1 pair each sizes 3 and 5 knitting needles
1 each sizes 3 and 5 circular needles

Back and front (alike)
Using smaller needles and A, cast on 96[102:106] sts.
Work 3in K1, P1 rib.
Next row Rib 9[12:14], *work twice into next st, rib 18, rep from * ending last rep rib 10[13:15]. 101[107:111] sts.
Change to larger needles and beg patt. Use small, separate balls of yarn for each color section, twist yarns when changing color to prevent a hole.
1st row (RS) K4[7:4]C, K2A, *with B, K5, yo, sl 1, K1, psso, K4, K2A*, rep from * to * using D instead of B, rep from * to * using C instead of B, rep from * to *, rep from * to * using C instead of B, rep from * to *

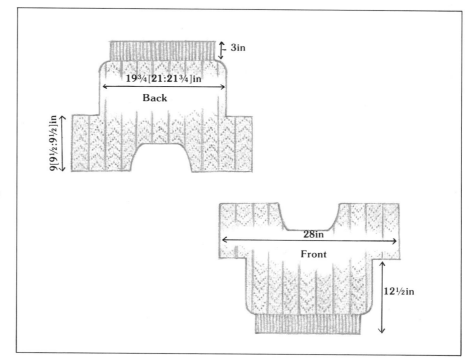

using D instead of B, rep from * to *, K4[7:9]C.
2nd and every other row K1, P to last st, K1 keeping sections of color as set.
3rd row K4[7:9]C, K2A, * with B, K3, K2 tog, yo, K1, yo, sl 1, K1, psso, K3, K2A*, rep from * to * using D instead of B, rep from * to * using C instead of B, rep from * to *, rep from * to * using C instead of B, rep from * to * using D instead of B, rep from * to *, K4[7:9]C.
5th row K4[7:9]C, K2A, *with B, K2, K2 tog, yo, K3, yo, sl 1, K1, psso, K2, K2A*, rep from * to *

using D instead of B, rep from * to * using C instead of B, rep from * to *, rep from * to * using C instead of B, rep from * to * using D instead of B, rep from * to *, K4[7:9]C.
7th row K4[7:9]C, K2A, *with B, K1, K2 tog, yo, K5, yo, sl 1, K1, psso, K1, K2A*, rep from * to * using D instead of B, rep from * to * using C instead of B, rep from * to *, rep from * to * using C instead of B, rep from * to * using D instead of B, rep from * to *, K4[7:9]C.
8th row As 2nd row.
These 8 rows form the patt. Cont in patt until work measures about

12½in, ending with a 4th patt row.
Shape sleeves
Next row Cast on 21[18:16] sts, work across these sts as foll: K1D, using D instead of B, work as given for 5th row from * to *, using C instead of B work as for 5th row from * to *, patt to end.
Next row Cast on 21[18:16] sts, work across these sts as foll: K1D, P11D, P2A, P11C, patt to end. 143 sts.
Keeping patt correct, work even until work measures 4¾in from beg of sleeve shaping, ending with a WS row.
Shape neck
Next row Patt 56, turn, leaving rem sts on a spare needle.
Complete left side of neck first.
Keeping patt correct, dec 1 st at neck

edge on foll 10 rows. 46 sts.
Work even until work measures 9[9½:9½]in from beg of sleeve shaping, ending with a WS row.
Bind off.
Return to sts on spare needle. Sl center 31 sts onto a st holder, join in appropriate yarn to next st, patt to end.
Complete to match first side of neck.

To finish
Join shoulder seams.
Collar
With RS of work facing, using smaller circular needle and A, pick up and K 30[32:32] sts down left side of front neck, K31 sts from front neck, pick up and K 30[32:32] sts up right side of front neck, 30[32:32] sts down right back neck.

K31 from center back neck, and pick up and K 30[32:32] sts up left back neck.
182[190:190] sts. Work in rounds of K1, P1 rib for 3in.
Change to larger circular needle and cont in rounds of rib until work measures 6in from beg.
Bind off loosely in rib.
Sleeve edgings
Using smaller needles and A, with RS of work facing, pick up and K 128 [132:136] sts evenly around sleeve edge.
Next row *K2 tog, P2 tog, rep from * to end. 64[66:68] sts.
Work 6 rows K1, P1 rib.
Bind off loosely in rib.
Join side and underarm seams (see Special Technique).
Roll collar to RS.

Special technique – edge-to-edge seam selvage

 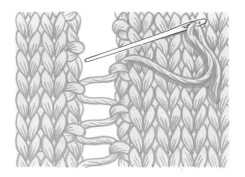 

1 *Thick yarns such as the summer cotton used for the sweater can produce bulky seams. These can be avoided by working an edge-to-edge seam. This requires a special selvage to be knitted in as the work progresses. Knit the first and last stitches on both right-side and wrong-side rows, thus producing a line of horizontal threads on both edges.*

2 *When the time comes to finish the garment, place the edges of the pieces to be joined facing each other, matching row to row. Thread a needle with matching yarn and secure it at one side of the bottom of the seam. Insert the needle up through the horizontal thread just above, then up through the one opposite. Continue lacing the thread from side to side.*

3 *Pull the thread to tighten and close up the seam as you work. Fasten it off securely when the seam is complete. This seam, which is almost invisible, can be worked with either the right or wrong side of the work facing.*

Fine Lace Collar

Introduce a little old-fashioned elegance into your life with
this exquisite lace collar. It transforms the plainest dress
into something special.

Size
Collar depth 7in after stretching

Gauge
40 sts and 64 rows to 4in over garter st on size 1 needles

Materials
1oz (approx 400yd) size 60 crochet cotton
1 pair size 1 knitting needles
1 small button

To make
Using knitting needles, cast on 39 sts.
Next 2 rows P.
Beg patt.
1st row (RS) P20, K4, (yo, P2 tog) twice, K4, yo, sl 1, K1, psso, (yo, P2 tog) twice, K1.
2nd row K1, (yo, P2 tog) 3 times, K4, (yo, P2 tog) twice, K4, P20.
3rd row P4, (yo, K2 tog) 8 times, K4, (yo, P2 tog) twice, K3, K2 tog, yo, K1, (yo, P2 tog) twice, yo, (P1, K1) into last st.
4th row K1, yo, K2, (yo, P2 tog) twice, K2, yo, P2 tog, K2, (yo, P2 tog) twice, K4, P20.
5th row P4, (yo, K2 tog) 8 times, K4, (yo, P2 tog) twice, K1, K2 tog, yo, K3, (yo, P2 tog) twice, yo, K3, (P1, K1) into last st, turn, K1, yo, K2, yo, P2 tog, turn, yo, P2 tog, yo, K3, (P1, K1) into last st.
6th row Bind off 5 sts, yo, P2 tog, K1, (yo, P2 tog) twice, K4, (yo, P2 tog) 3 times, K4, P20.
7th row P4, (yo, K2 tog) 8 times, K4, (yo, P2 tog) twice, yo, sl 1, K1, psso, K4, (yo, P2 tog) twice, (P1, K1) into next st, yo, P2 tog, yo, (P1, K1) into last st, make picot edge as foll: turn, K3, yo, P2 tog, turn, yo, P2 tog, yo, K2, yo, (P1, K1) into last st, – called make picot.
8th row Bind off 5 sts, yo, P2 tog, yo, K2, (yo, P2 tog) twice, K3, P2 tog tbl, yo, K1, (yo, P2 tog) twice, K4, P20.
9th row P4, (yo, K2 tog) 8 times,

K4, (yo, P2 tog) twice, K2, yo, sl 1, K1, psso, K2, (yo, P2 tog) twice, K2, (P1, K1) into next st, yo, P2 tog, yo, (P1, K1) into last st, make picot.
10th row Bind off 5 sts, yo, P2 tog, yo, K4, (yo, P2 tog) twice, K1, P2 tog tbl, yo, K3, (yo, P2 tog) twice, K4, P20.
11th row P4, (yo, K2 tog) 8 times, K4, (yo, P2 tog) twice, K4, yo, sl 1, K1, psso, (yo, P2 tog) twice, K4, (P1, K1) into next st, yo, P2 tog, yo, (P1, K1) into last st, make picot.
12th row Bind off 5 sts, yo, P2 tog, yo, K6, (yo, P2 tog) 3 times, K4, (yo, P2 tog) twice, K4, P20.
13th row P4, (yo, K2 tog) 8 times, K4, (yo, P2 tog) twice, K3, K2 tog, yo, K1, (yo, P2 tog) twice, K6, (P1, K1) into next st, yo, P2 tog, yo, (P1, K1) into last st, make picot.
14th row Bind off 5 sts, yo, P2 tog, yo, K8, (yo, P2 tog) twice, K2, yo, P2 tog, K2, (yo, P2 tog) twice, K4, P20.
15th row P4, (yo, K2 tog) 8 times, K4, (yo, P2 tog) twice, K1, K2 tog, yo, K3, (yo, P2 tog) twice, K8, (P1, K1) into next st, yo, P2 tog, yo, (P1, K1) into last st, make picot.
16th row Bind off 5 sts, yo, P2 tog, yo, P3 tog, K7, (yo, P2 tog) twice, K4, (yo, P2 tog) 3 times, K4, P20.
17th row P4, (yo, K2 tog) 8 times, K4, (yo, P2 tog) twice, yo, sl 1, K1, psso, K4, (yo, P2 tog) twice, K6, K2 tog, K1, yo, P2 tog, (P1, K1) into last st, make picot.
18th row Bind off 5 sts, yo, P2 tog, yo, P3 tog, K5, (yo, P2 tog) twice, K3, P2 tog tbl, yo, K1, (yo, P2 tog) twice, K4, P20.
19th row P4, (yo, K2 tog) 8 times, K4, (yo, P2 tog) twice, K2, yo, sl 1, K1, psso, K2, (yo, P2 tog) twice, K4, K2 tog, K1, yo, P2 tog, yo, (P1, K1) into last st, make picot.
20th row Bind off 5 sts, yo, P2 tog, yo, P3 tog, K3, (yo, P2 tog) twice, K1, P2 tog tbl, yo, K3, (yo, P2 tog) twice, K4, P20.

21st row P4, (yo, K2 tog) 8 times, K4, (yo, P2 tog) twice, K4, yo, sl 1, K1, psso, (yo, P2 tog) twice, K2, K2 tog, K1, yo, P2 tog, yo, (P1, K1) into last st, make picot.
22nd row Bind off 5 sts, yo, P2 tog, yo, P3 tog, K1, (yo, P2 tog) 3 times, K4, (yo, P2 tog) twice, K4, P20.
23rd row P4, (yo, K2 tog) 8 times, K4, (yo, P2 tog) twice, K3, K2 tog, yo, K1, (yo, P2 tog) twice, K2 tog, K1, yo, P2 tog, yo, (P1, K1) into last st, make picot.
24th row Bind off 5 sts, yo, P2 tog twice, (yo, P2 tog) twice, K2, yo, P2 tog, K2, (yo, P2 tog) twice, K4, P20.
25th row P4, (yo, K2 tog) 8 times, K4, (yo, P2 tog) twice, K1, K2 tog, yo, K3, (yo, P2 tog) twice, sl 1, K2 tog, psso, K1.
26th row K2 tog, (yo, P2 tog) twice, K4, (yo, P2 tog) 3 times, K4, P20.
27th row P4, (yo, K2 tog) 8 times, K4, (yo, P2 tog) twice, yo, sl 1, K1, psso, K4, (yo, P2 tog) twice, K1.
28th row K1, (yo, P2 tog) twice, K3, P2 tog tbl, yo, K1, (yo, P2 tog) twice, K4, P20.
29th row P4, (yo, K2 tog) 8 times, K4, (yo, P2 tog) twice, K2, yo, sl 1, K1, psso, K2, (yo, P2 tog) twice, K1.
30th row K1, (yo, P2 tog) twice, K1, P2 tog tbl, yo, K3, (yo, P2 tog) twice, K4, P20.
31st row P4, (yo, K2 tog) 8 times, K4, (yo, P2 tog) twice, K4, yo, sl 1, K1, psso, (yo, P2 tog) twice, K1.
32nd row K1, (yo, P2 tog) 3 times, K4, (yo, P2 tog) twice, K4, turn, K4, (yo, P2 tog) twice, K3, K2 tog, yo, K1, (yo, P2 tog) twice, yo, (P1, K1) into last st.
33rd row K1, yo, K2, (yo, P2 tog) twice, K2, yo, P2 tog, K2, (yo, P2 tog) twice, K4, P1, turn, P1, K4, (yo, P2 tog) twice, K1, K2 tog, yo, K3, (yo, P2 tog) twice, yo, K3, (P1, K1) into last st, turn, K1, yo, K2, yo, P2 tog, turn, yo, P2 tog, yo, K3, (P1, K1) into last st.
34th row Bind off 5 sts, yo, P2 tog,

K1, (yo, P2 tog) twice, K4, (yo, P2 tog) 3 times, K4, P2, turn, P2, K4, (yo, P2 tog) twice, yo, sl 1, K1, psso, K4, (yo, P2 tog) twice, (P1, K1) into next st, yo, P2 tog, yo, (P1, K1) into last st, make picot.

35th row Bind off 5 sts, yo, P2 tog, yo, K2, (yo, P2 tog) twice, K3, P2 tog tbl, yo, K1, (yo, P2 tog) twice, K4, P3, turn, P3, K4, (yo, P2 tog) twice, K2, yo, sl 1, K1, psso, K2, (yo, P2 tog) twice, K2, (P1, K1) into next st, yo, P2 tog, yo, (P1, K1) into last st, make picot.

36th row Bind off 5 sts, yo, P2 tog, yo, K4, (yo, P2 tog) twice, K1, P2 tog tbl, yo, K3, (yo, P2 tog) twice, K4, P4, turn, P4, K4, (yo, P2 tog) twice, K4, yo, sl 1, K1, psso, (yo, P2 tog) twice, K4, (P1, K1) into next st, yo, P2 tog, yo, (P1, K1) into last st, make picot.

37th row Bind off 5 sts, yo, P2 tog, yo, K6, (yo, P2 tog) 3 times, K4, (yo, P2 tog) twice, K4, P5, turn, P5,

K4, (yo, P2 tog) twice, K3, K2 tog, yo, K1, (yo, P2 tog) twice, K6, (P1, K1) into next st, yo, P2 tog, yo, (P1, K1) into last st, make picot.

38th row Bind off 5 sts, yo, P2 tog, yo, K8, (yo, P2 tog) twice, K2, yo, P2 tog, K2, (yo, P2 tog) twice, K4, P6, turn, P6, K4, (yo, P2 tog) twice, K1, K2 tog, yo, K3, (yo, P2 tog) twice, K8, (P1, K1) into next st, yo, P2 tog, yo, (P1, K1) into last st, make picot.

39th row Bind off 5 sts, yo, P2 tog, yo, P3 tog, K7, (yo, P2 tog) twice, K4, (yo, P2 tog) 3 times, K4, P5, turn, P5, K4, (yo, P2 tog) twice, yo, sl 1, K1, psso, K4, (yo, P2 tog) twice, K6, K2 tog, K1, yo, P2 tog, yo, (P1, K1) into last st, make picot.

40th row Bind off 5 sts, yo, P2 tog, yo, P3 tog, K5, (yo, P2 tog) twice, K3, P2 tog tbl, yo, K1, (yo, P2 tog) twice, K4, P4, turn, P4, K4, (yo, P2 tog) twice, K2, yo, sl 1, K1, psso, K2, (yo, P2 tog) twice, K4, K2 tog,

K1, yo, P2 tog, yo, (P1, K1) into last st, make picot.

41st row Bind off 5 sts, yo, P2 tog, yo, P3 tog, K3, (yo, P2 tog) twice, K1, P2 tog tbl, yo, K3, (yo, P2 tog) twice, K4, P3, turn, P3, K4, (yo, P2 tog) twice, K4, yo, sl 1, K1, psso, (yo, P2 tog) twice, K2, K2 tog, K1, yo, P2 tog, yo, (P1, K1) into last st, make picot.

42nd row Bind off 5 sts, yo, P2 tog, yo, P3 tog, K1, (yo, P2 tog) 3 times, K4, (yo, P2 tog) twice, K4, P2, turn, P2, K4, (yo, P2 tog) twice, K3, K2 tog, yo, K1, (yo, P2 tog) twice, K2 tog, K1, yo, P2 tog, yo, (P1, K1) into last st, make picot.

43rd row Bind off 5 sts, yo, (P2 tog) twice, (yo, P2 tog) twice, K2, yo, P2 tog, K2, (yo, P2 tog) twice, K4, P1, turn, P1, K4, (yo, P2 tog) twice, K1, K2 tog, yo, K3, (yo, P2 tog) twice, sl 1, K2 tog, psso, K1.

44th row K2 tog, (yo, P2 tog) twice, K4, (yo, P2 tog) 3 times, K4, turn, K4, (yo, P2 tog) twice, yo, sl 1, K1, psso, K4, (yo, P2 tog) twice, K1.

45th row K1, (yo, P2 tog) twice, K3, P2 tog tbl, yo, K1, (yo, P2 tog) twice, K4, P20.

46th row P20, K4, (yo, P2 tog) twice, K2, yo, sl 1, K1, psso, K2, (yo, P2 tog) twice, K1.

47th row K1, (yo, P2 tog) twice, K1, P2 tog tbl, yo, K3, (yo, P2 tog) twice, K4, P20.

48th–64th rows Rep 31st–47th rows once more.

The last 64 rows form the patt repeat.

Rep these 64 rows 4 more times.

Rep first–30th rows once more.

Next 2 rows P.

Bind off very loosely.

To finish

Make a line of running stitches at neck edge. Gather into required measurement. Curve collar, stretch, and pin into shape.

Starch and press.

Make a button loop at neck edge.

Sew on button to fasten.

Puff-sleeved Evening Top

Brighten up your nightlife in this gorgeous
glittering sweater knitted in fine gold yarn. The central panel,
with its pretty eyelet bow motif, is bordered by textured
panels in cables and blackberry stitch.

Sizes
To fit 32[34:36]in bust
Length 20in
Sleeve seam 6in

Note Instructions for larger sizes are in brackets []; where there is only one set of figures it applies to all three sizes.

Gauge
38 sts and 48 rows to 4in over st st on size 2 needles

Materials
11[12:12]oz fine metallic fingering yarn
1 pair each sizes 1 and 2 knitting needles
Cable needle

Back
*** Using smaller needles, cast on 138[142:146] sts. Work in K2, P2 rib as foll:
1st row *K2, P2, rep from * to last 2 sts, K2.
2nd row *P2, K2, rep from * to last 2 sts, P2.
Rep the last 2 rows until work measures 4½in from cast-on edge, ending with a 2nd row.
Next row P8[4:0], *P2, P twice into next st, rep from * to last 10[6:2] sts, P to end. 178[186:194] sts. ***
Beg patt.
1st row (WS) P1, *(K1, P1, K1) all into next st, P3 tog, rep from * to last st, P1.
2nd row K1, P to last st, K1.
3rd row P1, *P3 tog, (K1, P1, K1) all into next st, rep from * to last st, P1.
4th row As 2nd row.
These 4 rows form the patt. Cont in patt for a further 118 rows, ending with a 2nd patt row.
Shape armholes
Keeping patt correct, bind off 20 sts at beg of next 2 rows. 138[146:154] sts. Work first—2nd patt rows again.
Next row Bind off 4 sts, *P3 tog, (K1, P1, K1) all into next st, rep from * to last st, P1.
Next row Bind off 4 sts, P to last st, K1.
Rep the last 4 rows once more. 122 [130:138] sts.
Work even in patt for a further 50 rows. Bind off.

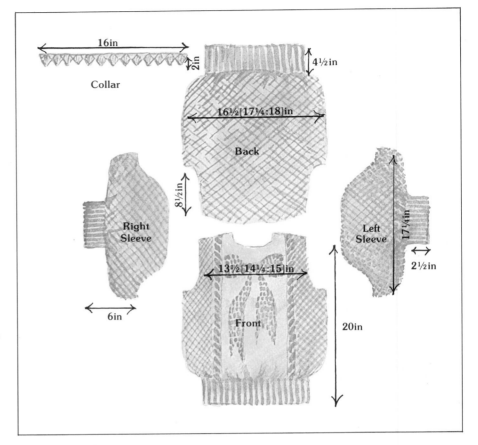

Front
Work as for back from *** to ***.
Beg patt.
1st row (WS) P1, *(K1, P1, K1) all into next st, P3 tog*, rep from * to * 9[10:11] more times, K2, P10, K2, P68, K2, P10, K2, **P3 tog, (K1, P1, K1) all into next st **, rep from ** to **, 9[10:11] more times, P1.
2nd row K1, P42[46:50], K10, P2, K68, P2, K10, P42[46:50], K1.
3rd row P1, *P3 tog, (K1, P1, K1) all into next st *, rep from * to * 9[10: 11] more times, K2, P10, K2, P68, K2, P10, K2, **(K1, P1, K1) all into next st, P3 tog **, rep from ** to ** 9[10:11] more times.
4th row K1, P42[46:50], sl next 5 sts onto cable needle and hold at back of work, K5, then K5 sts from cable needle – called C10B, P2, K68, P2, sl next 5 sts onto cable needle and hold at front of work, K5, then K5 sts from cable needle – called C10F, P42[46:50], K1.
5th row As first row.
6th row As 2nd row.
7th row As 3rd row.

8th row As 2nd row.
These 8 rows establish the side panel patt with the central panel in st st. Work the first row again.
Now maintaining side panel patt as set, beg working picture eyelets from chart.
1st row Patt 55[59:63], work first row from chart as foll: K45, yo, K2 tog, K21, patt to end.
2nd row Patt 55[59:63], work 2nd row from chart as foll: P68, patt to end.
3rd row Patt 55[59:63], K68, patt to end.
4th row Patt 55[59:63], P68, patt to end.
5th–8th rows Rep first–4th rows again.
9th row Patt 55[59:63], K45, (yo, K2 tog) twice, K19, patt to end.
Cont in this way until 113 rows have been worked from chart. (On 107th row refer to Special Technique for how to work a bold eyelet.)
Shape armholes
Keeping patt and chart correct, bind off 20 sts at beg of next 2 rows.

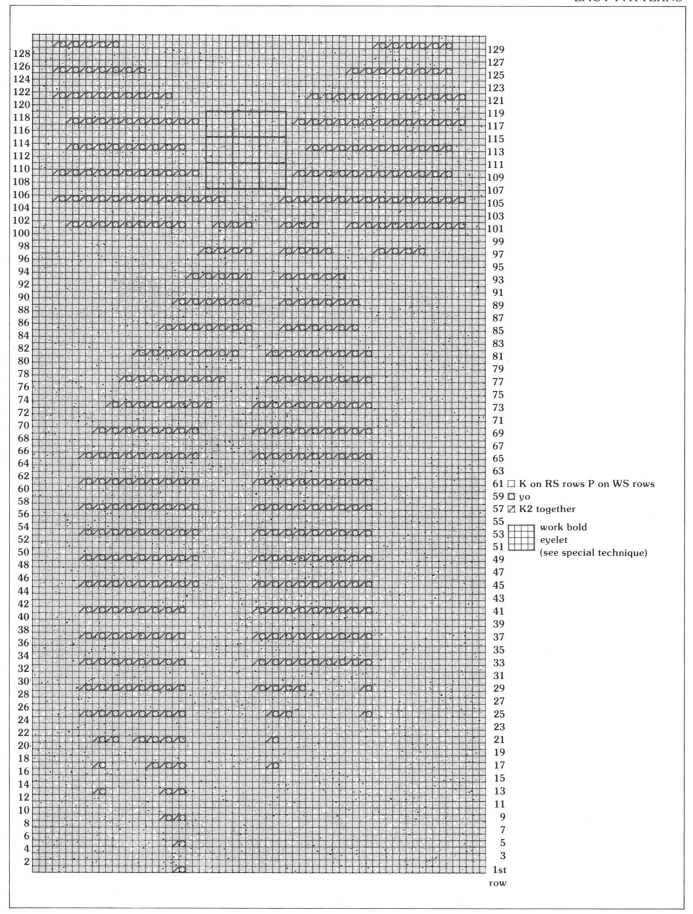

61 □ K on RS rows P on WS rows
59 ▨ yo
57 ▨ K2 together

work bold
eyelet
(see special technique)

138[146:174] sts.
Work 2 rows.
Bind off 4 sts at beg of next 2 rows.
Rep the last 4 rows once more.
132[130:138] sts.
Work a further 7 rows until chart is completed.
Now cont with side panel patt as set and central panel in st st.
Work 28 rows.

Shape neck
Next row Patt 57[61:65] and turn, leaving rem sts on a spare needle.
Complete left side of neck first.
Bind off 4 sts at beg of next row and 2 sts at beg of every other row once.
Work 1 row.
Dec 1 st at neck edge on next 5 rows and on every other row once.
35[39:43] sts.
Work even until work matches back to shoulder, ending at armhole edge.
Bind off
With RS of work facing return to sts on spare needle.
Join in yarn, bind off center 28 sts, patt to end.
Work 1 row.
Complete as for first side of neck.

Sleeves
Using smaller needles, cast on 94 sts.

Work in K2, P2 rib as for back for 2½in, ending with a 2nd row.
Change to larger needles.
Next row P1, *P twice into next st, rep from * to last st, P1. 186 sts.
Cont in patt as for back until work measures 6in, ending with a 2nd or 4th patt row.

Shape top
Keeping patt correct, bind off 20 sts at beg of next 2 rows. Bind off 4 sts at beg of every row until 106 sts rem.
Work even until work measures 9½in, ending with a 2nd or 4th patt row. Bind off 4 sts at beg of next 8 rows.
Next row P1, *P3 tog, rep from * to last st, P1.
Bind off.

Collar
Using larger needles, cast on 12 sts.
K 2 rows.
Beg patt.
1st row (RS) K twice into first st – called inc 1, K1, turn.
2nd and every other row K to end.
3rd row Inc 1, K3, turn.
5th row Inc 1, K5, turn.
7th row Inc 1, K7, turn.
9th row Inc 1, K9, turn.
11th row Inc 1, K11, turn.

13th row Inc 1, K13, turn.
15th row Inc 1, K15, turn.
17th row Inc 1, K17, turn.
19th row Inc 1, K19, turn.
21st row K22.
23rd row K2 tog, K19, turn.
25th row K2 tog, K17, turn.
27th row K2 tog, K15, turn.
29th row K2 tog, K13, turn.
31st row K2 tog, K11, turn.
33rd row K2 tog, K9, turn.
35th row K2 tog, K7, turn.
37th row K2 tog, K5, turn.
39th row K2 tog, K3, turn.
41st row K2 tog, K1, turn.
42nd–54th rows K.
These 54 rows form the patt. Rep them 12 more times.
Bind off.

To finish
Join shoulder seams.
Join side and sleeve seams.
Set in sleeves, gathering to form a puff top.
Join short ends of collar. Sew collar to neck edge, placing seam at center back neck.
Do not press. Remember to wash the finished top gently by hand in warm water and dry completely flat on a towel.

Special technique – working a bold eyelet

1 *The knot on the bow motif of this sweater is made from a series of bold eyelets worked over four stitches and four rows. On the first row, knit two together, take the yarn over the needle twice, then slip one, knit one, and pass the slipped stitch over.*

2 *On the second row, purl together the first stitch and the first yarn-over, knit together the second yarn-over and the second stitch.*

3 *On the third row, knit one, yarn-over twice, knit one. On the fourth row, purl together the first stitch, the first yarn-over and the strand below, then knit one and purl one, into the second yarn-over and strand below at the same time, then purl one.*

Elderberry Lace Sweater

A fluffy sweater knitted in an elderberry lace pattern that's
delicious enough to make your mouth water. It looks
equally good with dressy or casual clothes.

Sizes
To fit 32–34[36–38]in bust.
Length 23[25]in
Sleeve seam 17in
Note Instructions for larger size are in
brackets []; where there is only one
set of figures it applies to both sizes.

Gauge
28 sts and 38 rows to 4in over patt
on size 2 needles.

Materials
13[15]oz lightweight mohair-blend
yarn
1 pair each sizes 1 and 2 knitting
needles

Back
•• Using smaller needles, cast on
120[150] sts.
Next row (RS) (K1, P1) to end.
Next row (K1, P1) to end.
Cont in K1, P1 rib until work
measures 3in, ending with an RS row.
Next row Rib 12[15], pick up loop
lying between needles and K tbl –
called make 1 or M1 –, (rib 24[30],
M1) 4 times, rib to end. 125[155] sts.
Change to larger needles, beg patt.
1st row (RS) K3, *K2 tog, P3, K1,
yo, P8, (K1, yo, K1, yo, K1) all into
next st, turn, P5, turn, K2 tog tbl, K3
tog, pass first st over 2nd – called
make bobble or MB –, P8, yo, K1,
P3, ybk, sl 1 P-wise, K1, psso, K1,
rep from * to last 2 sts, K2.
2nd row K2, P2, *K3, P2, K8, P1
tbl, K8, P2, K3, P3, rep from * to
last 4 sts, P2, K2 instead of P3.
3rd row K4, *P2 tog, P1, K1, yo,
P5, MB, P3, K1, P3, MB, P5, yo,
K1, P1, P2 tog, K3, rep from * to
last st, K1.
4th row K2, P2, *K2, P2, K5, P1
tbl, K3, P1, K3, P1 tbl, K5, P2, K2,
P3, rep from * to last 4 sts, P2, K2
instead of P3.
5th row K4, *P2 tog, K1, yo, P2,
MB, (P3, K1) 3 times, P3, MB, P2,
yo, K1, P2 tog, K3, rep from * to last
st, K1.
6th row K2, P2, *K1, P2, K2, P1
tbl, (K3, P1) 3 times, K3, P1 tbl, K2,
P2, K1, P3, rep from * to last 4 sts,
P2, K2 instead of P3.
7th row K4, *K2 tog, yo, (P3, K1) 5
times, P3, yo, sl 1 P-wise, K1, psso,
K3, rep from * to last st, K1.

8th row K2, P4, *(K3, P1) 5 times,
K3, P7, rep from * to last 6 sts, P4,
K2 instead of P7.
9th row K3, *K2 tog, yo, P4, yo,
K1, P3, K1, P1, P2 tog, K1, P2 tog,
P1, K1, P3, K1, yo, P4, yo, sl 1
P-wise, K1, psso, K1, rep from * to
last 2 sts, K2.
10th row K2, P3, *K4, P2, K3, (P1,
K2) twice, P1, K3, P2, K4, P5, rep
from * to last 5 sts, P3, K2 instead of
P5.
11th row K2, K2 tog, *yo, P6, yo,
K1, P3, (K1, P2 tog) twice, K1, P3,
K1, yo, P6, yo, sl 1 P-wise, K2 tog,
psso, rep from * to last 4 sts, sl 1
P-wise, K1, psso, K2.
12th row K10, *P2, K3, (P1, K1)
twice, P1, K3, P2, K15, rep from *
to last 10 sts, K10 instead of K15.
13th row K2, *MB, P8, yo, K1, P3,
ybk, sl1 P-wise, K1, psso, K1, K2
tog, P3, K1, yo, P8, rep from * to
last 3 sts, MB, K2.
14th row K2, *P1 tbl, K8, P2, K3,
P3, K3, P2, K8, rep from * to last 3
sts, P1 tbl, K2.
15th row K3, P3, MB, P5, yo, K1,

P1, P2 tog, K3, P2 tog, P1, K1, yo,
P5, MB, P3, K1, rep from * to last 2
sts, K2.
16th row K2, *P1, K3, P1 tbl, K5,
P2, K2, P3, K2, P2, K5, P1 tbl, K3,
rep from * to last 3 sts, P1, K2.
17th row K3, *P3, K1, P3, MB, P2,
yo, K1, P2 tog, K3, P2 tog, K1, yo,
P2, MB, (P3, K1) twice, rep from *
to last 2 sts, K2.
18th row K2, * (P1, K3) twice, P1
tbl, K2, P2, K1, P3, K1, P2, K2, P1
tbl, K3, P1, K3, rep from * to last 3
sts, P1, K2.
19th row K3, * (P3, K1) twice, P3,
yo, sl 1 P-wise, K1, psso, K3, K2
tog, yo, (P3, K1) times, rep from * to
last 2 sts, K2.
20th row K2, * (P1, K3) 3 times,
P7, (K3, P1) twice, K3, rep from * to
last 3 sts, P1, K2.
21st row K3, * P2 tog, P1, K1, P3,
K1, yo, P4, yo, sl 1 P-wise, K1,
psso, K1, K2 tog, yo, P4, yo, K1,
P3, K1, P1, P2 tog, K1, rep from *
to last 2 sts, K2.
22nd row K2, * P1, K2, P1, K3, P2,
K4, P5, K4, P2, K3, P1, K2, rep

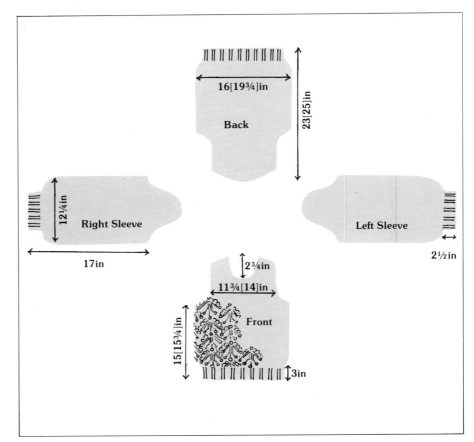

Back
16[19¾]in
23[25]in

Right Sleeve
12¼in
17in

Left Sleeve
2½in

Front
2¾in
11¾[14]in
15[15¾]in
3in

from * to last 3 sts, P1, K2.
23rd row K3, * P2 tog, K1, P3, K1, yo, P6, yo, sl 1 P-wise, K2 tog, psso, yo, P6, yo, K1, P3, K1, P2 tog, K1, rep from * to last 2 sts, K2.
24th row K2, * P1, K1, P1, K3, P2, K15, P2, K3, P1, K1, rep from * to last 3 sts, P1, K2.
These 24 rows form the elderberry lace patt. Cont in patt until work measures 15[15¾]in, ending with a WS row.
Shape armholes
Keeping patt correct, bind off 6 sts at beg of next 2 rows.
Dec 1 st at each end of next 5[9] rows, then dec 1 st at each end of every other row until 93[111] sts rem **.

Work even until work measures 23[25]in, ending with a WS row.
Shape shoulders
Keeping patt correct, bind off 8[9] sts at beg of next 4 rows, then 9[10] sts at beg of next 2 rows. Leave rem 43[55] sts on a spare needle.

Front
Work as for back from ** to **.
Work even until work measures

20[22½]in, ending with a WS row.
Shape left front neck
Next row Patt 35 [44] sts, P2 tog, turn, leaving rem sts on a spare needle.
Dec 1 st at neck edge on every row until 25[28] sts rem.
Work even until front matches back exactly to beg of shoulder shaping, ending with a WS row.
Shape shoulder
Keeping patt correct, bind off 8[9] sts at beg of next and every other row once. Work 1 row.
Bind off rem 9[10] sts.
Shape right front neck
Return to sts on spare needle and beg at neck edge, slip 19 sts onto a holder. Rejoin yarn to rem sts, P2 tog, patt to end.
Complete to match left side, reversing shapings.

Sleeves (alike)
Using smaller needles, cast on 56[62] sts and work in K1, P1 rib as for back for 2½in.
Next row Rib 9[15], M1, (rib 1, M1) 38[32] times, rib to end. 95 sts.
Change to larger needles and cont in

patt as for back until work measures 17in, ending with a WS row.
Shape top
Keeping patt correct, bind off 6 sts at beg of next 2 rows.
Dec 1 st at each end of next and every foll 4th row until 79[65] sts rem. Work 1 row.
Dec 1 st at each end of next and every other row until 31 sts rem. Work 1 row. Bind off.

To finish
Do not press.
Join right shoulder seam.
Neck border
Using smaller needles and with RS facing, pick up and K 24 sts down left side of neck, K19 sts from stitch holder, pick up and K 24 sts up right side of neck, then K43[55] from spare needle. 110[122] sts.
Work in K1, P1 rib as for back for 2¾in. Bind off in rib.
Join left shoulder and neck border seam.
Fold neck border in half to WS and slip stitch loosely in place.
Set in sleeves.
Join side and sleeve seams.

Special technique – working a crew neckband

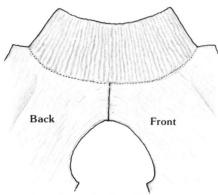

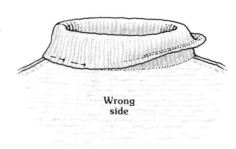

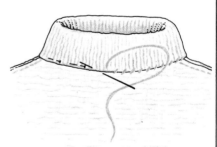

1 *Join the right shoulder seam, Pick up the number of stitches specified in the pattern around the neck edge. Work the ribbing to twice the desired depth of neckband. Bind off very loosely in rib.*

2 *Join the left shoulder seam and the neckband seam. Fold the neckband in half to the wrong side of the garment. Pin the bound-off edge to the inner neck edge.*

3 *Thread a tapestry needle with matching yarn and slipstitch the bound-off edge in place.*

Lace Paneled Sweater

Splurge on ultra-luxurious silk for this superb sweater with
its asymmetrical combination of stitch patterns – strictly
for the experienced knitter and would-be designer!

Size
To fit 32–34in bust
Length 23½in
Sleeve seam 20½in

Gauge
20 sts and 26 rows to 4in over st st
on size 5 needles

Materials
44oz silk knitting worsted-weight yarn
1 pair size 2 knitting needles, sizes 2
and 5 circular needles

Note The sweater is knitted in one
piece, starting at the wrist of one
sleeve, and the work is divided for
the front and back. The following
stitch patterns are used. It is advisable
to knit samples of one or two repeats
to become familiar with the patterns
before starting the work. The pattern
repeats are given between * * and
extra stitches have been included for
the first pattern row where necessary
in the instructions to balance the
pattern. Make sure that these extra
stitches are taken into consideration
on the sleeve shaping.

A Bobble stitch pattern
1st–3rd rows K.
4th row (WS) P.
5th row *K5, (K1, yo, K1, yo, K1)
all into next st, turn, P5, turn, K5,
turn, P2 tog, P1, P2 tog, turn, sl 1,
K2 tog, psso – called MB –, rep from
* to end.
6th row P.
7th–9th rows K.
10th row P. These 10 rows form the
pattern repeat (6 repeat stitches).

B Fan pattern
1st row (RS) K1, *yo, sl 1, K1, psso,
K5*, yo, K2 tog.
2nd and every other row P.
3rd row K1, *yo, K1, sl 1, K1, psso,
K4*, yo, K2 tog.
5th row K1, *yo, K2, sl 1, K1, psso,
K3*, yo, K2 tog.
7th row K1, *yo, K3, sl 1, K1, psso,
K2*, yo, K2 tog.
9th row K1, *yo, K4, sl 1, K1, psso

K1* yo, K2 tog.
11th row K1, *yo, K5, sl 1, K1,
psso*, yo, K2 tog.
12th row P.
These 12 rows form the pattern
repeat. (1 edge stitch, 7 repeat
stitches, 2 edge stitches).

C Triangular leaf pattern
1st row K1, yo, sl 1, K1, psso, K1,
*K2, K2 tog, yo, K1, yo, sl 1, K1,
psso, K1*, K2, K2 tog, yo, K1.
2nd and every other row P.
3rd row K1, yo, K1, sl 1, K1, psso,
*K1, K2 tog, K1, yo, K1, yo, K1, sl
1, K1, psso*, K1, K2 tog, K1, yo,
K1.
5th row K1, yo, K2. *sl 1, K2 tog,
psso, K2, yo, K1, yo, K2*, sl 1, K2
tog, psso, K2, yo, K1.
7th row K2, K2 tog, yo, *K1, yo,
sl 1, K1, psso, K3, K2 tog, yo*, K1,
yo, sl 1, K1, psso, K2.
9th row K1, K2 tog, K1, yo, *K1,
yo, K1, sl 1, K1, psso, K1, K2 tog,
K1, yo*, K1, yo, K1, sl 1, K1, psso,
K1.
11th row K2 tog, K2, yo, *K1, yo,
K2, sl 1, K2 tog, psso, K2, yo*, K1,
yo, K2, sl 1, K1, psso.
12th row P.
These 12 rows form the pattern
repeat.
(4 edge stitches, 8 repeat stitches, 5
edge stitches).

D Diamond stitch
1st row (RS) K1*, P1, K1, P1, K1,
P2, K1, P1, K1, P1*, K1.
2nd and every other row P1, *K1,
P1, K1, P1, K2, P1, K1, P1, K1*,
P1.
3rd row K1, *P1, yo, P3 tog, yo,
P2, yo, P3 tog, yo, P1*, K1.
5th row As first row.
7th row K1, *P2 tog, yo, P1, yo, P2
tog, P2 tog, yo, P1, yo, P2 tog*, K1.
These 8 rows from the pattern repeat
(10 repeat stitches).

E Curved leaf pattern
1st row *P2, K5, K2 tog, yo, K1,
yo, K2*, P2.
2nd row *K2, P5, P2 tog, P4*, K2.

3rd row *P2, K3, K2 tog, K1, yo,
K1, yo, K3*, P2.
4th row *K2, P7, P2 tog, P2*, K2.
5th row *P2, K1, K2 tog, K2, yo,
K1, yo, K4*, P2.
6th row *K2, P9, P2 tog *, K2.
These 6 rows form the pattern
repeat. (12 repeat stitches, 2 edge
stitches).

Sweater
Sleeve
Using pair of needles, cast on 36 sts
and work 15 rows in K1, P1 rib.
Change to larger circular needle and
work in rows.
Next row P to end, inc 8 sts evenly
across the row. 44 sts.
Cont in bands of patt, *at the same
time*, inc 1 st at each end of every
6th row.
1st–10th rows Work in bobble stitch
pattern A (7 repeats of 6 sts, 2 edge
sts).
11th–34th rows Work in fan pattern
B (2 edge sts, 6 repeats of 7 sts, 2
edge sts in 11th row).
35th–44th rows Work in bobble
stitch pattern A.
45th–80th rows Work in triangular
leaf pattern stitch C (5 edge sts, 6
repeats of 8 sts, 5 edge sts in 45th
row).
81st–90th rows Work in bobble
stitch pattern A (11 repeats of 6 sts,
4 edge sts in 81st row).
91st–114th rows Work in diamond
stitch pattern D (1 edge st, 6 repeats
of 12 sts, 1 edge st in 91st row).
115th row K.
116th row K, inc 1 st at each end.
84 sts.
117th row K2, *MB, K5*, rep from
* to last 4 sts, MB, K3.
118th row P, inc 1 st at each end.
119th row K.
120th row P, inc 1 st at each end.
88 sts.

Front and back
121st row Cast on 54 sts, K across
these sts, K88 from sleeve, cast on
54 sts. 196 sts.
122nd row P.

123rd–132nd rows Work in bobble stitch pattern A (2 edge stitches, 32 repeats of 6 sts in bobble row, 2 edge sts).
133rd row K4, *MB, K5*, rep from * to end.
134th row P.
135th–137th rows K.
138th row P.
139th row K.
140th row P.

Neck
141st row K92 and leave these sts on a spare needle, bind off 12 sts, K92. Work front and back separately as foll:
142nd row P.
143rd–160th rows **Work in curved leaf pattern stitch E (3 edge sts, 7 repeats of 12 sts, 5 edge sts)
161st–170th rows Work in bobble stitch pattern A (15 repeats of 6 sts, 2 edge sts)
171st–206th rows Work in fan pattern stitch B (4 edge sts, 12 repeats of 7 sts, 4 edge sts).
207th–216th rows Work in bobble stitch pattern A (15 repeats of 6 sts, 2 edge sts). **
Cut yarn and leave these sts on a spare needle.
With WS of work facing return to sts on spare needle, join in yarn at neck edge. Work as from ** to ** again.

Joining back and front
217th row K92, cast on 12 sts and K92 from spare needle. 196 sts.
218th row P.
219th–230th rows Work in triangular leaf stitch pattern C (6 edge sts, 23 repeats of 8 sts, 6 edge sts).
221st–237th rows Work first–7th rows of bobble stitch pattern A (32 repeats of 6 sts, 5 edge sts).

Sleeve
238th row Bind off 54 sts, K142.
239th row Bind off 54 sts, K88.
240th row P, dec 1 st at each end. 86 sts.
241st row K1, *MB, K5, rep from * to last st, K1.
242nd row P, dec 1 st at each end. 84 sts.

243rd row K.
244th row K, dec 1 st at each end.
245th row K.
246th row P, dec 1 st at each end. 80 sts. Now cont in patt, *at the same time*, dec 1 st at each end of every foll 6th row.
247th row K1, *MB, K5, rep from * to last st, K1.
248th row P.
249th–250th rows K.
251st–266th rows Work in diamond stitch pattern D (4 edge sts, 6 repeats of 12 sts, 6 edge sts).
267th–276th rows Work in bobble stitch pattern A (12 repeats of 6 sts, 2 edge sts).
277th–282nd rows Work in curved leaf pattern E (4 edge sts, 5 repeats of 12 sts, 6 edge sts).
283rd–292nd rows Work in bobble stitch pattern A (11 repeats of 6 sts, 2 edge sts).
293rd–316th rows Work 2 repeats in fan pattern B (1 edge st, 9 repeats of 7 sts, 2 edge sts).
317th–326th rows Work in bobble stitch pattern A (9 repeats of 6 sts, 4 edge sts).
327th–350th rows Work in triangular leaf pattern C (7 edge sts, 5 repeats of 8 sts, 7 edge sts).
351st–358th rows Work first–8th rows of bobble stitch pattern A (7 repeats of 6 sts, 2 edge sts).
Next row K to end, dec 8 sts evenly across the row. 36 sts.
Change to pair of needles, work 15 rows in K1, P1 rib. Bind off in rib.

To finish
With RS of work facing, using pair of needles, pick up and K 39 sts around front neck edge.
1st row (WS) P1, *K1, P1, rep from * to end.
2nd row K1, *P1, K1, rep from * to end.
Rep last 2 rows 3 more times. Bind off in rib. Work back neck to match. Using pair of needles, pick up and K 64 sts evenly from back lower edge. Work 20 rows in K1, P1 rib. Bind off in rib and work front lower edge to match. Sew row ends of neckbands to sts on shoulders.
Join side and underarm seams.

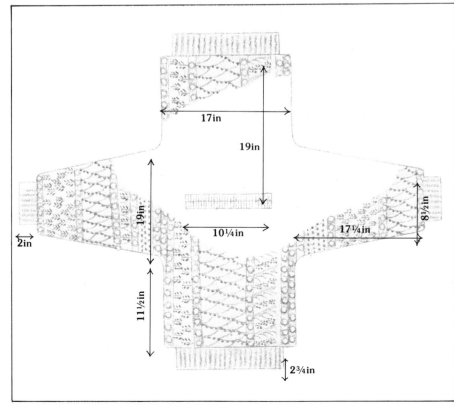

Color Patterns

Working color patterns into knitting is surprisingly easy. It involves using several different-colored yarns within the same row – often as few as two but sometimes a great many more. Handling these yarns may seem awkward at first but very quickly improves with practice. One of the most important techniques – used in Fair Isle-type patterns – is to carry the yarns correctly across the back of the work, either stranding the yarns or weaving them in (see page 24).

Once these techniques have been mastered you will be able to work beautiful all-over patterns like the paisley cardigan on page 98 and the harlequin sweater on page 114, or those with bold pictorial or abstract motifs like the jacket on page 118 and the fireworks sweater (page 111).

There is also a type of color-patterned knitting in which amazing geometric patterns can be produced using only one color to a row. This is "mosaic" knitting, and there is an example of it on page 121. It is one of a large family of patterns that combine different-colored yarns and slip-stitch techniques (see page 23) with some strikingly attractive results.

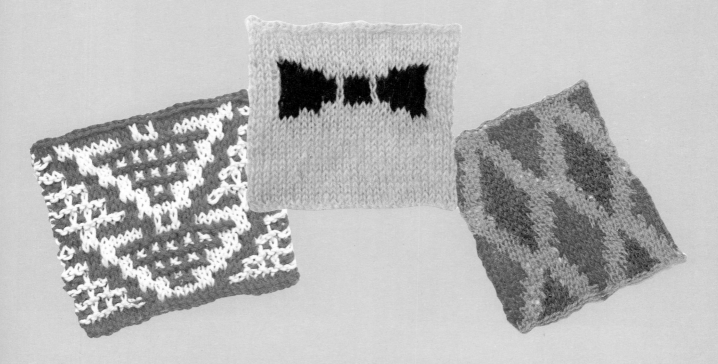

Jacquard Sweater and Legwarmers

This beautifully patterned sweater set is made in quick-to-knit bulky yarn. To make it even easier the dots are duplicate-stitched afterward.

Sizes

Sweater
To fit 34−36[38−40]in bust
Length 24½[24¾]in
Sleeve seams 15½in
Legwarmers
Width around calf 14in

Note Instructions for the larger size are in brackets []; where there is only one set of figures it applies to both sizes.

Gauge

13½ sts and 15 rows to 4in over st st on size 10 needles

Materials

9[13]oz Icelandic yarn in main color (A)
9[13]oz in first contrasting color (B)
6oz in each of 5 contrasting colors (C), (D), (E), (F) and (G)
1 pair each sizes 8 and 10 knitting needles

Back

**Using smaller needles and A, cast on 62[68] sts.
1st row K2[0], *P2, K2, rep from * to end.
2nd row *P2, K2, rep from * to last 2[0] sts, P2[0].
Rep the last 2 rows 5 more times. Inc 1 st at end of last row. 63[69] sts.
Change to larger needles.
Beg patt.
Beg with a K row work 20 rows st st. Now cont in st st, working from chart (page 97) reading K rows from right to left and P rows from left to right.
Work 30 rows, ending with a P row.
Shape armholes

Keeping patt correct, bind off 3 sts at beg of next 2 rows and 2[3] sts at beg of foll 4 rows. 49[51] sts.
Work even until the 52 rows of chart have been completed.**
Cont in F only and st st until work measures 9[9¼]in from beg of armhole shaping, ending with a P row.
Shape shoulders
Bind off 13 sts at beg of next 2 rows. Leave the rem 23[25] sts on a spare needle.

Front

Work as for back from ** to **.
Cont in F only and st st until work measures 6¼[6¾]in from beg of armhole shaping, ending with a P row.
Divide for neck
Next row Patt 18 sts and turn,

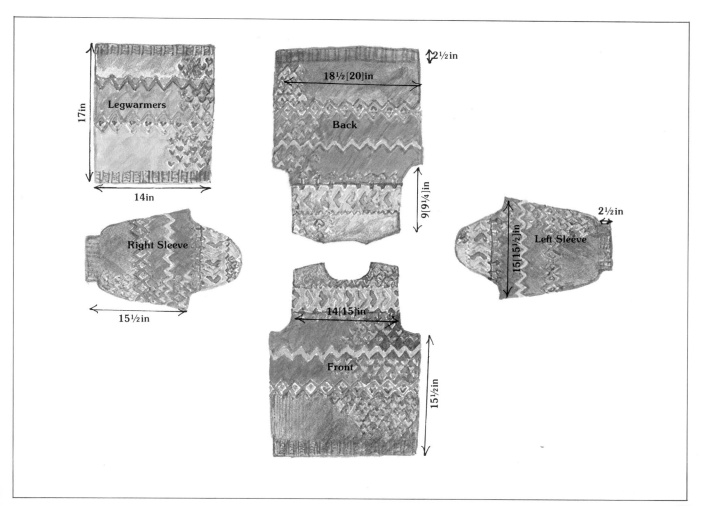

leaving rem sts on a spare needle, patt to end.
Complete left side of neck first.
****Next row Patt to end.
Next row Bind off 3 sts, patt to end.
Next row Patt to end.
Next row Bind off 2 sts, patt to end.
Work even until work matches back to shoulder shaping, ending at armhole edge.

Shape shoulder
Bind off rem 13 sts.****
Return to sts on spare needle. With RS of work facing, sl center 13[15] sts onto a stitch holder, join in yarn to next st, patt to end.
Complete to match first side of neck, working from **** to ****.

Sleeves
Using smaller needles and A, cast on 28 sts.
Work 11 rows K2, P2 rib.
Next row Rib 5, (work into front and back of next st − called M1 −, rib 1) 8 times, M1, rib to end. 37 sts.
Change to larger needles and cont in patt as for back from *** to ***, at the same time, inc 1 st at each end of the 7th[5th] row and every foll 6th row until there are 51[53] sts.
Work even until 30 rows have been worked from chart, ending with a P row.

Shape sleeve top
Keeping patt correct, bind off 3 sts at beg of next 2 rows and 2[3] sts at beg of foll 2 rows. Dec 1 st at each end of the next and every other row until 21[19] sts rem, ending with a P row.
Bind off 2 sts at beg of next 2 rows and 3[2] sts at beg of next 2 rows.
Bind off rem 11 sts.

Legwarmers
Using smaller needles and G, cast on 48 sts.
Work 8 rows in K2, P2 rib. Inc 1 st at end of law row. 49 sts.
Change to larger needles.
Beg patt.
Beg with a K row work 20 rows st st. Now cont in st st, working from chart, reading K rows from right to left and P rows from left to right. Use G instead of A, F instead of B, A instead of C and B instead of D.
Work 21 rows ending with a K row.

Beg with a P row cont in E only and work 11 rows in st st. Dec 1 st at end of last row. 48 sts.
Change to smaller needles and work 8 rows K2, P2 rib. Bind off in rib.

To finish
Join left shoulder seam of sweater. With RS of work facing, using smaller needles and F, pick up and K 12 sts down left side of neck, K across the 13[15] sts at center front, pick up and K 12 sts up right side of neck, K across the 23[25] sts on back neck. 60[64] sts.
Work 13 rows in K2, P2, rib. Bind off loosely in rib.
Join right shoulder and neckband seam.
Fold neckband to WS and slipstitch down. Set in sleeves. Join side and sleeve seams. Duplicate stitch single stitches for dots on the blank areas of the pattern on every 4th stitch of every 4th row, staggering them above each other.
Join side seams of legwarmers.
Duplicate stitch dots as desired.

Special technique – duplicate stitching dots

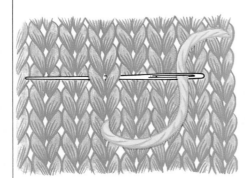

1 It is usually easier to duplicate stitch widely spaced dots than to knit them in. Thread a tapestry needle with the chosen yarn. Secure the end of the yarn at the back of the work. Bring the yarn to the front through the base of the stitch. Insert the needle from right to left as shown.

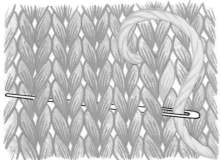

2 Pull the yarn through. Push the point of the needle through the base of the stitch and bring it out at the base of the stitch at the next dot position, working from right to left.

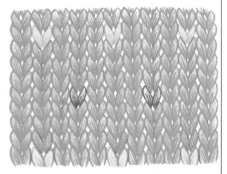

3 Continue in this way working dots in the chosen colors as desired. On the basic sweater the dots are worked every 4th row on every 4th stitch in contrasting colors and staggered above each other as shown in the photograph.

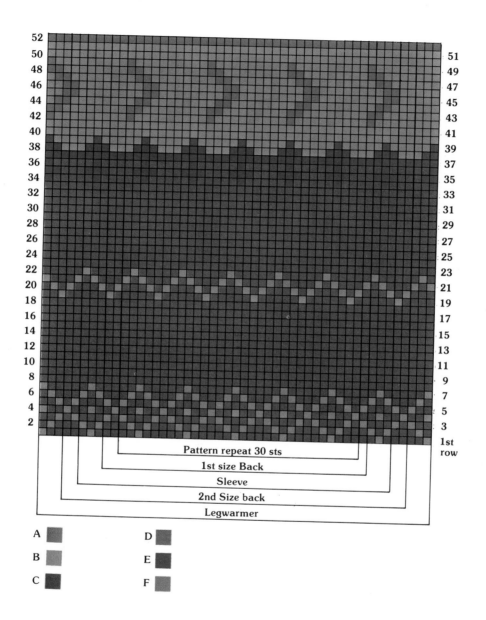

52
50
48
46
44
42
40
38
36
34
32
30
28
26
24
22
20
18
16
14
12
10
8
6
4
2

51
49
47
45
43
41
39
37
35
33
31
29
27
25
23
21
19
17
15
13
11
9
7
5
3
1st
row

Pattern repeat 30 sts

1st size Back

Sleeve

2nd Size back

Legwarmer

A D

B E

C F

Paisley Cardigan

A string of tiny flowers buttons up this scoop-necked
cardigan worked in a pretty paisley pattern. The sleeves are
beautifully puffed at the top and taper to the wrist.

Sizes
To fit 30[32:34:36]in bust
Length 19½[19½:21:21]in
Sleeve seam 15[15¾:16½:17½]in

Note Instructions for the larger sizes are in brackets []; where there is only one set of figures it applies to all sizes.

Gauge
29 sts and 29 rows to 4in over patt on size 3 needles

Materials
8[8:9:11]oz Shetland wool in main color (A)
4[4:5:5]oz in first contrasting color (B)
5[5:6:6]oz in 2nd contrasting color (C)

1 pair each sizes 2 and 3 knitting needles
13[13:14:14] buttons

Back
Using larger needles and A, cast on 118[126:136:142] sts.
**Work 6 rows K1, P1 rib.
Beg with a K row cont in st st and patt from chart 1. Read K rows from right to left, P rows from left to right.
Cont until work measures 11[11:11½:11½]in, ending with a P row.**
Shape armholes
Keeping patt correct, bind off 4 sts at beg of next 2 rows, 3 sts at beg of next 2 rows and 2 sts at beg of next 2 rows.
Dec 1 st at beg of next 2 rows.
98[106:116:122] sts.

Work even until work measures 19½[19½:21:21]in, ending with a P row.
Shape shoulders
Bind off 24[28:33:36] sts at beg of next 2 rows.
Bind off rem 50 sts.

Right front
Using larger needles and A, cast on 56[60:64:68] sts.
Work as for back from ** to **, working patt from chart 2.
Shape armhole
Next row Bind off 4 sts, patt to end.
Next row Patt to end.
Next row Bind off 3 sts, patt to end.
Next row Patt to end.
Next row Bind off 2 sts, patt to end.
Next row Patt to end.
Next row Work 2 tog, patt to end.

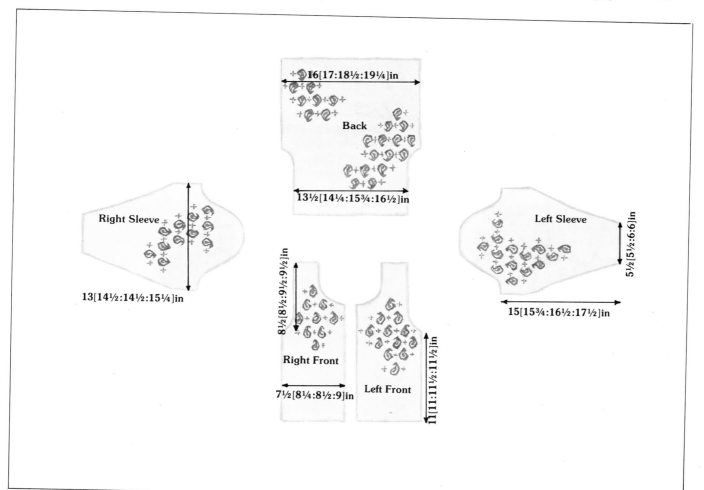

46[50:54:58] sts.
Work even until work measures
15[15:15¾:15¾]in, ending with a K
row.
Shape neck
Next row Bind off 9 sts patt to end.
Next row Patt to end.
Next row Bind off 7[7:6:7] sts, patt
to end.
Next row Patt to end.
Next row Bind off 6 sts, patt to end.
24[28:33:36] sts.
Work even until work matches back
to shoulder shaping, ending at
armhole edge.
Shape shoulder
Bind off rem sts.

Left front
Work as for right front, working patt
from chart 3, reversing shaping.

Sleeves
Using larger needles and A, cast on
42[42:44:44] sts. Work 6 rows rib.
Change to st st and work in patt from
chart 1. Inc 1 st at each end of every
foll 4th row until there are
60[60:64:64] sts. Now inc 1 st at
each end of every other row until
there are 102[108:108:112] sts.
Work even until work measures
15[15¾:16½:17½]in, ending with a
P row.
Shape sleeve top
Bind off 4 sts at beg of next 2 rows
and 2 sts at beg of next 2 rows.
Dec 1 st at each end of next and
every other row until 54[66:54:62]
sts rem, ending with a P row.
Bind off 2 sts at beg of next
8[14:8:12] rows, then 4 sts at beg of
next 2 rows.
Bind off rem 30 sts.

To finish
Join shoulder seams.
Neckband
With RS of work facing, using smaller
needles and A, pick up and K
53[53:55:55] sts up right side of
neck, pick up and K 50 across back
neck, pick up and K 53[53:55:55]
sts down left side of neck. 156
[156:160:160] sts.
Work 5 rows K1, P1 rib.
Bind off in rib.
Buttonhole band
With RS of work facing, using smaller
needles and A, pick up and K
115[115:123:123] sts evenly along
front and neckband edge.
1st row (WS) P1, *K1, P1, rep from
* to end.
2nd row K1, *P1, K1, rep from * to
end.
Rep the first row again.
Buttonhole row Rib 3, (yo, work 2
tog, rib 7) 12[12:13:13] times, yo,
work 2 tog, rib to end.
Rib 4 more rows. Bind off in rib.
Button band
Work as for buttonhole band omitting
buttonholes.
Join side and sleeve seams.
Set in sleeves gathering sleeve top to
form puff.
Sew on buttons.

Special technique – picking up stitches from shaped and vertical edges

1 On a shaped edge, insert a needle from front to back through a bound-off stitch or the last stitch in a row. Take the yarn knitwise around the point of the needle and draw a loop through. On shaped edges one stitch is picked up for every two rows.

2 On vertical edges, insert a needle from front to back through the first stitch in a row. Take the yarn around the point of the needle knitwise and draw a loop through. Generally, on vertical edges, one stitch is picked up for every row.

3 Similarly, stitches can be picked up and purled along shaped or vertical edges. In this case work with the wrong side of the fabric facing.

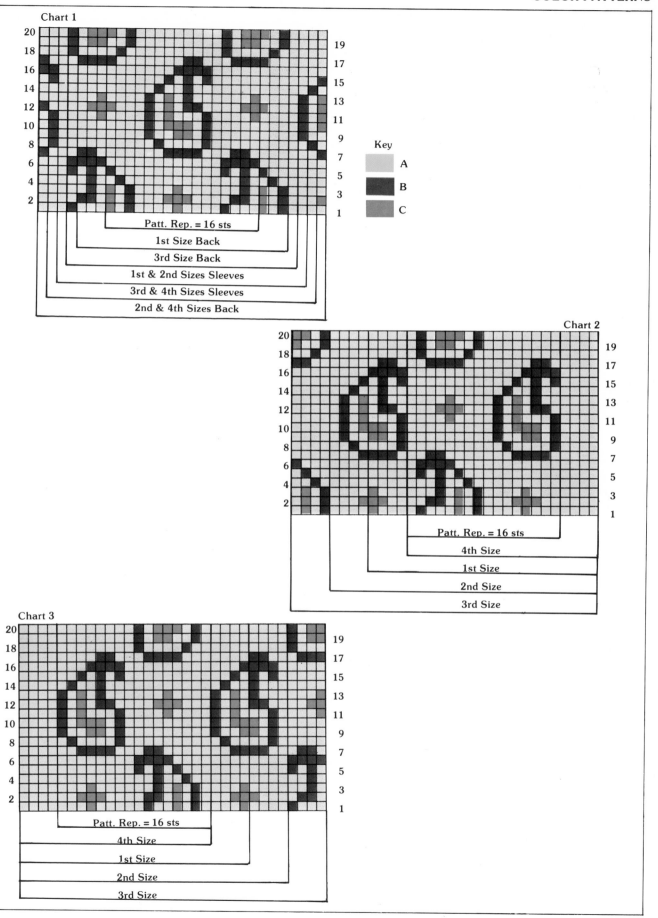

Chart 1

Patt. Rep. = 16 sts
1st Size Back
3rd Size Back
1st & 2nd Sizes Sleeves
3rd & 4th Sizes Sleeves
2nd & 4th Sizes Back

Key
A
B
C

Chart 2

Patt. Rep. = 16 sts
4th Size
1st Size
2nd Size
3rd Size

Chart 3

Patt. Rep. = 16 sts
4th Size
1st Size
2nd Size
3rd Size

Slipstitch Sweater

The light crunchy textures of a three-color slipstitch pattern and warm autumnal colors made this shawl-collared sweater an all-weather favorite for men and women.

Sizes
To fit 38[40:42]in chest/bust
Length 24¾[25¼:25½]in
Sleeve seam 19[19:19½]in
Note Instructions for larger sizes are in brackets []; where there is only one set of figures it applies to all sizes.

Gauge
22 sts and 31 rows to 4in over patt on size 5 needles

Materials
350[400:450]g double knitting yarn or 15[17:19]oz knitting worsted in main color (A)
175[225:275]g or 8[9:11]oz, respectively, in contrasting color (B)
125[175:175]g or 6[8:8]oz, respectively, in contrasting color (C)
1 pair each sizes 3 and 5 knitting needles

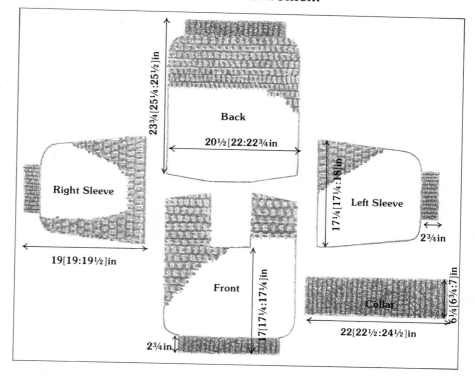

Back
**Using smaller needles and A, cast on 104[112:116] sts.
Work in K2, P2 rib for 2¾in
Next row Rib 12[16:18], *work twice into next st, rib 7, rep from * to last 4[8:10] sts, K to end. 115[123:127] sts. Using larger needles, beg patt.
Sl all sl sts with yarn on WS of work.
1st row (RS) With A, K.
2nd row With A, P.
3rd row With B, K3, *sl 1, K3, rep from * to end.
4th row With B, P3, *sl 1, P3, rep from * to end.
5th row With C, K1, *sl 1, K3, rep from * ending last rep K1.
6th row With C, K1, *sl 1, K3, rep from * ending last rep K1.
7th and 8th rows As 3rd and 4th rows.
9th row As 5th row but with A.
10th row With A, P1, *sl 1, P3, rep from * ending last rep P1.
11th–12th rows As first–2nd rows.
13th row With B, K1, *sl 1, K3, rep from * ending last rep K1.
14th row With B, P1, *sl 1, P3, rep from * ending last rep P1.
15th row With C, K3, *sl 1, K3, rep from * to end.
16th row With C, K3, *sl 1, K3, rep from * to end.

17th and 18th rows As 13th and 14th rows.
19th row As 15th row but with A.
20th row With A, P3, *sl 1, P3, rep from * to end. These 20 rows form the patt.** Cont in patt until work measures 24¾[25¼:25½]in, ending with a WS row.
Shape shoulders
Keeping patt correct, bind off 13[14:15] sts at beg of next 4 rows, then 14[15:14] sts at beg of next 2 rows. Bind off rem 35[37:39] sts.

Front
Work as for back from ** to **.
Cont in patt until work measures 17[17¼:17¼]in ending with a WS row.
Shape neck
Next row Patt 40[43:44], bind off 35[37:39], patt to end.
Work right side of neck first.
Work even until work matches back to shoulder shaping, ending at armhole edge.
Shape shoulder
Bind off 13[14:15] sts at beg of next and every other row once. Work 1 row. Bind off rem 14[15:14] sts.

With WS of work facing, return to sts for left side of neck. Join in yarn and complete to match first side, reversing shaping.

Sleeves
Using smaller needles and A, cast on 56 sts. Work 2¾in K2, P2 rib.
Next row Rib 5[5:1], *work twice into next st, rib 1, rep from * to last 5[5:1] sts, rib to end. 79[79:83] sts. Change to larger needles.
Cont in patt as given for back, inc 1 st at each end of the next and every foll 12th row until there are 97[97:101] sts. Work even until work measures 19[19:19½]in, ending with WS row. Bind off.

Collar
Using smaller needles and A, cast on 172[176:192] sts. Work K2, P2 rib for 6¼[6¾:17]in. Bind off in rib.

To finish
Join shoulder seams. Mark 8½[8½:9]in down from shoulders. Set in sleeves. Join side and sleeve seams. Sew on collar.

Bow and Suspenders Sweater

This intriguing *trompe l'oeil* design is really easy to knit,
but it's likely to attract some second glances from
fascinated passers-by.

Sizes

To fit 34[36:38]in bust
Length 21¼[21½:22]in
Sleeve seam 17[17:17¾]in
Note Instructions for the larger sizes are in brackets []; where there is only one set of figures it applies to all sizes.

Gauge

22 sts and 28 rows to 4in over st st on size 5 needles

Materials

350[350:400]g double knitting yarn or 15[15:17]oz of knitting worsted in main color (A)
50g or 2oz, respectively, in each of 3 contrasting colors (B), (C) and (D)
1 pair sizes 3 and 5 knitting needles
Size 3 circular needle
6 buttons

Front

**Using smaller needles and B, cast on 91[97:103] sts.
1st row K1, *P1, K1, rep from *.
2nd row P1, *K1, P1, rep from *.
Rep the last 2 rows for 2¾in, ending with a first row.
Next row Rib 4[6:9], pick up loop between st just worked and next st, and work into back of it, − called M1 −, (rib 7, M1) 12 times, rib 3[7:10]. 104[110:116] sts.
Change to larger needles and beg with a K row work 2 rows st st.**
Cont to work in st st, reading patt from chart A as foll:
1st row K15[18:21] B, K first row from chart A, K24B, K first row from chart A, K15[18:21] B.
2nd row P15[18:21] B, P 2nd row from chart A, P24B, P 2nd row from chart A, P15[18:21] B.
These 2 rows establish the position of the suspender thongs.
Cont until the 22 rows of chart A have been worked.
Next row K24[27:30]A, 7D, 42A, 7D, 24[27:30] A.
Next row P24[27:30]A, 7D, 42A, 7D, 24[27:30] A.
The last 2 rows establish the position of the suspenders.
Rep the last 2 rows 28 more times.
Shape armholes
Keeping patt correct as set, bind off 7[7:8] sts at beg of next 2 rows. Dec 1 st at each end of the next and every other row until 74[78:82] sts rem.

Work 1[1:3] rows straight.
Work even, keeping patt correct as set, and beg patt from chart B as foll:
Next row Patt 26[28:30] A, K first row from chart B, patt 26[28:30] A.
Next row Patt 26[28:30] A, P 2nd row from chart B, patt 26[28:30] A.
These 2 rows establish the position of the bow tie. Cont as set until the 8 rows of chart B have been worked.
Keeping the patt for suspenders correct work 4 rows straight.
Shape neck
Next row Patt 32[32:34] sts, turn, leaving rem sts on a spare needle, patt to end.
Complete left side of neck first.
Keeping patt correct, dec 1 st at neck edge on the next and every other row until 22[23:24] sts rem, ending at armhole edge.
Shape shoulder
Bind off 7 sts at the beg of next and every other row once.
Patt 1 row. Bind off rem 8[9:10] sts.

With RS of work facing return to sts on spare needle.
Sl center 10[12:14] sts onto a stitch holder, join in yarn to next st, patt to end. Patt 1 row.
Complete to match first side of neck reversing shapings.

Back

Work as for front from ** to **.
Cont to work in st st, reading patt from chart A as foll:
Next row K40[43:46] B, K first row from chart A, K39[42:45] B.
Next row P39[42:45] B, P 2nd row from chart A, P40[43:46] B.
The last 2 rows establish the position of the suspenders thong.
Cont until the 22 rows of chart A have been worked.
Next row K49[52:55] A, 7D, 48[51:54] A.
Next row P48[51:54] A, 7D, 49[52:55] A.
Rep the last 2 rows once more.

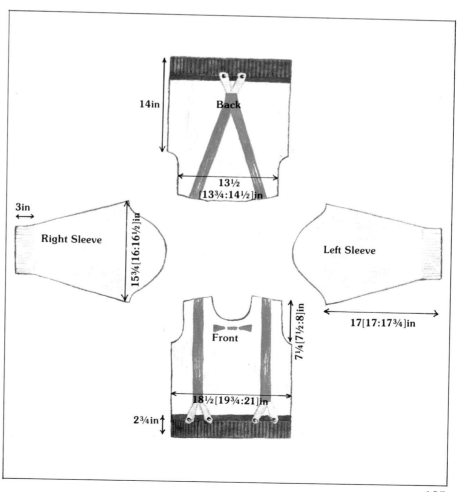

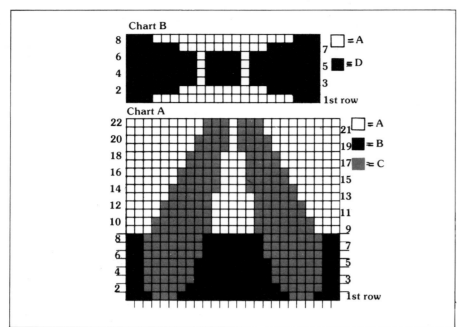

Chart B

= A
= D

1st row

Chart A

= A
= B
= C

1st row

Next row K48[51:54]A, 8D, 48[51:54] A.
Next row P48[51:54] A, 8D, 48[51:54] A.
Rep the last 2 rows once more.
Next row K47[50:53] A, 10D, 47[50:53] A.
Next row P47[50:53] A, 10D, 47[50:53] A.
Rep the last 2 rows once more, then the first of them again.
Next row P46[49:52] A, 12D, 46[49:52] A.
Next row K46[49:52] A, 12D, 46[49:52] A.
Rep the last 2 rows once more.
Next row P45[48:51] A, 14D, 45[48:51] A.
Next row K45[48:51] A, 14D, 45[48:51] A.
Rep the last 2 rows once more.
Next row P44[47:50] A, 7D, 2A, 7D, 44[47:50] A.
Next row K44[47:50] A, 7D, 2A, 7D, 44[47:50] A.
Rep the last 2 rows once more.
Next row P43[46:49] A, 7D, 4A, 7D, 43[46:49] A.
Next row K43[46:49] A, 7D, 4A, 7D, 43[46:49] A.
Rep the last 2 rows once more.
Next row P42[45:48]A, 7D, 6A, 7D, 42[45:48] A.
Next row K42[45:48] A, 7D, 6A, 7D, 42[45:48] A.
Rep the last 2 rows once more, then

the first of them again.
Next row K41[44:47] A, 7D, 8A, 7D, 41[44:47] A.
Next row P41[44:47] A, 7D, 8A, 7D, 41[44:47] A.
Rep the last 2 rows once more, then the first of them again.
Next row P40[43:46] A, 7D, 10A, 7D, 40[43:46] A.
Next row K40[43:46] A, 7D, 10A, 7D, 40[43:46] A.
Rep the last 2 rows once more.
Next row P39[42:45] A, 7D, 12A, 7D, 39[42:45] A.
Next row K39[42:45] A, 7D, 12A, 7D, 39[42:45] A.
Rep the last 2 rows once more, then the first of them again.
Next row K38[41:44] A, 7D, 14A, 7D, 38[41:44] A.
Next row P38[41:44] A, 7D, 14A, 7D, 38[41:44] A.
Rep the last 2 rows once more.
Next row K37[40:43] A, 7D, 16A, 7D, 37[40:43] A.
Next row P37[40:43] A, 7D, 16A, 7D, 37[40:43] A.
Rep the last 2 rows once more, then the first of them again.
Next row P36[39:42] A, 7D, 18A, 7D, 36[39:42] A.
Shape armholes
Next row Bind off 7[7:8] sts, K29[32:34] A, 7D, 18A, 7D, 36[39:42] A.
Next row Bind off 7[7:8] sts,

P29[32:34] A, 7D, 18A, 7D, 29[32:34] A.
Keep patt for suspenders correct by moving them to the armhole edges by 1 st on the 2nd then on every foll 5th and then 4th row as before.
At the same time, dec 1 st at each end of the next and every other row until 74[78:82] sts rem.
Work even in patt until there are 9[11:13] sts in A at armhole edge. Then cont as set until work measures same as front to shoulder shaping, ending with a P row.
Shape shoulders
Bind off 7 sts at beg of next 4 rows and 8[9:10] sts at beg of next 2 rows. Leave rem 30[32:34] sts on a stitch holder.

Sleeves
Using smaller needles and A, cast on 40[42:44] sts and work in K1, P1 rib for 3in.
Change to larger needles and cont in st st, inc 1 st at each end of the next and every foll 4th row until there are 88[90:92] sts.
Work even until work measures 17[17:17¾]in ending with a P row.
Shape top
Bind off 7[7:8] sts at beg of next 2 rows. Dec 1 st at each end of the next and every foll 3rd row until 38 sts rem.
Bind off.

To finish
Join shoulder seams.
With RS of work facing, using circular needle and A, join in yarn to center of sts on front stitch holder, K5[6:7], pick up and K 22 sts up right side of neck, K30[32:34] sts on back neck, pick up and K 22 sts down left side of neck, then K5[6:7] sts from front stitch holder. 84[88:92] sts. Mark first st for beg of round.
Work in rounds of K1, P1 rib for 1¼in, ending at the end of a round. Now work in rows for another 2in. Bind off in rib. Join side and sleeve seams.
Set in sleeves, gathering fullness to form a puff top.
Sew the buttons to the suspender thongs.
Lightly press corners of collar to form wings.

Patterned Two-piece

Put on the style in this super-sophisticated, unusual
two-piece combining a pocketed vest and classic cardigan
in an interesting positive-negative color scheme.

Sizes
To fit 32[34:36:38]in bust
Vest length 22[22½:23:23½]in
Cardigan length 26[26½:27:27½]in
Sleeve seam 17[17:17¼:17¼]in
Note Instructions for larger sizes are in brackets []; where there is only one set of figures it applies to all sizes.

Gauge
Vest:
31 sts and 34 rows to 4in over patt on size 3 needles
Cardigan:
19 sts and 24 rows to 4in over patt on size 6 needles

Materials
Vest
225[225:275:275]g four-ply yarn or 9[10:12:12]oz sport-weight yarn in main color (A)
75[75:100:100]g or 3[3:5:5]oz, respectively, in contrasting color (B)
1 pair each sizes 2 and 3 knitting needles
6 buttons

Cardigan
21[21:23:23]oz knitting worsted in main color (C)
7[7:8:8]oz in contrasting color (D)
1 pair each sizes 4 and 6 knitting needles
7 buttons

Vest

Back
Using smaller needles and A, cast on 103[109:115:123] sts.
Work in K1, P1 rib as foll:
1st row (RS) K1, *P1, K1, rep from * to end.
2nd row P1, *K1, P1, rep from * to end.
Rep the last 2 rows for 3in ending with a first row.
Next row Rib 11[12:13:15], pick up loop between last st worked and next st and work into back of it – called M1 –, (rib 2, M1) 41[43:45:47] times, rib to end 145[153:161:171] sts.
Change to larger needles and work in st st foll patt from Chart 1, working edge sts as shown and rep the 12 patt sts across the row.
Cont in patt until work measures 13½[13½:13½:13¾]in, ending with a WS row.
108

Shape armholes
Keeping patt correct, bind off 7 sts at beg of next 2 rows.
Dec 1 st at each of the next 9[9:11:11] rows, then at each end of every other row until 99[103:105:113] sts rem.
Work even until work measures 22[22½:23:23½]in, ending with a WS row.

Shape shoulders
Bind off 8[9:8:9] sts at beg of next 4 rows and 9[8:9:10] sts at beg of next 2 rows.
Bind off rem 49[51:55:57] sts.

Pocket lining
Using larger needles and A, cast on 31 sts. Beg with a K row cont in st st until work measures 4in, ending with a P row. Leave these sts on a spare needle.

Left front
**Using smaller needles and A, cast on 51[55:57:61] sts.
Work in K1, P1 rib as for back for 3in, ending with a first row.

Next row Rib 6[8:7:8], M1, (rib 2, M1) 20[20:22:23] times, rib to end. 72[76:80:85] sts.**
Change to larger needles and work in st st foll patt from Chart 2.
Cont in patt until work measures 7in, ending with a WS row.

Place pocket
Next row Patt 16[18:20:22], sl next 41 sts onto a stitch holder, patt across 31 sts of pocket lining *at same time* inc 10 sts evenly, patt to end.
Cont in patt until work matches back to underarm, ending with a WS row.

Shape armhole and neck
Next row Bind off 7 sts, patt to last 2 sts, K2 tog.
Next row Patt to end.
Dec 1 st at armhole edge on next 9[9:11:11] rows then on every other row and *at the same time*, dec 1 st at neck edge on the next and every other row until 36[36:35:38] sts rem.
Keeping armhole edge straight cont to dec at neck edge on every foll 3rd row until 25[26:25:28] sts rem.
Work even until work matches back to shoulder shaping, ending with a WS row.

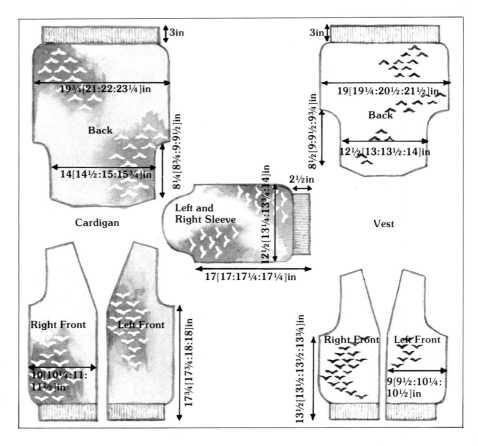

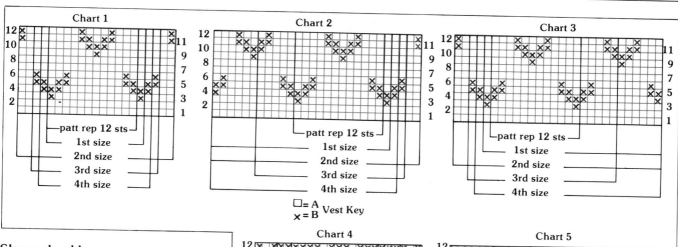

Chart 1   Chart 2   Chart 3

patt rep 12 sts — 1st size — 2nd size — 3rd size — 4th size

□ = A
✗ = B   Vest Key

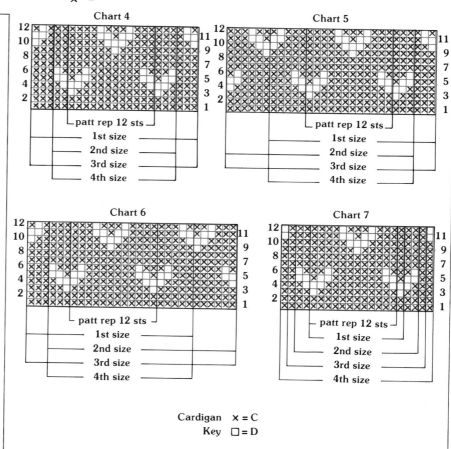

Chart 4   Chart 5

patt rep 12 sts — 1st size — 2nd size — 3rd size — 4th size

Chart 6   Chart 7

patt rep 12 sts — 1st size — 2nd size — 3rd size — 4th size

Cardigan   ✗ = C
Key   □ = D

Shape shoulder
Bind off 8[9:8:9] sts at beg of next and every other row once. Work 1 row. Bind off rem 9[8:9:10] sts.

Right front
Work as for left front from ** to **.
Change to larger needles and work in st st foll patt from Chart 3.
Complete to match left front, omitting pocket and reversing shapings.

To finish
Press as appropriate for yarn used.
Join shoulder seams.
Pocket edging
With RS of work facing, using smaller needles, join in A to 41 sts on stitch holder.
1st row K1, *P1, K1, rep from * to end.
2nd row P1, *K1, P1, rep from * to end.
Rep the last 2 rows 3 more times.
Bind off in rib.
Catch down pocket edging and pocket lining.
Button band
Using smaller needles and A, cast on 11 sts.
1st row (RS) K2, *P1, K1, rep from * to last st, K1.
2nd row *K1, P1, rep from * to last st, K1.
Rep the last 2 rows until band, when slightly stretched, fits up left front edge to center back neck.
Bind off in rib.
Buttonhole band
Sew on button band. Mark the position of six buttonholes, the first to come ¾in from lower edge, the last ¾in below front neck shaping, with

the others evenly spaced between.
Using smaller needles and A, cast on 11 sts.
Work as for button band making buttonholes opposite markers as foll:
1st row (RS) Rib 5, bind off 2, rib 4.
2nd row Rib 4, cast on 2, rib 5.
Sew on buttonhole band, joining to button band at center back neck.
Armbands
With RS of work facing, using smaller needles and A, pick up and K

114[118:124:130] sts evenly around the armhole edge.
Work 10 rows K1, P1 rib. Bind off in rib.
Join side seams. Sew on button.

Cardigan

Back
Using smaller needles and C, cast on 81[85:91:97] sts and work in K1, P1

rib as for vest back for 3in, ending with a first row.
Next row Rib 8[5:8:4], M1, (rib 5[5:5:6], M1) 13[15:15:15] times, rib to end. 95[101:107:113] sts.
Change to larger needles and work in st st foll patt from Chart 4. Cont in patt until work measures approx 17¾[17¾:18:18]in from cast-on edge, ending with a WS row.
Shape armholes
Keeping patt correct, bind off 5 sts at beg of next 2 rows. Dec 1 st at each end of the next 3[3:5:5] rows, then on every other row until 69[71:73:77] sts rem.
Work even until work measures 26[26½:27:27½]in, ending with a WS row.
Shape shoulders
Bind off 6[6:6:7] sts at beg of next 4 rows and 7[7:7:6] sts at beg of next 2 rows.
Bind off rem 31[33:35:37] sts.

Left front
***Using smaller needles and C, cast on 39[41:45:47] sts and work in K1, P1 rib as for vest back for 3in, ending with a first row.
Next row Rib 2[5:5:4], M1, (rib 5[4:5:5], M1) 7[8:7:8] times, rib to end. 47[50:53:56] sts. ***
Change to larger needles and work in st st foll patt from Chart 5. Cont in patt until work matches back to underarm, ending with a WS row.

Shape armhole and neck
Next row Bind off 5 sts, patt to last 2 sts, K2 tog.
Next row Patt to end.
Dec 1 st at armhole edge on the next 3[3:5:5] rows then on every other row *at the same time*, dec 1 st at neck edge on the next and every other row until 19[19:19:20] sts rem.
Work even until work matches back to shoulder shaping, ending with a WS row.
Shape shoulder
Bind off 6[6:6:7] sts at beg of next and every other row once.
Work 1 row.
Bind off rem 7[7:7:6] sts.

Right front
Work as for left front from *** to ***.
Change to larger needles and working in patt from Chart 6 complete to match left front reversing shapings.

Sleeves
Using smaller needles and C, cast on 38[40:42:44] sts and work in K1, P1 rib for 2½in.
Next row Rib 8[8:9:10], M1, (rib 1, M1) 22[24:24:24] times, rib to end. 61[65:67:69] sts.
Change to larger needles and work in st st foll patt from Chart 7. Cont in patt until work measures approx 17[17:17¼:17¼]in from cast-on

edge, ending with a 6th[6th:8th:8th] patt row.
Shape top
Keeping patt correct, bind off 5 sts at beg of next 2 rows.
1st size only
Dec 1 st at each end of the next and foll 4th row. Work 1 row. 47 sts.
All sizes
Dec 1 st at each end of the next and every other row until 21 sts rem, ending with a WS row. Bind off.

To finish
Press as appropriate for yarn used. Join shoulder, side and sleeve seams. Set in sleeves.
Button band
Using smaller needles and C, cast on 9 sts. Work as for button band of vest.
Buttonhole band
Sew on button band. Mark the position of seven buttonholes, the first to come ¾in from lower edge, the last ¾in below front neck shaping, with the others evenly spaced between.
Using smaller needles and C, cast on 9 sts.
Work as for button band making buttonholes opposite markers as foll:
1st row (RS) Rib 4, bind off 2, rib 3.
2nd row Rib 3, cast on 2, rib 4.
Sew on buttonhole band, joining to button band at center back neck.
Sew on buttons.

Special technique – working an armband

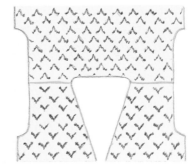

1 The vest has armbands which are knitted onto the main pattern pieces. Begin by joining the shoulder seams.

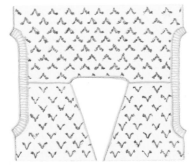

2 With the right side of the work facing, pick up and knit the required stitches evenly around the armhole edge. Work in single rib to the required depth. Bind off in rib.

3 Finish by joining the side seams. Join the ribbed waistband and armband with a flat seam. Join the stockinette stitch parts with an invisible seam.

Fireworks Sweater

**Set a few sparks alight with this stunning design – a perfect
example of the effectiveness of sharp, bright colors on a
black background**

Size
To fit 32–37in bust
Length 25½in
Sleeve seam 16in

Gauge
17 sts and 25 rows to 4in over st st
on size 8 needles

Materials
16oz knitting worsted in main color
(A)
2oz each in 7 contrasting colors
1 pair each sizes 5 and 8 knitting
needles
Set of size 5 double-pointed needles

Back
*Using smaller needles and A, cast
on 71 sts. Work in K1, P1 rib as foll:
1st row K1, (P1, K1) to end.
2nd row P1, (K1, P1) to end.
Rep last 2 rows 9 more times.
Change to larger needles. Beg with a
K row cont in st st working from chart
inc 10 sts evenly across first row.
81 sts. Cont until 98 rows have been
worked in st st, ending with a P row.
Shape raglan armholes
Dec 1 st at each end of next and
every other row until 33 sts rem,
ending with a P row. Bind off.

Front
Work as for back from * to *.
Shape raglan armholes
Dec 1 st at each end of next and
every other row until 77 sts rem,
ending with a P row.
Divide for neck
Next row K2 tog, patt 36, turn,
leaving rem sts on a spare needle.
Cont to dec at armhole edge as
before, *at the same time*, dec 1 st at
neck edge on the next, then *every
foll 4th and 2nd row* until 1 st rem.
Fasten off.
With RS of work facing, sl center st
onto a safety pin, join in yarn to next
st, patt to last 2 sts, K2 tog.
Complete to match first side of neck.

Sleeves
Using smaller needles and A, cast on
35 sts. Work 15 rows K1, P1 rib.
Change to larger needles and st st
working patt from chart, inc 10 sts
evenly across first row. 45 sts. Inc 1
st at each end of foll 9th and every
foll 10th row until there are 61 sts.

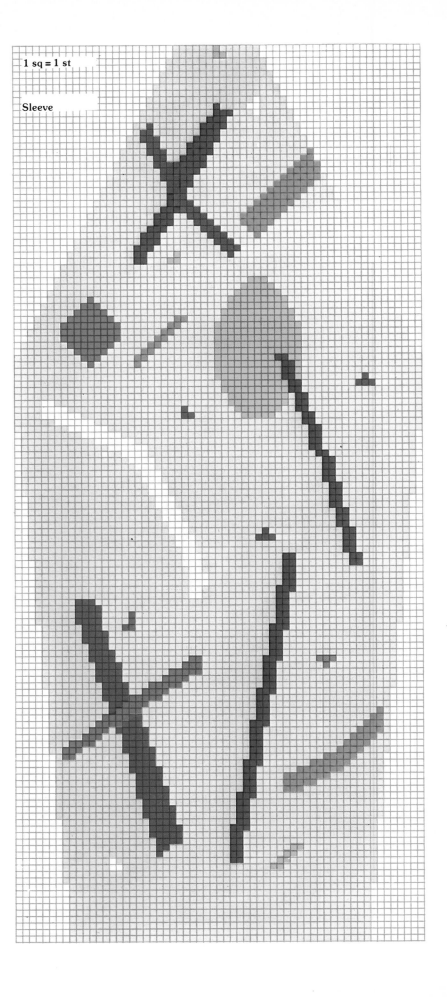

1 sq = 1 st

Sleeve

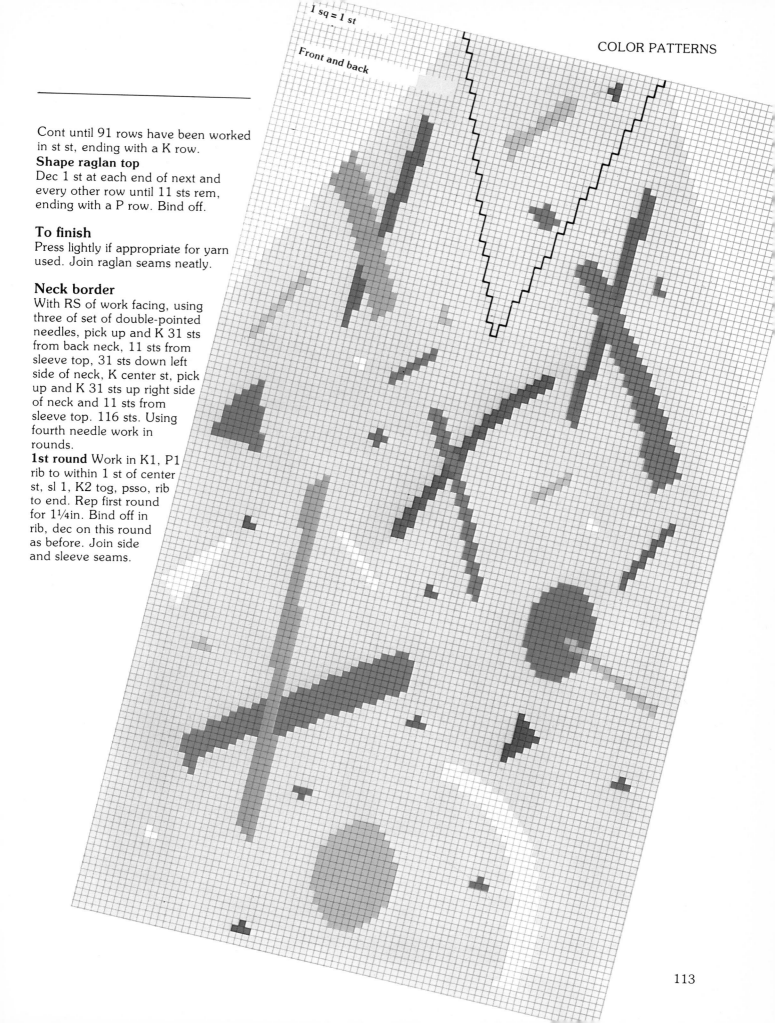

1 sq = 1 st

Front and back

Cont until 91 rows have been worked
in st st, ending with a K row.

Shape raglan top
Dec 1 st at each end of next and
every other row until 11 sts rem,
ending with a P row. Bind off.

To finish
Press lightly if appropriate for yarn
used. Join raglan seams neatly.

Neck border
With RS of work facing, using
three of set of double-pointed
needles, pick up and K 31 sts
from back neck, 11 sts from
sleeve top, 31 sts down left
side of neck, K center st, pick
up and K 31 sts up right side
of neck and 11 sts from
sleeve top. 116 sts. Using
fourth needle work in
rounds.

1st round Work in K1, P1
rib to within 1 st of center
st, sl 1, K2 tog, psso, rib
to end. Rep first round
for 1¼in. Bind off in
rib, dec on this round
as before. Join side
and sleeve seams.

Harlequin Pullover and T-shirt

Join the carnival spirit with this original, multicolored pullover, finished with flattering ruffles at the neck and waist. The child's T-shirt is simply made from two rectangles.

Pullover

Sizes

To fit 30[32:34]in bust
Length, excluding ruffle, 19[20½:22]in
Sleeve seam 17in
Note Instructions for the larger sizes are in brackets []; where there is only one set of figures, it applies to all sizes.

Gauge

26 sts and 25 rows to 4in over patt on size 5 needles

Materials

8[9:10]oz sport-weight yarn in main color (A)
6oz each in two contrasting colors (B) and (C)
1 pair size 5 knitting needles
Size 5 circular needle

Back

**Using pair of needles and B, cast on 202[214:230] sts.
Next row K.
Change to C.
Next row P.
Next row K.
Change to A.
Beg with a P row, cont in st st.
Work 18 rows.
Next row *P2 tog, rep from * to end. 101[107:115] sts.
Using small separate balls of B and C, beg patt from chart, twisting yarns when changing colors to prevent a hole. Read RS rows (odd-numbered) from right to left and WS rows (even-numbered) from left to right.
Cont until work measures 11½[13:14½]in, ending with a P row.

Shape armholes

Keeping patt correct, bind off 6 sts at beg of next 2 rows and 5 sts at beg of foll 2 rows. Dec 1 st at each end of next 1[2:4] rows. 77[81:85] sts.**
Work even until work measures 19[20½:22]in from beg, ending with a WS row.

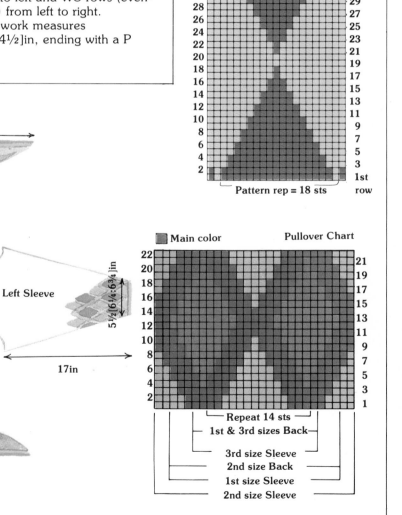

T-shirt chart (page 117)

Pattern rep = 18 sts

Main color   Pullover Chart

Repeat 14 sts
1st & 3rd sizes Back
3rd size Sleeve
2nd size Back
1st size Sleeve
2nd size Sleeve

30½[32¼:34½]in

Back

7½in

12[12¼:13]in

Right Sleeve

13[13¾:14½]in

Left Sleeve

5½[6¼:6¾]in

Front

11½[13:14½]in

15¼[16:17¼]in

17in

Shape shoulders
Bind off 8 sts at beg of next 2 rows and 15[17:19] sts at beg of foll 2 rows. Bind off rem sts.

Front
Work as for back from ** to **.
Work even until work measures 16[17¾:19¼]in, ending with a WS row.
Shape neck
Next row Patt 33[35:37], bind off 11 sts, patt to end.
Complete right side of neck first.
Next row Patt to end.
***Next row** Bind off 5 sts, patt to end.
Next row Patt to end.
Next row Bind off 3 sts, patt to end.
Next row Patt to end.
Dec 1 st at neck edge on next and every other row once. 23[25:27] sts.
Work even until work matches back to shoulder shaping, ending at armhole edge.
Shape shoulder
Bind off 8 sts at beg of next row.
Work 1 row.
Bind off rem 15[17:19] sts.
With WS of work facing return to sts for left side of neck.
Complete to match right side of neck, working from *** to end.

Sleeves
Using pair of needles and A, cast on 37[41:45] sts.
Beg with a K row cont in st st. Work 3 rows.
Change to C. K 2 rows.
Change to B.
Next row P.
Next row K.
Change to A.
Form hem
Next row *P next st and corresponding st of cast-on row tog, rep from * to end.
Using small separate balls of B and C beg patt from chart, *at the same time*, inc 1 st at each end of the 3rd and every foll 4th row until there are 87[91:95] sts.
Work even until work measures 17in from hem, ending with a P row.
Shape sleeve top
Keeping patt correct, bind off 3 sts at beg of next 2 rows and 2 sts at beg of foll 2 rows.
Dec 1 st at each end of foll 5th row.

Patt 2 rows.
Dec 1 st at beg of next 16 rows.
Bind off 2 sts at beg of foll 4 rows.
Dec 1 st at beg of foll 2 rows.
Bind off 2 sts at beg of foll 2 rows.
Dec 1 st at beg of next 6 rows.
Bind off.

To finish
Press pieces.
Join right shoulder seam.
Neck ruffle
With WS of work facing, using circular needle and A, pick up and 88[100:112] sts around neck. Work in rows as foll:
Next row *P into front and back of next st, rep from * to end. 176[200:224] sts.
Beg with a K row work 9 rows st st.
Next row *P into front and back of next st, rep from * to end. 352[400:448] sts.
Change to C, beg with a K row and work 2 rows st st. Change to B.
Next row K.
Bind off P-wise.
Join left shoulder and collar.
Set in sleeves, gathering cap to form puff. Join side and sleeve seams.

Special technique – knitted-in hem

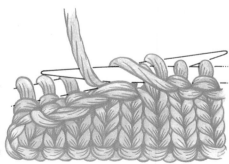

1 *The sleeves on the sweater have knitted-in hems. Work the underside of the hem in stockinette stitch beginning and ending with a knit row. Knit the next row. This row forms the fold line of the hem.*

2 *Continue in stockinette stitch for the same number of rows as for the underside, beginning and ending with a knit row.*

3 *On the next row purl each stitch together with the corresponding stitch in the cast-on edge, thus completing the hem.*

T-shirt
Size
To fit 25in chest
Length 18in

Gauge
23 sts and 31 rows to 4in over patt on size 3 needles.

Materials
5oz sport-weight cotton yarn in each of 2 contrasting colors (A) and (B)
1 pair each sizes 2 and 3 knitting needles

Back and front (alike)
Using smaller needles and A, cast on 74 sts. Work in K1, P1 rib for 2¾in, ending with a WS row. Inc 1 st at end of last row. 75 sts.
Change to larger needles. Join in B. Work 114 rows in diamond patt from chart on page 115, marking each end of 76th row for armholes.
Cont in A only, work 8 rows K1, P1 rib. Bind off in rib.

To make up
Sew shoulder seams together 20 sts in from each end.
Armbands
Using smaller needles and A, pick up and K 80 sts between markers. Work in K1, P1 rib for 5 rows. Bind off in rib. Sew side seams together.

Atlas Jacket

A colorful map of the world enlives this warm and stylish jacket, knitted in a bulky yarn and suitable for a man or woman.

Sizes
To fit 34[36:38]in chest/bust
Length 24[25:26]in
Sleeve seam 18[18½:19¼]in
Note Instructions for larger sizes are in brackets []; where there is only one set of figures it applies to all sizes.

Gauge
14 sts and 19 rows to 4in over st st on size 10 needles

Materials
27[27:29]oz Icelandic yarn in main color (A)
2oz in each of 5 contrasting colors (B), (C), (D), (E) and (F)
Five 1in-diameter buttons – 3 in A, 1 in B and 1 in E
1 pair each sizes 8 and 10 knitting needles

Back
Using smaller needles and A, cast on 76[80:84] sts.
Work 14 rows in K1, P1 rib.
Change to larger needles and beg with a K row cont in st st working in patt from chart for the back section given on page 120, reading K rows from right to left and P rows from left to right.
Work 62[66:70] rows.
Shape armholes
Bind off 6 sts at beg of next 2 rows.
Dec 1 st at beg of the next and every row until 56 sts rem.
Work even until 102[106:110] rows have been worked from chart.
Shape shoulders
Bind off 16 sts at beg of next 2 rows.
Bind off rem 24 sts.

Left front
Using smaller needles and A, cast on 41[43:45] sts.
1st row P1, *K1, P1, rep from * to last 6 sts, K6.
32nd row K7, *P1, K1, rep from *.
Woman's version only
Rep first and 2nd rows 6 more times.
Man's version only
Rep first and 2nd rows once more.
1st buttonhole row P1, *K1, P1, rep from * to last 6 sts, K2, bind off 2 sts, K2.

2nd buttonhole row K2, cast on 2 sts, K3, *P1, K1, rep from * to end.
Rep first and 2nd rows 4 more times.
Both versions
Change to larger needles.
Next row Working from chart K to last 6 sts, K6.
Next row K6, working from chart P to end.
Cont in this way, keeping front edge sts in garter st, working patt and buttonholes for man's version as shown on chart.
Work a further 60[64:68] rows.
Shape armhole
Bind off 6 sts at beg of next row.
Work 1 row. Dec 1 st at beg of next and every other row until 31 sts rem.
Work even until 89[93:97] rows have been worked from chart.
Shape neck
Bind off 11 sts at beg of next row.
Work 1 row.
Dec 1 st at beg of next and every other row until 16 sts rem.
Work even until 102[106:110] rows have been worked from chart.
Shape shoulder
Bind off rem sts.

Right front
Using smaller needles and A, cast on 41[43:45] sts.
1st row K6, *P1, K1, rep from * to last st, P1.
2nd row *K1, P1, rep from * to last 7 sts, K7.
Man's version only
Rep first and 2nd rows 6 more times.
Woman's version only
Rep first and 2nd rows once more.
1st buttonhole K2, bind off 2 sts, K2, *P1, K1, rep from * to last st, P1.
2nd buttonhole *K1, P1, rep from * to last 5 sts, K3, cast on 2 sts, K2.
Rep first and 2nd rows 4 more times.
Both versions
Change to larger needles.
Next row K6, working from chart, K to end.
Next row Working from chart, P to last 6 sts, K6.
Cont in this way, keeping front edge sts in garter st and working patt and buttonholes for woman's version as

shown on chart.
Work a further 61[65:69] rows.
Shape armhole
Bind off 6 sts at beg of next row.
Work 1 row.
Dec 1 st at beg of next and every other row until 31 sts rem.
Work even until 88[92:96] rows have been worked from chart.
Shape neck
Bind off 11 sts at beg of next row.
Work 1 row.
Dec 1 st at beg of next and every other row until 16 sts rem.
Work even until 103[107:111] rows have been worked from chart.
Shape shoulder
Bind off rem sts.

Sleeves
Using smaller needles and A, cast on 38 sts. Work 14 rows K1, P1 rib.
Change to larger needles and beg with a K row work in st st and patt from chart, for left sleeve only.
Work 2[6:10] rows. Inc 1 st at each end of the next and every foll 6th row until there are 56 sts. Work even until 70[74:78] rows have been worked from chart.
Shape sleeve top
Bind off 6 sts at beg of next 2 rows.
Dec 1 st at beg of every foll row until 14 sts rem.
Bind off.

Collar
Using larger needles and A, cast on 6 sts. Cont in garter st (every row K).
Work 2 rows.
Inc 1 st at the beg of the next and every other row until there are 14 sts.
Work even until 60 rows have been worked from cast-on edge. Dec 1 st at the beg of the next and every other row until 6 sts rem.
Work 2 rows.
Bind off.

To finish
Press lightly if appropriate for yarn used.
Join shoulder, side, and sleeve seams. Set in sleeves.
Sew shaped edge of collar to neck edge. Sew on buttons.

**Jacket
charts**

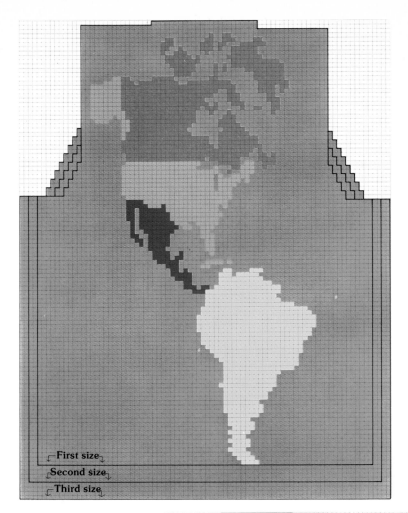

First size
Second size
Third size

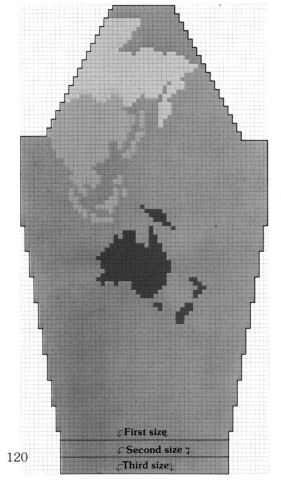

First size
Second size
Third size

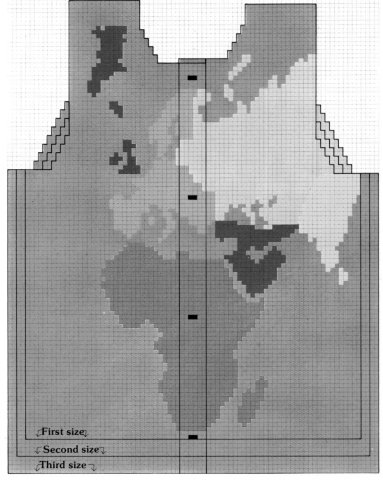

First size
Second size
Third size

Mosaic Sweater

Perfect for a warm spring day, this stunning sweater is knitted in cool cotton. The stitch pattern may look intricate, but it's very easy to knit – only one color is used in each row.

Sizes
To fit 32–34[36–38]in bust
Length 22[22½]in
Sleeve seam 4½in
Note Instructions for the larger size are in brackets []; where there is only one figure it applies to both sizes.

Gauge
22 sts and 36 rows to 4in over patt on size 5 needles

Materials
15[16]oz thick cotton yarn such as Pingouin Coton Naturel 8 Fils in main color (A)
8[10]oz contrasting color (B)
1 pair each sizes 3 and 5 knitting needles
3 buttons

Back
On all RS rows sl all the sl sts with yarn at back of work and on all WS rows sl all the sl sts with the yarn at front of work.
**Using smaller needles and A, cast on 82[90] sts and work 3in in K1, P1 rib.
Next row Rib 1, work twice into next st – called inc 1 –, *rib 3, inc 1, rep from * to end. 103[113] sts.
Change to larger needles.
Next row P.
Beg patt.
1st row (RS) With B, K7[12], *sl 2, K7, sl 2, K15, rep from * ending last rep K7[12].
2nd row With B, K7[12], *sl 2, P7, sl 2, K15, rep from * ending last rep K7[12].
3rd row With A, K2, sl 1, K1[K1, (sl 1, K1) 4 times], sl 1, K4, sl 2, K3, sl 2, K4, (sl 1, K1) 3 times, *(sl 1, K1) twice, sl 1, K4, sl 2, K3, sl 2, K4, (sl 1, K1) 3 times, rep from * ending last rep (sl 1, K1) twice, K1[sl 1, K1) 5 times] instead of (sl 1, K1) 3 times.
4th row With A, K1, (K1, sl 1) twice, [(K1, sl 1), 5 times], P4, sl 2, K3, sl 2, P4, (sl 1, K1) 3 times, *(sl 1, K1) twice, sl 1, P4, sl 2, K3, sl 2, P4, (sl 1, K1) 3 times, rep from * ending last rep (sl 1, K1) twice, K1[sl

1, K1) 5 times] instead of (sl 1, K1) 3 times.
5th row With B, K5[10], *sl 2, K4, sl 1, K1, sl 1, K4, sl 2, K11, rep from * ending last rep K5[10].
6th row With B, K5[10], *sl 2, P4, sl 1, K1, sl 1, P4, sl 2, K11, rep from * ending last rep K5[10].
7th row With A, K2, sl 1[(K1, sl 1) 4 times], K4, sl 2, K7, sl 2, K4, (sl 1, K1) twice, *sl 1, K1, sl 1, K4, sl 2, K7, sl 2, K4, (sl 1, K1) twice, rep from * ending last rep sl 1, K2[(sl 1, K1) 4 times] instead of (sl 1, K1) twice.
8th row With A, K2, sl 1[(K1, sl 1) 4 times], P4, sl 2, K7, sl 2, P4, (sl 1, K1) twice, *sl 1, K1, sl 1, P4, sl 2, K7, sl 2, P4, (sl 1, K1) twice, rep from * ending last rep sl 1, K2[(sl 1, K1) 4 times] instead of (sl 1, K1) twice.
9th row With B, K3[8], *sl 2, K4, (sl 1, K1) 3 times, sl 1, K4, sl 2, K7, rep from * ending last rep K3[8].
10th row With B, K3[8], *sl 2, P4, (sl 1, K1) 3 times, sl 1, P4, sl 2, K7, rep from * ending last rep K3[8].
11th row With A, K1[K3, sl 1, K1, sl 1], K4, sl 2, K11, sl 2, K4, sl 1, K1, *sl 1, K4, sl 2, K11, sl 2, K4, sl 1, K1, rep from * ending last rep K1[sl 1, K1, sl 1, K3] instead of sl 1, K1.
12th row With A, K1[K3, sl 1, K1, sl 1], P4, sl 2, K11, sl 2, P4, sl 1, K1, *sl 1, P4, sl 2, K11, sl 2, P4, sl 1, K1, rep from * ending last rep K1[sl 1, K1, sl 1, K3] instead of sl 1, K1.
13th row With B, K1, [K1, sl 2, K3], *sl 2, K4, (sl 1, K1) 5 times, sl 1, K4, sl 2, K3, rep from * ending last rep K1[K3, sl 2, K1] instead of K3.
14th row With B, K1[P1, sl 2, K3], *sl 2, P4, (sl 1, K1) 5 times, sl 1, P4, sl 2, K3, rep from * ending last rep K1[K3, sl 2, P1] instead of K3.
15th row With A, K3[8], *sl 2, K15, sl 2, K7, rep from * ending last rep K3[8].
16th row With A, P3[8], *sl 2, K15, sl 2, P7, rep from * ending last rep P3[8].
17th row With B, K1[K3, sl 1, K1, sl 1], K8, sl 2, K3, sl 2, K8, sl 1, K1,

*sl 1, K8, sl 2, K3, sl 2, K8, sl 1, K1, rep from * ending last rep K1[sl 1, K1, sl 1, K3] instead of sl 1, K1.
18th row With B, K1, [P3, sl 1, K1, sl 1], P8, sl 2, P3, sl 2, P8, sl 1, K1, *sl 1, P8, sl 2, P3, sl 2, P8, sl 1, K1, rep from * ending last rep K1[sl 1, K1, sl 1, P3] instead of sl 1, K1.
19th row With A, K1[K1, sl 2, K3], *sl 2, K8, sl 1, K1, sl 1, K8, sl 2, K3, rep from * ending last rep K1[K3, sl 2, K1] instead of K3.
20th row With A, P1[P1, sl 2, P3], *sl 2, P8, sl 1, K1, sl 1, P8, sl 2, P3, rep from * ending last rep P1[P3, sl 2, P1] instead of P3.
These 20 rows form the patt. **Rep these 20 rows 6 more times, then work first–18th rows again.
Beg yoke
1st–2nd rows With A, K.
3rd–4th rows With B, K1, *sl 1, K1, rep from * to end.
These 4 rows form the yoke patt.
Rep the last 4 rows 3[4] more times, then first–2nd rows again.
Shape shoulders
Keeping patt correct, bind off 9[10]

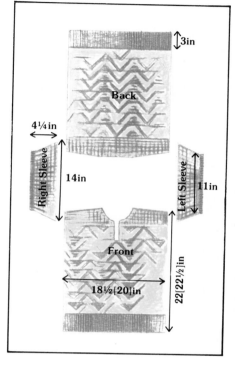

(Back) 3in, Back, 4¼in, Right Sleeve, 14in, Left Sleeve, 11in, Front, 18½[20]in, 22[22½]in

121

sts at beg of next 8 rows. Leave the rem 31[33] sts on a stitch holder.

Front

Work as for back from ** to **. Rep these 20 rows 5 more times, then first–8th[1st–12th] rows again.

Divide for neck

Next row Patt 49[54] sts, bind off 5 sts, patt to end.

Complete right side of neck first. Work even until the 20 patt rows have been worked 7 times in all.

1st size only

Work first–16th rows again.

Shape neck

Next row (RS) Bind off 2 sts, patt to end.

Dec 1 st at neck edge on next row. Change to yoke patt as on back. Rep the last 2 rows once.

2nd size only

Work first–18th rows again. Change to yoke patt as on back.

Shape neck

Next row (RS) Bind off 2 sts, patt to end.

Dec 1 st at neck edge on next row. Rep last 2 rows once.

Both sizes

Dec 1 st at neck edge on every other row 4[5] times, then on 2 foll 4th rows.

Shape shoulder

Dec 1 st at neck edge on next row. Bind off 9[10] sts at beg of next row and on every other row twice. Work 1 row. Bind off rem 9[10] sts. Return to sts for left side of neck. With WS of work facing, join in yarn and patt to end.

Complete to match first side of neck, reversing shapings.

Sleeves

Using smaller needles and A, cast on 52[56] sts. Work 8 rows K1, P1 rib.

Next row Rib 2[4], inc 1, *rib 2, inc 1, rep from * to last 1[3] sts, rib to end. 69[73] sts.

Change to larger needles.

1st–2nd rows With A, K.

3rd–4th rows With B, K1, *sl 1, K1, rep from * to end.

The last 4 rows form the patt. Cont in patt inc 1 st at each end of the next and every foll 4th row until there are 83[87] sts. Work even for 6 more rows. Bind off.

To finish

Join shoulder seams.

Neck border

Using smaller needles and A, with RS of work facing, pick up and K 24 sts from right neck edge, K across 31[33] sts on back neck, pick up and K 24 sts down left side of neck. 79[81] sts.

Next row P1, *K1, P1, rep from *.

Next row K1, *P1, K1, rep from *.

Rep the last 2 rows twice more. Bind off in rib.

Right front border

Using smaller needles and A, with RS of work facing, pick up and K 26 sts down right neck border and front edge.

Work 3 rows K1, P1 rib.

1st buttonhole row Rib 4, *bind off 2 sts, rib 6, rep from * ending last rep rib 4.

2nd buttonhole row Rib 4, *cast on 2 sts, rib 6, rep from * ending last rep rib 4.

Rib 2 rows. Bind off in rib.

Left front border

Work to match right front border omitting buttonholes.

Lap the right front border over left and catch the row ends together sewing to bound-off sts at center front. Place the center of bound-off edge of sleeve at shoulder seam and set in sleeve. Join side and sleeve seams. Sew on buttons.

Special technique – working a simple mosaic

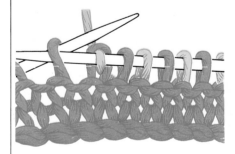

1 *This stitch is used on the sleeves and yoke of the sweater. With color A knit the first two rows (odd-numbered rows are right-side rows). With color B knit the third row, slipping every other stitch purlwise with the yarn at the back of the work.*

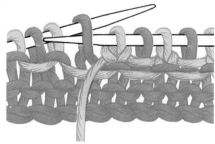

2 *With color B knit the fourth row, slipping purlwise the stitches that were slipped the previous row, but this time with the yarn held at the front (that is, the wrong side) of the work.*

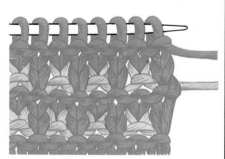

3 *Repeat these four rows to form the pattern. All mosaic stitches are based on the same principles: the yarn color is changed every two rows, the slip stitches are taken over two rows and are slipped with the yarn in front on wrong-side rows and at the back on right-side rows.*

Zigzag Jacket

Make yourself a genuine coat of many colors in a sizzling
zigzag pattern. This one has an interesting double-
breasted front and a graceful shawl collar.

Sizes
To fit 32–34[36–38]in bust
Length 25[26]in
Sleeve seam 17in

Note Instructions for larger size are in brackets []; where there is only one set of figures it applies to both sizes.

Gauge
21 sts and 23 rows to 4in over patt on size 5 needles

Materials
400[450]g double knitting yarn (see page 9) or 17[19]oz of knitting worsted in main color (A)
175[225]g or 6[9]oz, respectively, in each of contrasting colors (B) and (C)
100g or 4oz, respectively, each of contrasting colors (D) and (E)
1 pair each sizes 4 and 5 knitting needles
4 buttons

Back
Using smaller needles and A, cast on 104[114] sts. Work 2in K1, P1 rib. Change to larger needles.
Beg with a K row cont in st st and patt from chart on page 126. Use small, separate balls of yarn for each color area, twist yarns when changing color to prevent a hole.
Work 90 rows.
Shape armholes
Bind off 4[5] sts at beg of next 2 rows.
Dec 1 st at each end of next and every other row until 82[88] sts rem. Work even until work measures 7¾[8¾]in from beg of armhole shaping, ending with a WS row.
Shape shoulders
Bind off 9 sts at beg of next 4 rows and 7[10] sts at beg of foll 2 rows. Bind off rem 32 sts.

Pocket lining (make 2)
Using larger needles and A, cast on 24 sts. Work in st st for 4¾in, ending with a P row. Leave these sts on a spare needle.

Left front
Using smaller needles and A, cast on 36[41] sts. Work 2in K1, P1 rib.

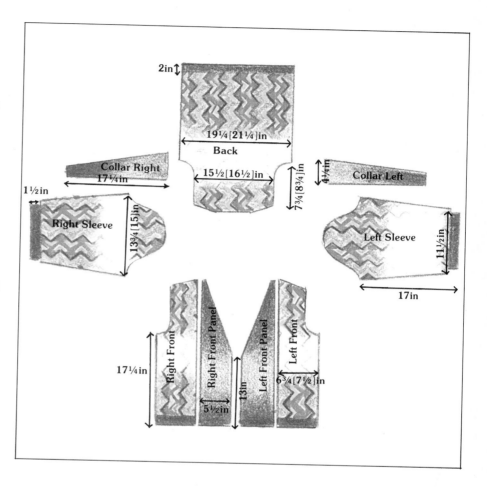

Change to larger needles.
Beg with a K row cont in patt from chart until work measures 6¾in, ending with a WS row.
Place pocket
Next row Patt 6 sts, sl next 24 sts onto a st holder and patt across pocket lining sts on spare needle, patt to end.
Cont in patt until work matches back to armhole, ending with a P row.
Shape armhole
Bind off 4[5] sts at beg of next row.
Dec 1 st at armhole edge on every other row until 25[28] sts rem. Work even until work matches back to shoulder shaping, ending at armhole edge.
Shape shoulder
Bind off 9 sts at beg of next and every other row once.
Work 1 row. Bind off rem 7[10] sts.

Right front
Work as for left front from ** to **.

Change to larger needles.
Beg with a K row cont in st st and patt from chart until work measures 6¾in, ending with a WS row.
Place pocket
Next row Patt 6[11] sts, sl next 24 sts onto a st holder, patt across pocket lining sts on spare needle, patt to end.
Cont in patt until work matches back to armhole, ending with a K row.
Shape armhole
Bind off 4[5] sts at beg of next row.
Dec 1 st at armhole edge on next and every other row until 25[28] sts rem.
Complete to match left front.

Sleeves
Using smaller needles and A, cast on 62 sts. Work 1½in K1, P1 rib.
Change to larger needles.
Beg with a K row cont in st st and patt from chart. Inc and work into patt 1 st at each end of the 11th and every foll 12th[9th] row until there

are 74[80] sts. Work even until work measures aprox 17in, ending with an 18th patt row.

Shape top

Bind off 4[5] sts at beg of next 2 rows.

Dec 1 st at each end of next and every other row until 50 sts rem, then at each end of every row until 18 sts rem.

Bind off.

Right front panel

Using smaller needles and A, cast on 36 sts.

Work 4¾in K1, P1 rib.

1st buttonhole row Rib 7, bind off 2 sts, rib 18 including st used in binding off, bind off 2 sts, rib to end.

2nd buttonhole row Rib to end, casting on 2 sts over those bound off in previous row.

Cont in rib until work measures 8½in. Work first and 2nd buttonhole rows again.

Now cont in rib until work measures 13in, ending at front edge.

Shape front edge

Bind off 12 sts at beg of next row.

Dec 1 st at front edge on 3 foll 4th[6th] rows, then on every foll 4th row until 2 sts rem.

Work 2 tog and fasten off.

Left front panel

Work to match right front panel, omitting buttonholes.

Collar (make 2 pieces)

Using smaller needles and A, cast on 106[110] sts.

Work 14 rows K1, P1 rib.

Next row Rib to last 2 sts, turn.

Next row Sl 1, rib to end.

Next row Rib to last 4 sts, turn.

Next row Sl 1, rib to end.

Cont in this way until the row "rib to last 10 sts, turn" has been worked.

Next row Sl 1, rib to end.

Next row Rib to last 20 sts, turn.

Next row Sl 1, rib to end.

Next row Rib to last 30 sts, turn.

Next row Sl 1, rib to end.

Next row Rib to last 40 sts, turn.

Next row Sl 1, rib to end.

Next row Rib to end across all sts on needle. Bind off.

To finish

Press if appropriate for yarn used.

Pocket edgings

Using smaller needles and A, K across 24 sts left on st holder. Work ¾in K1, P1 rib. Bind off in rib.

Sew down pocket linings on WS and edgings on RS.

Join shoulder, side, and sleeve seams.

Set in sleeves. Sew front panels to front edges. Join center back neck seam of collar. Sew shaped edge of collar to neck edge, joining short ends to bound-off sts at front edge.

Sew on buttons and reinforce buttonholes.

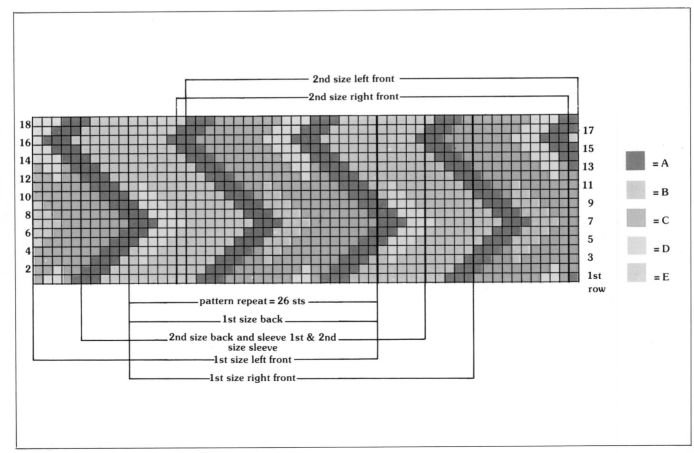

Folk Knitting

Knitting has a long history, going back, some say, as far as the ancient Egyptians. During that time several countries have developed their own particular knitting style – whether it be in the form of color patterns, like Fair Isle and Scandinavian knitting, or a special kind of texture or stitch pattern, like those found in traditional Aran garments. In some cases (Guernsey knitting, for example) it is the shape of a garment and the yarn used for it that is distinctive; in others it is a special style of decoration – the brightly colored yarn embroidery on Tyrolean garments is an example of this last kind.

One of the most interesting features of folk knitting styles is that they are becoming more, rather than less, popular with the passage of time, and there is a great demand for them to be authentic in every detail. All the patterns in the following pages are based on traditional patterns and use a wide range of stitches and motifs from all over the world, from Scotland to Peru.

Aran Sweater

The highly textured stitch patterns used in this classic sweater come from the Aran Islands, off the west coast of Ireland. The thick, crunchy fabric is specially designed to withstand the cruelest winter weather.

Size
To fit 32–34[36–38:40–42]in bust/chest.
Length 24[26½:27½]in
Sleeve length 17[18:18½]in
Note Instructions for larger sizes are in brackets []; where there is only one set of figures it applies to all sizes.

Gauge
22 sts and 28 rows to 4in over Irish moss st on size 6 needles.

Materials
30[33:37]oz knitting worsted or fisherman yarn
1 pair each sizes 4 and 6 knitting needles
1 cable needle

Irish moss stitch
Work over an even number of sts.
1st and 2nd rows (RS) *K1, P1, rep from * to end.
3rd and 4th rows *P1, K1, rep from * to end.
Rep these 4 rows.

Back
**Using smaller needles, cast on 113[123:131] sts. Work in K1, P1 rib for 2in.
Change to larger needles and work in patt as foll:
1st row K1, (P1, K1) 4[6:8] times, P2, K4, *P2, C3B, K3, P5, Tw3B, K1, Tw3F, P5, C3B, K3, P2, *K1, (P1, K1) 8[9:9] times, rep from * to * once, K4, P2, K1, (P1, K1) 4[6:8] times.
2nd row P1, (K1, P1) 4[6:8] times, K2, P4, *K2, P6, K5, P2, K1, P1, K1, P2, K5, P6, K2, *P1, (K1, P1) 8[9:9] times, rep from * to * once, P4, K2, P1, (K1, P1) 4[6:8] times.
3rd row P1, (K1, P1) 4[6:8] times, P2, C4B, *P2, K3, C3F, P4, Tw3B, K1, P1, K1, Tw3F, P4, K3, C3F, P2, *P1, (K1, P1) 8[9:9] times, rep from * to * once, C4B, P3, (K1, P1) 4[6:8] times.
4th row K1, (P1, K1) 4[6:8] times, K2, P4, *K2, P6, K4, P2, (K1, P1) twice, K1, P2, K4, P6, K2, *K1, (P1, K1) 8[9:9] times, rep from * to * once, P4, K3, (P1, K1) 4[6:8] times.
5th row K1, (P1, K1) 4[6:8] times, P2, K4, *P2, C3B, K3, P3, Tw3B, (K1, P1) twice, K1, Tw3F, P3, C3B, K3, P2, *K1, (P1, K1) 8[9:9] times, rep from * to * once K4, P2, K1, (P1, K1) 4[6:8] times.
6th row P1, (K1, P1) 4[6:8] times, K2, P4, *K2, P6, K3, P2, (K1, P1) 3 times, K1, P2, K3, P6, K2, *P1, (K1, P1) 8[9:9] times, rep from * to * once, P4, K2, P1, (K1, P1) 4[6:8] times.

Aran abbreviations

CN – cable needle
C4F – **cable 4 front** (sl next 2 sts onto CN and leave at front of work, K2, then K2 from CN).
C4B – **cable 4 back** (sl next 2 sts onto CN and leave at back of work, K2, then K2 from CN).
C3F – **cable 3 front** (sl next st onto CN and leave at front of work, K2, then K1 from CN).
C3B – **cable 3 back** (sl next 2 sts onto CN and leave at back of work, K1, then K2 from CN).
Tw3F – **twist 3 front** (sl next 2 sts onto CN and leave at front of work, P1, then K2 from CN).
Tw3B – **twice 3 back** (sl next st onto CN and leave at back of work, K2, then P1 from CN).
Tw5B – **twist 5 back** (sl next 3 sts onto cable needle and leave at back of work, K2, then P1, K2 from CN).
Cr3B – **cross 3 back** (sl next st onto CN and leave at back of work, K2, then K1 from CN).
Tw2B – **twist 2 back** (sl next st onto CN and leave at back of work, K1 tbl, then P1 from CN).
Tw2F – **twist 2 front** (sl next st onto CN and leave at front of work, P1, then K1 tbl from CN).
C2Ftbl – **cable 2 front through back of loop** (sl next st onto CN and leave at front of work, K1 tbl, then K1 tbl from CN).
C2Btbl – **cable 2 back through back of loop** (sl next st onto CN and hold at back of work, K1 tbl then K1 tbl from CN).
C2F P-wise – **cable 2 front purlwise** (sl next st onto CN and leave at front of work, P1, then P1 from CN).
C2Ftbl P-wise – **cable 2 front through back of loop purlwise** (sl next st onto to CN and leave at front of work, P1 tbl; P1 tbl from CN).

7th row P1, (K1, P1) 4[6:8] times, P2, C4B, *P2, K3, C3F, P2, Tw3B, (K1, P1) 3 times, K1, Tw3F, P2, K3, C3F, P2, *P1, (K1, P1) 8[9:9] times, rep from * to * once, C4B, P3, (K1, P1) 4[6:8] times.

8th row K1, (P1, K1) 4[6:8] times, K2, P4, *K2, P6, K2, P2, (K1, P1) 4 times, K1, P2, K2, P6, K2, *K1, (P1, K1) 8[9:9] times, rep from * to * once, P4, K3, (P1, K1) 4[6:8] times.

9th row K1, (P1, K1) 4[6:8] times, P2, K4, *P2, C3B, K3, P2, K3, (P1, K1) 4 times, K2, P2, C3B, K3, P2, *K1, (P1, K1) 8[9:9] times, rep from * to * once, K4, P2, K1, (P1, K1) 4[6:8] times.

10th row P1, (K1, P1) 4[6:8] times, K2, P4, *K2, P6, K2, P3, (K1, P1) 4 times, P2, K2, P6, K2, *P1, (K1, P1) 8[9:9] times, rep from * to * once, P4, K2, P1, (K1, P1) 4[6:8] times.

11th row P1, (K1, P1) 4[6:8] times, P2, C4B, *P2, K3, C3F, P2, Tw3F, (K1, P1) 3 times, K1, Tw3B, P2, K3, C3F, P2, *P1, (K1, P1) 8[9:9] times, rep from * to * once, C4B, P3, (K1, P1) 4[6:8] times.

12th row K1, (P1, K1) 4[6:8] times, K2, P4, *K2, P6, K3, P3, (K1, P1) 3 times, P2, K3, P6, K2, *K1, (P1, K1) 8[9:9] times, rep from * to * once, P4, K3, (P1, K1) 4[6:8] times.

13th row K1, (P1, K1) 4[6:8] times, P2, K4, *P2, C3B, K3, P3, Tw3F, (K1, P1) twice, K1, Tw3B, P3, C3B, K3, P2, *K1, (P1, K1) 8[9:9] times, rep from * to * once, K4, P2, K1, (P1, K1) 4[6:8] times.

14th row P1, (K1, P1) 4[6:8] times, K2, P4, *K2, P6, K4, P3, (K1, P1) twice, P2, K4, P6, K2, *P1, (K1, P1) 8[9:9] times, rep from * to * once, P4, K2, P1, (K1, P1) 4[6:8] times.

15th row P1, (K1, P1) 4[6:8] times, P2, C4B, *P2, K3, C3F, P4, Tw3F, K1, P1, K1, Tw3B, P4, K3, C3F, P2, *P1, (K1, P1) 8[9:9] times, rep from * to * once, C4B, P3, (K1, P1) 4[6:8] times.

16th row K1, (P1, K1) 4[6:8] times, K2, P4, *K2, P6, K5, P3, K1, P3, K5, P6, K2, *K1, (P1, K1) 8[9:9] times, rep from * to * once, P4, K3, (P1, K1) 4[6:8] times.

17th row K1, (P1, K1) 4[6:8] times, P2, K4, *P2, C3B, K3, P5, Tw3F, K1, Tw3B, P5, C3B, K3, P2, *K1, (P1, K1) 8[9:9] times, rep from * to * once, K4, P2, K1, (P1, K1) 4[6:8] times.

18th row P1, (K1, P1) 4[6:8] times, K2, P4, *K2, P6, K6, P5, K6, P6, K2, *P1, (K1, P1) 8[9:9] times, rep from * to * once, P4, K2, P1, (K1, P1) 4[6:8] times.

19th row P1, (K1, P1) 4[6:8] times, P2, C4B, *P2, K3, C3F, P6, Tw5B, P6, K3, C3F, P2, *P1, (K1, P1) 8[9:9] times, rep from * to * once, C4B, P3, (K1, P1) 4[6:8] times.

20th row K1, (P1, K1) 4[6:8] times, K2, P4, *K2, P6, K6, P2, K1, P2, K6, P6, K2, *K1, (P1, K1) 8[9:9] times, rep from * to * once, P4, K2, K1, (P1, K1) 4[6:8] times.

These 20 rows form patt.

Cont in patt until work measures 16[16½:17½]in, ending with a WS row.

Shape armholes

Keeping patt correct, bind off 6[7:8] sts at beg of next 2 rows.

Dec 1 st at each end of next 5 rows.

Dec 1 st at each end of every other row 4[2:3] times. 83[95:99] sts.**

Work even in patt until work measures 8[10:10]in from beg of armhole shaping, ending with a WS row.

Shape shoulders

Keeping patt correct, bind off 7 sts at beg of next 6 rows. Bind off 4[7:8] sts at beg of next 2 rows. Leave rem 33[39:41] sts on a stitch holder.

Front

Work as for back from ** to **.

Work even in patt until work measures 5¾[6½:7¾]in from beg of armhole shaping, ending with a WS row.

Shape left front neck

Next row Patt 34[37:38] sts, turn, leaving rem sts on a spare needle.

***Dec 1 st at neck edge on next row and on every other row 8 times. 25[28:29] sts.

Shape left shoulder

Bind off 7 sts at beg of next row and on every other row twice. Work 1 row. Bind off rem 4[7:8] sts.***

Shape right front neck and shoulder

Return to sts on spare needle, sl next 15[21:23] sts onto a stitch holder. On rem 34[37:38] sts patt to end of row.

Complete to match left front and shoulder from *** to ***, reversing all shapings.

Sleeves (alike)

Using smaller needles, cast on 43 [49:53] sts. Work in K1, P1 rib for 3in, inc 1 st at each end of last row 45[51:55] sts.

Change to larger needles and work in patt as foll:

1st row (P1, K1) 0[1:2] times, K0[1:1], P2, K4, P2, C3B, K3, P5, Tw3B, K1, Tw3F, P5, C3B, K3, P2, K4, P2, K0[1:1], (P1, K1) 0[1:2] times.

2nd row (P1, K1) 0[1:2] times, P0[1:1], K2, P4, K2, P6, K5, P2, K1, P1, K1, P2, K5, P6, K2, P4, K2, P0[1:1], (K1, P1) 0[1:2] times.

3rd row (P1, K1) 0[1:2] times, P2[3:3], C4B, P2, K3, C3F, P4, Tw3B, K1, P1, K1, Tw3F, P4, K3, C3F, P2, C4B, P2[3:3], (K1, P1) 0[1:2] times.

4th row (K1, P1) 0[1:2] times, K2[3:3], P4, K2, P6, K4, P2, (K1, P1) twice, K1, P2, K4, P6, K2, P4, K2[3:3], (P1, K1) 0[1:2] times.

5th row (K1, P1) 0[1:2] times, K0[1:1], P2, K4, P2, C3B, K3, P3, Tw3B, (K1, P1) twice, K1, Tw3F, P3, C3B, K3, P2, K4, P2, K0[1:1], (P1, K1) 0[1:2] times.

6th row (P1, K1) 0[1:2] times, P0[1:1], K2, P4, K2, P6, K3, P2, (K1, P1) 3 times, K1, P2, K3, P6, K2, P4, K2, P0[1:1], (K1, P1) 0[1:2] times.

7th row (P1, K1) 0[1:2] times, P2[3:3], C4B, P2, K3, C3F, P2, Tw3B, (K1, P1) 3 times, K1, Tw3F, P2, K3, C3F, P2, C4B, P2[3:3], (K1, P1) 0[1:2] times.

8th row (K1, P1) 0[1:2] times, K2[3:3], P4, K2, P6, K2, P2, (K1, P1) 4 times, K1, P2, K2, P6, K2, P4, K2[3:3], (P1, K1) 0[1:2] times.

9th row (K1, P1) 0[1:2] times, K0[1:1], P2, K4, P2, C3B, K3, P2, K3, (P1, K1) 4 times, K2, P2, C3B, K3, P2, K4, P2, K0[1:1], (P1, K1) 0[1:2] times.

10th row (P1, K1) 0[1:2] times, P0[1:1], K2, P4, K2, P6, K2, P3, (K1, P1) 4 times, P2, K2, P6, K2, P4, K2, P0[1:1], (K1, P1) 0[1:2] times.

11th row (P1, K1) 0[1:2] times,

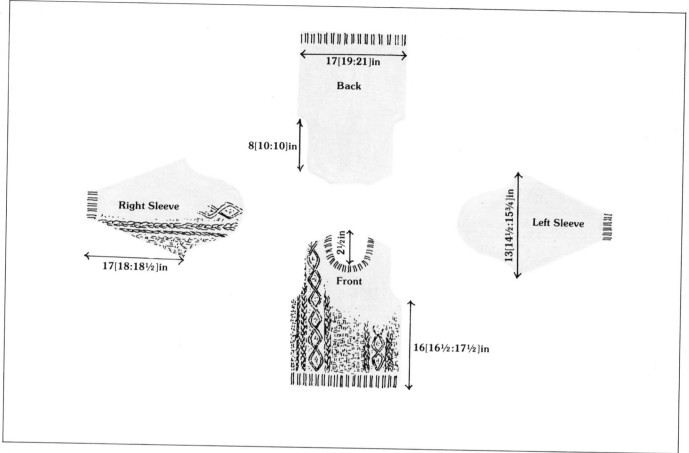

Right Sleeve

17[18:18½]in

Back

17[19:21]in

8[10:10]in

2½in

Front

16[16½:17½]in

Left Sleeve

13[14½:15¾]in

P2[3:3], C4B, P2, K3, C3F, P2, Tw3F, (K1, P1) 3 times, K1, Tw3B, P2, K3, C3F, P2, C4B, P2[3:3], (K1, P1) 0[1:2] times

12th row (K1, P1) 0[1:2] times, K2[3:3], P4, K2, P6, K3, P3, (K1,P1) 3 times, P2, K3, P6, K2, P4, K2[3:3], (P1, K1) 0[1:2] times.

13th row (K1, P1) 0[1:2] times, K0[1:1], P2, K4, P2, C3B, K3, P3, Tw3F, (K1, P1) twice, K1, Tw3B, P3, C3B, K3, P2, K4, P2, K0[1:1], (P1, K1) 0[1:2] times.

14th row (P1, K1) 0[1:2] times, P0[1:1], K2, P4, K2, P6, K4, P3, (K1, P1) twice, P2, K4, P6, K2, P4, K2, P0[1:1], (K1, P1) 0[1:2] times.

15th row (P1, K1) 0[1:2] times, P2[3:3], C4B, P2, K3, C3F, P4, Tw3F, K1, P1, K1, Tw3B, P4, K3, C3F, P2, C4B, P2[3:3], (K1, P1) 0[1:2] times.

16th row (K1, P1) 0[1:2] times, K2[3:3], P4, K2, P6, K5, P3, K1, P3, K5, P6, K2, P4, K2[3:3], (P1, K1) 0[1:2] times.

17th row (K1, P1) 0[1:2] times,

K0[1:1], P2, K4, P2, C3B, K3, P5, Tw3F, K1, Tw3B, P5, C3B, K3, P2, K4, P2, K0[1:1], (P1, K1) 0[1:2] times.

18th row (P1, K1) 0[1:2] times, P0[1:1], K2, P4, K2, P6, K6, P5, K6, P6, K2, P4, K2, (K1, P1) 0[1:2] times.

19th row (P1, K1) 0[1:2] times, P2[3:3], C4B, P2, K3, C3F, P6, Tw5B, P6, K3, C3F, P2, C4B, P2[3:3], (K1, P1) 0[1:2] times.

20th row (K1, P1) 0[1:2] times, K2[3:3], P4, K2, P6, K6, P2, K1, P2, K6, P6, K2, P4, K2[3:3], (P1, K1) 0[1:2] times.

These 20 rows form patt. Cont in patt for 4 rows.

Keeping patt correct and working the extra sts into the patt, inc 1 st at each end of next and every foll 4th row until there are 73[79:79] sts on needle, then inc 1 st at each end of every foll 5th row until there are 77[87:93] sts on needle.

Work even until sleeve measures 17[18:18½]in from beg.

Shape sleeve top

Keeping patt correct, bind off 6[7:8] sts at beg of next 2 rows.

Dec 1 st at each end of next 5 rows.

Dec 1 st at each end of every other row until 29[33:33] sts rem.

Work 1 row.

Bind off 3 sts at beg of next 6 rows.

Bind off rem 11[15:15] sts.

To finish

Press lightly on WS as appropriate for yarn used. Join left shoulder.

Neckband

With RS facing, using smaller needles, pick up and K 33[39:41] sts from back neck stitch holder, 26 sts from left side front neck, 15[21:23] sts from center front neck, 26 sts from right side front neck 100[112:116] sts.

Work in K1, P1, rib for 2½in.

Bind off in rib.

Join right shoulder seam. Fold neckband in half onto wrong side and slipstitch in place. Set in sleeves. Join side and sleeve seams.

Shetland Lace Shawl

**This beautiful lace shawl, made in the traditional manner,
makes a fabulous fashion accessory but is soft enough for baby.**

Size
Approx 60in square after stretching

Gauge
26 sts and 34 rows to 4in over st st on size 6 needles

Materials
8oz fine, two-ply Shetland laceweight or fingering yarn
1 pair size 6 knitting needles

To make
Cast on 3 sts.
Work center
1st row (WS) Yo, K3.
2nd row Yo, K4.
3rd row Yo, K5.
Cont in this way inc 1 st at beg of every row until there are 12 sts. Place a marker at beg of next row, to denote the beg of RS rows.
Beg patt.
Next row (RS) Yo, K3, K2 tog, yo, K1, yo, K2 tog, K4.
Next row Yo, K13.
Next row Yo, K3, K2 tog, yo, K3, yo, K2 tog, K4.
Next row Yo, K15.
Next row Yo, K6, yo, sl 1, K2 tog, psso, yo, K7.
Next row Yo, K to end.
Rep last row 6 more times so ending with a WS row (marker is at beg of next row). 24 sts.
Next row Yo, *K3, K2 tog, yo, K1, yo, K2 tog, K4, rep from * to end.
Next row Yo, K to end.
Next row Yo, *K3, K2 tog, yo, K3, yo, K2 tog, K2, rep from * to last 2 sts, K2.
Next row Yo, K to end.
Next row Yo, *K6, yo, sl 1, K2 tog, psso, yo, K3, rep from * to last 4 sts, K4.
Next row Yo, K to end.
Rep last row 6 more times. 36 sts.
Cont in this way, rep the last 12 rows until there are 120 sts, ending with a WS row.
Next row Yo, *K3, K2 tog, yo, K1, yo, K2 tog, K4, rep from * to end.
Next row Yo, K to end.
Next row Yo, *K3, K2 tog, yo, K3, yo, K2 tog, K2, rep from * to last 2 sts, K2.
Next row Yo, K3 tog, K to end.

Next row Yo, K3 tog, K3, yo, sl 1, K2 tog, psso, yo, K5, *K4, yo, sl 1, K2 tog, psso, yo, K5, rep from * to end.
Next row Yo, K3 tog, K to end.
Rep the last row 6 more times. 114 sts.
Next row Yo, K3 tog, *K4, K2 tog, yo, K1, yo, K2 tog, K3, rep from * to last 3 sts, K3.
Next row Yo, K3 tog, K to end.
Next row Yo, K3 tog, *K2, K2 tog, yo, K3, yo, K2 tog, K3, rep from * to last st, K1.
Next row Yo, K3 tog, K to end.
Next row Yo, K3 tog, K3, yo, sl 1, K2 tog, psso, yo, K5, *K4, yo, sl 1, K2 tog, psso, yo, K5, rep from * to end.
Next row Yo, K3 tog, K to end.
Rep last row 6 more times. 102 sts.
Cont in this way, rep the last 12 rows until 6 sts rem.
Next row Yo, K3 tog, K to end.
Rep last row twice more, 3 sts.
Next row K3 tog, fasten off, but do not break yarn.

First side border
**With RS of work facing, pick up and K 60 sts from first side of center square as foll:
Pick up and K 1, yo, (pick up and K 2, yo) 29 times, pick up and K 1. 90 sts.
Next row K. **
Beg border patt.
1st row (RS) Yo, K3, yo, sl 1, K2 tog, psso, yo, *K3, yo, K2 tog, K2, yo, sl 1, K2 tog, psso, yo, rep from * to last 4 sts, K4.
2nd and foll alt rows Yo, K to end.
3rd row Yo, K2, *K2 tog, yo, K3, yo, K2 tog, K3, rep from * to end.
5th row Yo, K2, *K2 tog, yo, K5, yo, K2 tog, K1, rep from * to last 2 st, K2.
7th row Yo, K1, *yo, sl 1, K2 tog, psso, yo, K3, yo, K2 tog, K2, rep from * to last 5 sts, yo, sl 1, K2 tog, psso, yo, K2.
9th row Yo, *K2 tog, yo, K3, yo, K2 tog, K3, rep from * to last 8 sts, K2 tog, yo, K3, yo, K2 tog, K1.
11th row Yo, *K2 tog, yo, K5, yo, K2 tog, K1, rep from * to end.
13th row Yo, K2 tog, yo, *K3, yo,

K2 tog, K2, yo, sl 1, K2 tog, psso, yo, rep from * to last 10 sts, K3, yo, K2 tog, K2, yo, K2 tog, K1.
15th row Yo, *K3, yo, K2 tog, K3, K2 tog, yo, rep from * to last 4 sts, K4.
17th row Yo, *K5, yo, K2 tog, K1, K2 tog, yo, rep from * to last 6 sts, K6.
19th row Yo, *K3, yo, K2 tog, K2, yo, sl 1, K2 tog, psso, yo, rep from * to last 8 sts, K3, yo, K2 tog, K3.
21st row Yo, K1, *yo, K2 tog, K3, K2 tog, yo, K3, rep from * to last 9 sts, yo, K2 tog, K3, K2 tog, yo, K2.
23rd row Yo, K3, *yo, K2 tog, K1, K2 tog, yo, K5, rep from * to last 9 sts, yo, K2 rog, K1, K2 tog, yo, K4.
25th row Yo, K1, *yo, K2 tog, K2, yo, sl 1, K2, tog, psso, yo, K3, rep from * to last 3 sts, yo, K2 tog, K1.
27th row Yo, K4, *K2 tog, yo, K3, yo, K2 tog, K3, rep from * to last 2 sts, K2.
29th row Yo, K1, *yo, K2 tog, K1, K2 tog, yo, K5, rep from * to last 7 sts, yo, K2 tog, K1, K2 tog, yo, K2.
30th row As 2nd row.
31st–61st rows Rep first-30th rows once, then first row again.
62nd row Yo, K to end, turn and cast on 16 sts for lace edging.

First side edging
Next row K15, K tog last st and first st of border – called join 2 tog – turn. Beg point.
1st row Sl 1, K1, yo, K2 tog, K8, yo, K2 tog, yo, K2.
2nd row K14, yo, K2 tog, join 2 tog.
3rd row Sl 1, K1, yo, K2 tog, K2, K2 tog, yo, K1, yo, K2 tog, K2, yo, K2 tog, yo, K2.
4th row K15, yo, K2 tog, join 2 tog, turn.
5th row Sl 1, K1, yo, K2 tog, K1, K2 tog, yo, K3, yo, K2 tog, K2, yo, K2 tog, yo, K2.
6th row K16, yo, K2 tog, join 2 tog, turn.
7th row Sl 1, K1, yo, K2 tog, K3, yo, sl 1, K2 tog, psso, yo, K5, yo, K2 tog, yo, K2.
8th row K17, yo, K2 tog, join 2 tog, turn.
9th row Sl 1, K1, yo, K2 tog, K12, yo, K2 tog, yo, K2.

10th row Bind off 5 sts loosely, K13 (including st used in binding off), yo, K2 tog, join 2 tog, turn.
These 10 rows form the first point.
Rep these 10 rows until all the border sts have been worked, ending with a WS row.
Sl these sts onto a stitch holder.
Second side border
Work as for first side border from **
to **.
***Now cont in patt from first-61st rows as for first side border, joining second border to first side on every other row as foll:
2nd and every other row Yo, K to last st, K1 tog with corresponding row end of first border.
62nd row As 2nd row, then sl sts for edging from stitch holder onto end of needle.

Second side edging
Keeping patt correct, cont edging from first side.
Third side border and edging
Work as first side border from ** to **. work as second side from *** to ***.
Fourth side border
Work as for first side border from ** to **. Beg patt.
1st row (RS) Yo, K3, yo, sl 1, K2 tog, psso, yo, *K3, yo, K2 tog, K2, yo, sl 1, K2 tog, psso, yo, rep from * to last 4 sts, K3, K1 tog with corresponding row end of first border.
2nd and foll alt rows Yo, K to last st, K1 tog with corresponding row end of third border.
Cont in this way, working patt as for first side of border joining at the end

of every row until 61st row has been worked.
62nd row As 2nd row, then sl sts for edging from stitch holder onto end of needle.
Fourth side edging
Keeping patt correct, cont edging from third side. Graft rem 16 sts to cast-on sts of edging.

To finish
Roll shawl in a damp towel. Fold a twin bed sheet into a square 60in × 60in on a thickly carpeted floor or a folded blanket. Place the damp shawl on the sheet and pin out the work through the holes in the points of the edging in line with the edges of the square.
Leave the shawl until it is completely dry.

Special technique – constructing the shawl

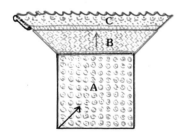

1 Work the center square (A) from corner to corner. Pick up stitches along one side and work the inner border (B). Cast on stitches for the edging (C) onto the last row of the border and work the edging, knitting into border stitches on every other row, thus joining the edging and border invisibly. When all the border stitches have been worked off, leave the edging stitches on a stitch holder.

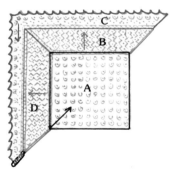

2 Now pick up stitches along the second side of the center and work the inner border (D) as before, but this time knitting into the row ends of the first border (B) on every other row, thus joining B and D invisibly. When the border is complete, slip the stitches from the stitch holder onto the end of the needle and work second side edging (E) as first side edging.

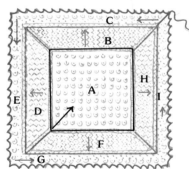

3 Work third side border (F) and edging (G) as instructed for the second side. Work the fourth side border (H) as before but knitting into the row ends from the first border on one side and the third border on the other side. Work the edging (I) as before, grafting the last row to the cast-on stitches. In this way the shawl is constructed entirely without seams or ugly joinings.

Shetland Lace Dress

This pretty little dress has been knitted in stockinette stitch
with panels of eyelets and a Shetland lace edging. It is
quite simple to work, despite its intricate appearance.

Size
To fit 23½in chest
Length 17in

Gauge
28 sts and 40 rows to 4in over st st on size 2 needles

Materials
8oz size 5 silky cotton yarn such as Phildar Perlé No. 5
1 pair each sizes 2 and 5 knitting needles
5yd narrow ribbon
3 small buttons

Back
**Using smaller needles, cast on 155 sts.
1st row (RS) K.
2nd row P.
3rd–5th rows K.
6th row P.
7th row *K2 tog, yo, rep from * to last st, K1.
8th–11th rows As 2nd–5th rows.
12th row P to last 2 sts, P2 tog. 154 sts.
13th row K1, *yo, P2 tog, rep from * to last st K1.
14th–22nd rows As 13th row.
23rd row K.
24th, 25th and 26th rows P.
27th row Inc 1, K to end. 155 sts.
28th row P2, *yo, P2 tog, rep from * to last st, P1.
29th–31st rows As 23rd–25th rows.
Beg with a P row, cont in st st until work measures 9in, ending with a P row. (This length may be altered as desired.)
Next row K8, *K2 tog, rep from * to last 9 sts, K9. 86 sts.
Next 3 rows P.
Next row K.

Next row P1, *yo, P2 tog, rep from * to last st, P1.
Next row K.
Next 2 rows P.**
Beg with a P row, cont in st st until work measures 15in, ending with a P row. Bind off, marking center 36 sts for back neck.

Front
Work as for back from ** to **. Beg with a P row, cont in st st for 4in, ending with a P row.
Shape neck
Next row K28, bind off next 30 sts, K to end. Complete right side of neck first. Cont in st st, dec 1 st at neck edge on next 3 rows. 25 sts. Work even until work measures 15in, ending with a P row. Bind off. With WS of work facing rejoin yarn to sts for left side of neck. Complete to match first side.

Hem edging
Using larger needles cast on 7 sts and work edging patt as foll:
1st row K.
2nd row P.
3rd row Sl 1 P-wise, K2, yo, K2 tog, yo twice, K2 tog.
4th row Yo, K2, P1, K2, yo, K2 tog, K1.
5th row Sl 1 P-wise, K2, yo, K2 tog, K4.
6th row K6, yo, K2 tog, K1.
7th row Sl 1 P-wise, K2, yo, K2 tog, yo twice, K2 tog, yo twice, K2 tog.
8th row (K2, P1) twice, K2, yo, K2 tog, K1.
9th row Sl 1 P-wise, K2, yo, K2 tog, K6.
10th row K8, yo, K2 tog, K1.
11th row Sl P-wise, K2, yo, K2 tog, (yo twice, K2 tog) 3 times.

12th row (K2, P1) 3 times, K2, yo, K2 tog, K1.
13th row Sl 1 P-wise, K2, yo, K2 tog, K9.
14th row Bind off 7 sts, K4 including st used in binding off, yo, K2 tog, K1.
The 3rd–14th rows form the patt rep.
Rep the 3rd–14th rows until edging measures approx 46in, ending with a 14th patt row.
Bind off.

Armhole edgings
Using larger needles, cast on 7 sts and work as for hem edging for approx 9in, ending with a 14th patt row. Bind off.

To finish
Press all pieces as appropriate for yarn used.
Join left shoulder seam.
With RS facing, using smaller needles, beg at right back neck marker, pick up and K 94 sts around neck edge.
Next row Cast on 2 sts, bind off 3 sts, *transfer st on RH needle to LH needle, cast on 2 sts, bind off 3 sts, rep from * to end.
Fasten off.
Join right shoulder for ¾in at armhole edge.
Mark armholes 4½in down from shoulder on back and front.
Join side seams, leaving opening for armholes.
Sew on sleeve and hem edgings.
Work button loops on right front shoulder edge and sew on buttons.
Thread ribbon through eyelets, bringing ends out at center front waist to tie.

Shetland Classics

You can put together a whole wardrobe of beautiful classics
from this cleverly constructed composite pattern. A back,
front, and sleeves (long or short) makes a pullover; with a
front opening and sleeves it's a cardigan; omit the sleeves
and it's a vest.

Sizes
To fit 32[34:36:38]in bust
Length 21[21¼:22:22½]in
Long sleeve seam 17¼in
Short sleeve seam 6in

Note Instructions for larger sizes are in brackets []; where there is only one set of figures it applies to all sizes.

Gauge
30 sts and 29 rows to 4in over patt on size 3 needles

Materials
Vest
6[6:8:8]oz Shetland fingering yarn in main color (A)
3oz in contrasting color (B)
1oz in each of 9 contrasting colors (C, D, E, F, G, H, J, L, M)
Cardigan
9[9:10:10]oz in main color (A)
2oz in contrasting color (B)
1oz in each of 9 contrasting colors (C, D, E, F, G, H, J, L, M)
Short-sleeved pullover
10[10:11:11]oz in main color (A)
2oz in contrasting color (B)
1oz in each of 9 contrasting colors (C, D, E, F, G, H, J, L, M)
(add 3oz in main color for long-sleeved version)
1 pair each sizes 2 and 3 knitting needles
10[10:11:11] buttons (for vest or cardigan)

Vest

Back
****Using smaller needles and A, cast on 113[121:129:135] sts. Work in K1, P1 rib as foll:

1st row (RS) K1, *P1, K1, rep from * to end.
2nd row P1, *K1, P1, rep from * to end.
Rep the last 2 rows from 2¾in, ending with a first row.
Next row Rib 4[8:4:7], (work twice into next st – called inc 1 –, rib 6[6:7:7]) 15 times, inc 1, rib to end. 129[137:145:151] sts.
Change to larger needles and beg with a K row cont in st st working color patt from chart on page 141. Read K rows from right to left and P rows from left to right. Cont in patt until work measures 13in, ending with a P row.

Shape armholes
Keeping patt correct, bind off 8[8:10:10] sts at beg of next 2 rows. Dec 1 st at each end of next and every other row until 101[107:107:113] sts rem.
**Work even until work measures 8[8¼:9:9½]in from beg of armhole shaping, ending with a K row.

Shape shoulders
Next row P86[91:91:96], turn.
Next row K71[75:75:79], turn.
Next row P55[58:58:61], turn.
Next row K39[41:41:43], turn.
Next row P39[41:41:43]. Leave these sts on a spare needle.

Pocket linings (make 2)
Using larger needles and A, cast on 25 sts. Beg with a K row cont in st st. Work 23 rows, inc 1 st at each end of last row. 27 sts.
Leave these sts on a spare needle.

Left front
Using smaller needles and A, cast on 67[71:75:77] sts. Work K1, P1 rib as

for back for 2¾in, ending with first row.
Next row Rib 11 and sl these sts onto a safety pin, rib 4[6:8:6], (inc 1, rib 5) 8[8:8:9] times, inc 1, rib to end. 65[69:73:76] sts.
Change to larger needles and beg with a K row cont in st st and patt from chart on page 141 thus: beg reading chart at S[T:U:V], work 1[5:9:2] sts at beg of row, then rep 32 patt sts twice.
Cont until work measures 5in, ending with a P row.

Place pocket
Next row Patt 19[21:23:24], with A, K1, (P1, K1) 13 times, patt to end.
Next row Patt 19[21:23:25], with A, P1, (K1, P1) 13 times, patt to end.
Rep the last 2 rows once more.
Next row Patt 19[21:23:24], with A, bind off in rib 27 sts, patt to end.
Next row Patt 19[21:23:25], patt across sts of one pocket lining, patt to end. Cont in patt until work measures same as back to underarm, ending at side edge.

Shape armhole
Bind off 8[8:10:10] sts at beg of next row. Dec 1 st at armhole edge on every other row until 51[54:54:57] sts rem. Work even until work measures 5½[6:6¾:7]in from beg of armhole shaping, ending at front edge.

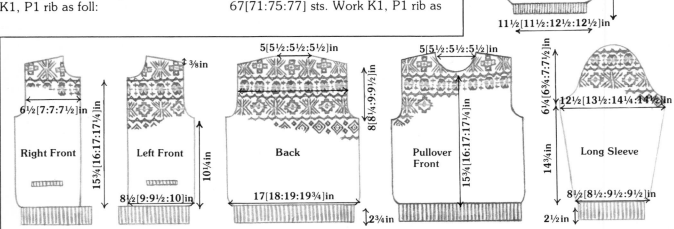

Shape neck

Next row Bind off 11 sts, patt to end.
Dec 1 st at neck edge on every row until 31[33:33:35] sts rem.
Work even until back and shoulder shaping match, ending at neck edge.

Shape shoulder

Next row Patt 16[17:17:18], turn.
Next row Patt to end.
Leave these sts on a spare needle.

Right front

Using smaller needles and A, cast on 67[71:75:77] sts.
Work in K1, P1 rib as for back for ⅜in, ending with a 2nd row.
1st buttonhole row Rib 4, bind off 3 sts, rib to end.
2nd buttonhole row Rib to end, casting on 3 sts over those bound off in previous row.
Cont in rib until work measures 2in from base of previous buttonhole, ending with a 2nd row. Work the 2 buttonhole rows again, then cont in rib until work measures 2¾in from cast-on edge, ending with a first row.
Next row Rib 3[5:7:5], (inc 1, rib 5) 8[8:8:9] times, inc 1, rib 4[6:8:6], turn and leave rem 11 sts on a safety pin. 65[69:73:76] sts.

Change to larger needles. Beg with a K row, cont in st st and patt from chart on page 141 thus: beg reading chart at S, work 1 st at beg of row, rep 32 patt sts twice, then work 0[4:8:11] sts, finishing at W[X:Y:Z]. Complete to match left front, reversing placing of pocket on 4th size and all shapings.

To finish

Graft shoulder seams.

Armbands

With RS of work facing, using smaller needles and A, pick up and K 117[123:133:139] sts evenly around armhole edge.
Beg with a 2nd row work in K1, P1 rib as for back for 9 rows. Bind off in rib.

Button band

With RS of work facing, using smaller needles and A, join yarn to inner edge of sts on safety pin on left front. Work in K1, P1 rib as set until band is long enough, when slightly stretched, to fit up front edge to neck, ending with a WS row. Break yarn, leave these sts. Mark position of 9[9:10:10] buttons, two on waistband opposite buttonholes already worked, one

1½in above waistband, one 1½in below neck edge and others evenly spaced between.

Buttonhole band

With WS or work facing, using smaller needles and A, join yarn to inner edge of sts on safety pin. Cont in rib as set making buttonholes opposite markers until band measures same as button band, ending with WS row. Do not break yarn.

Neckband

With RS of work facing, using smaller needles and A, rib across sts of buttonhole band, pick up and K 26 sts up right side of neck, K across 39[41:41:43] sts on back neck, pick up and K 26 sts down right side neck, then rib across 11 sts on button band. 113[115:115:117] sts. Beg with 2nd row work 3 rows ribbing as for back. Work 2 buttonhole rows again. Rib 4 more rows. Bind off in rib. Join side seams. Catch down pocket linings. Sew on front bands and buttons.

Cardigan

Back, pocket linings, left front and right front

Work as for vest.

Special technique – shaping with turning rows

1 The shoulders are shaped by working turning rows. On the first row of shoulder shaping purl the required number of stitches, then turn the work so that the knit side is facing you, leaving the remaining stitches on the right-hand needle. Wrap yarn around first stitch on right-hand needle thus: yarn forward, slip one from right-hand needle, yarn back, slip stitch back onto right-hand needle.

2 Knit the required number of stitches, then turn the work so that the purl side is facing you, with the remaining stitches on the needle. Wrap yarn around first stitch on right-hand needle thus: yarn back, slip one from right-hand needle, yarn forward, slip stitch back onto right-hand needle. Purl the required number of stitches back to right shoulder. Then turn again, wrapping yarn around first stitch on right-hand needle.

3 Knit the required number of stitches back. This point marks the inner edge of the left shoulder. Now turn, wrap yarn around first stitch on right-hand needle as before and purl the required number of stitches back. This point marks the inner edge of the right shoulder. Leave the stitches on a spare needle. Working turning rows in this way makes it possible to graft the shoulders invisibly when finishing.

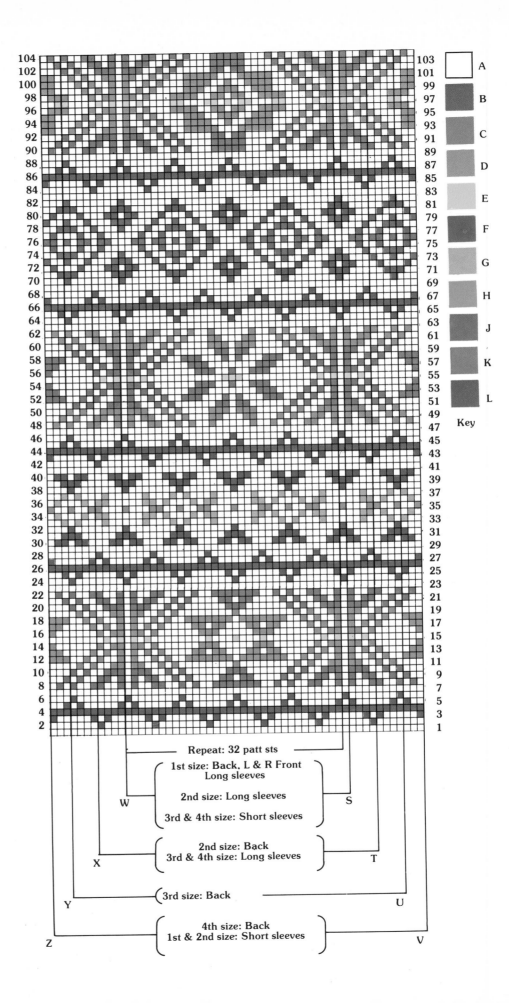

Repeat: 32 patt sts

1st size: Back, L & R Front
Long sleeves

2nd size: Long sleeves

3rd & 4th size: Short sleeves

2nd size: Back
3rd & 4th size: Long sleeves

3rd size: Back

4th size: Back
1st & 2nd size: Short sleeves

Key

A
B
C
D
E
F
G
H
J
K
L

Long sleeves

Using smaller needles and A, cast on 57[59:61:63] sts.
Work in K1. P1 rib as for back for 2½in, ending with a first row.
Next row Rib 4[7:3:4] *inc 1, rib 6[8:4:5], rep from * to last 4[7:3:5] sts, inc 1, rib to end. 65[65:73:73] sts.
Change to larger needles and beg with a 129th row cont in st st and patt from chart, inc and work into patt 1 st at each end of 6th[9th:5th:5th] row and every foll 6th[5th:5th:5th] row until there are 97[101:107:111] sts. Work even until work measures approx 17¼in, from ending with same patt row as back at underarm.

Shape top

Keeping patt correct, bind off 8[8:10:10] sts at beg of next 2 rows.
Dec 1 st at each end of next and every foll 4th row until 77[81:81:85] sts rem, then at each end of every other row until 55[55:53:57] sts rem.
Now dec 1 st at each end of every row until 25[25:27:27] sts rem.
Bind off.

To finish

Graft shoulder seams. Join side and sleeve seams. Set in sleeves. Catch down pocket linings. Sew on front bands and buttons.

Pullover

Back

Work as for back of vest.

Front

Work as for back of vest from ** to **.
Work even until work measures 5½[6:6¾:7]in from beg of armhole shaping, ending with a P row.

Shape neck

Next row Patt 38[40:40:42] and turn, leaving rem sts on a spare needle.
Complete left side of neck first.
Dec 1 st at neck edge on every row until 31[33:33:35] sts rem.
Work even until work matches back to shoulder shaping, ending at neck edge.

Shape shoulder

Next row Patt 16[17:17:18], turn.
Next row Patt to end.
Leave these sts on a spare needle.

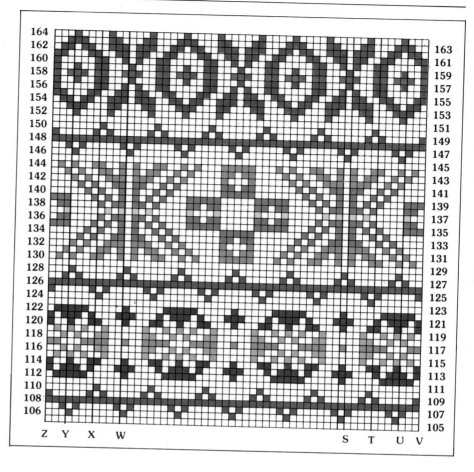

With RS of work facing return to sts for right side of neck. Sl center 25[27:27:29] sts onto a spare needle, join yarn to next st, patt to end.
Complete to match first side of neck.

Short sleeves

Using smaller needles and A, cast on 79[81:89:91] sts. Work in K1, P1 rib as for back or 1¼in, ending with a first row.
Next row Rib 4[8:6:5], *inc 1, rib 9[12:10:15], rep from * to last 5[8:6:6] sts, inc 1, rib to end. 87[87:97:97] sts.
Change to larger needles and beg with a 41st row cont in patt from chart, inc and work into patt 1 st at each end of the 5th and every foll 4th row until there are 97[101:107:111] sts.
Work even until work measures approx 6in ending with same patt row as back at underarm.

Shape top

Work as for long sleeves on cardigan.

Shoulder pads (make 2)

Using larger needles and A, cast on 38 sts.
Work in K1, P1 rib, dec 1 st at each end of the 3rd and every other row until 2 sts rem.
Work 2 tog and fasten off.

To finish

Neckband

Graft right shoulder seam.
With RS of work facing, using smaller needles and A, pick up and K 19 sts down left side of neck, K across 25[27:27:29] sts at center front, pick up and K 19 sts up right side of neck, K across 39[41:41:43] sts on back neck, inc 1 st at center. 103[107:107:111] sts.
Beg with a 2nd row work in K1, P1 rib as for back. Work 9 rows.
Bind off in rib.
Graft left shoulder seam and join neckband.
Join side and sleeve seams. Set in sleeves. Sew in shoulder pads.

Fair Isle Sleeveless Sweater

Knitted in marvelous muted earth colors, this neat
sleeveless pullover looks good on men and women, and
with clever accessorizing can be worn in town or country.

Sizes
To fit 32–34[36–38]in chest/bust
Length 23½[25½]in

Note Instructions for larger size are in brackets []; where there is one set of figures it applies to both sizes.

Gauge
32 sts and 28 rows to 4in over Fair Isle patt on size 4 needles

Materials
12oz Shetland fingering yarn in main color (A)
1oz in each of 5 contrasting colors
1 pair each sizes 2 and 4 knitting needles
Size 2 circular needle

Back
Using smaller needles and A, cast on 144[168] sts. Work in K1, P1 rib for 2¾[3]in, ending with a WS row. Change to larger needles and beg with a K row cont in st st working 45 rows in patt from chart on page 144. Read odd-numbered rows as K rows and even-numbered rows as P rows. Now repeat chart reading odd-numbered rows as P rows and even-numbered rows as K rows. These 90 rows form the patt. Work in patt until work measures 14½[15]in, ending with a WS row.
Shape armholes
Bind off 7[8] sts at beg of next 2 rows. Dec 1 st at each end of the foll 9[10] rows, then at each end of every other row 3 times. 106[126] sts.
Work even until work measures 23½[25½]in, ending with a WS row. Leave these sts on a spare needle.

Front
Work as for back from * to *.
Shape armhole and neck
Next row Bind off 7[8] sts, patt 63[74], K2 tog, turn, leaving rem sts on a spare needle, patt to end.
Complete left side of neck first.
**Dec 1 st at armhole edge on the foll 9 rows and then on every other row 3 times, *at the same time*, dec 1 st at neck edge on the next and every row until 24[26] sts rem.
Work even until work measures 23½[25½]in, ending with a WS row. Leave these sts on a spare needle.**
Return to sts for right side of neck.
With RS of work facing, join yarn to next st, K2 tog, patt to end.
Next row Bind off 7[8] sts, patt to end.
Complete as for left side of neck from ** to **.

To finish
With RS of work facing, beg at armhole edge, graft 24[26] sts from front shoulders to back.
Neck border
With RS of work facing, using circular needle and A, beg at center front,

Special technique – grafting stockinette stitch

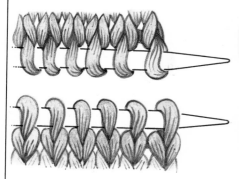

1 *This technique is used to join the shoulder seams of the pullover. Place the edges to be joined on a flat surface with the stitches facing each other. Thread a tapestry needle with a length of yarn at least four times the width of the edge.*

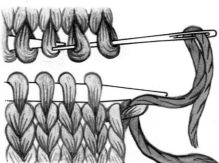

2 *Insert the needle through the first stitch on the lower edge from the back, then through the first stitch on the upper edge through the front, then through the second stitch on the upper edge from the back, withdrawing the knitting needle from each stitch as you work.*

3 *Insert the needle through the first stitch on the lower edge from the front, then the second stitch on the lower edge from the back, then the second stitch on the upper edge from the front, then the third stitch on the upper edge from the back. Continue in this way across the row.*

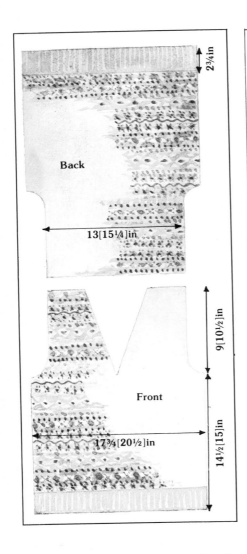

Back

2¾in

13[15¼]in

9[10½]in

Front

17¾[20½]in

14½[15]in

pick up and K 60[72] sts up right side of neck, K across the 58[74] sts on back neck, pick up and K 60[72] sts down left side of neck. 178[218] sts. Work backward and forward.

1st row (WS) P2 tog, *K2, P2, rep from * to last 4 sts, K2, P2 tog.

2nd row P2 tog, P1, *K2, P2, rep from * to last 5 sts, K2, P1, P2 tog. Cont in this way, keeping K2, P2 rib correct and dec 1 st at each end of every row. Work a further 11[13] rows. Bind off in rib, dec on this row as before.

Arm borders

With RS facing, using smaller needles and A, pick up and K 120[144] sts around armhole edge. Work 11 rows K2, P2 rib. Bind off in rib. Press as appropriate for yarn used.

Join side seams and front neckband.

144

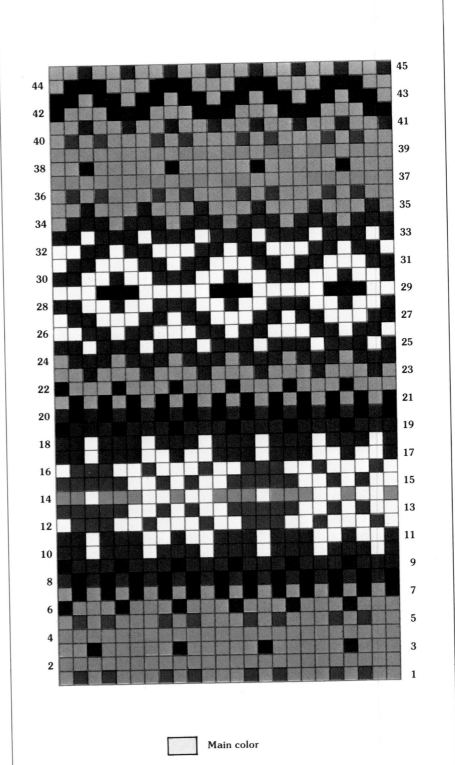

Main color

Checkered Accessories

Round off your wardrobe with this classic collection of
accessories – socks, gloves, scarf, and beret – all knitted
on four needles in traditional patterns from Sanquhar in
Scotland.

Sizes
Gloves 7½in around hand above thumb
Fingerless gloves 7½in around hand above thumb
Beret to fit an average head
Ankle socks length of foot 8¾in (adjustable)
Long socks length of foot 10in (adjustable)
Length of leg to heel (top turned down) 19in
Scarf length excluding fringe 60in

Gauge
28 sts and 28 rows to 4in over patt on size 4 needles
32 sts and 40 rows to 4in over st st on size 2 needles

Materials
Gloves
1oz Shetland fingering yarn in each of 2 colors (A) and (B)
Fingerless gloves
1oz in each of 2 colors (C) and (D)
Beret
2oz in main color (A)
1oz in contrasting color (B)
Ankle socks
2oz in main color (A)
1oz in contrasting color (B)
Long socks
5oz in main color (C)
1oz in contrasting color (D)
Scarf
11oz in main color (C)
6oz in contrasting color (D)
1 set each sizes 2, 3 and 4 double-pointed knitting needles

Gloves
Right glove
* * *Using smallest needles and A, cast on 44 sts and divide onto 3 needles.
(With spare contrast yarn, mark next st as first st of round.)
Using 4th needle work in rounds of K1. P1 rib for 2½in.
Next round Rib 2, pick up loop between last st and next st on LH needle and work into the back of it – called M1, (rib 6, M1) 7 times. 52 sts.
Change to largest needles and cont in st st, beg patt from chart 1 as foll (read every round from right to left):
1st round K1A, *K1B, K1A, rep from * to last 27 sts, patt first round

146

from chart 1.
2nd round K1B, *K1A, K1B, rep from * to last 27 sts, patt 2nd round from chart 1.
These 2 rows establish the patt for the palm with the back of hand worked from chart.
Keeping chart correct, work a further 13 rounds.* *
Place thumb
Next round K1, sl next 11 sts onto a safety pin, cast on 11 sts, patt to end. Work 11 rounds.

1st finger
Change to medium-size needles and A.
Next round K8, sl next 37 sts onto a length of yarn, cast on 2 sts, K7. 17 sts.* * *
K 30 rounds.
Shape top
Next round K1, *K2 tog, rep from * to end.
K one round.
Break off yarn and thread it through rem sts, draw up tightly and fasten off.
2nd finger
Join yarn to next st of round.
Next round K6, cast on 2 sts, K last 7 sts of round, pick up and K 2 sts from base of first finger. 17 sts.
K 36 rounds.
Complete as for first finger.
* * * *3rd finger
Join yarn to next st of round.
Next round K6, cast on 2 sts, K last 6 sts of round, pick up and K 2 sts from base of 2nd finger. 16 sts.* * * *
K 30 rounds.
Shape top
Next round *K2 tog, rep from * to

end.
K one round.
Thread yarn through rem sts, draw up and fasten off.
4th finger
Join yarn to rem sts.
Next round K12, pick up and K 2 sts from base of 3rd finger. 14 sts.
K 26 rounds.
Complete as for 3rd finger.
Thumb
With RS of work facing, using medium-size needles and A, K 11 sts from safety pin, then pick up and K 11 sts from cast-on sts. 22 sts.
K 26 rounds.
Complete as 3rd finger.

Left glove
Work as for right glove from * * * to * *.
Place thumb
Next round Patt 13, sl next 11 sts onto a safety pin, cast on 11 sts, patt to end.
Work 11 rounds.
1st finger
Change to medium-size needles and A.
Next round K17, sl these sts onto a length of yarn, K15, cast on 2 sts, leave rem sts on a length of yarn.
Complete as for first finger of right glove.
2nd finger
Next round Sl last 6 sts from first length of yarn onto needle, join in A. Pick up and K 2 sts from base of first finger, K7 sts from second length of yarn, cast on 2 sts. 17 sts.
Complete as for 2nd finger of right glove.
3rd finger
Next round Sl last 6 sts from first length of yarn onto needle, join in A. Pick up and K 2 sts from base of 2nd finger, K6 sts from second length of yarn, cast on 2 sts. 16 sts.
Complete as for 3rd finger of right glove.
4th finger
Next round Sl last 5 sts on first length of yarn onto needle, join in A, pick up and K 2 sts from base of 3rd finger, K 7 sts rem on second length of yarn. 14 sts.
Complete as 4th finger of right glove.
Thumb
Work as for right glove.

Fingerless gloves
Right fingerless glove
Work as for right glove from * * * to
* * *, working from chart 2.
Next round K7, K2 tog, K8, 16 sts.
K 4 rounds. Work 3 rounds K1, P1
rib.
Bind off loosely in rib.
2nd finger
Join in yarn to next st of round.
Next round K6, cast on 2 sts, K last
7 sts of round, pick up and K 2 sts
from base of first finger. 17 sts.
Next round K15, K2 tog, 16 sts.
Complete as first finger.
3rd finger
Work as 3rd finger of right glove from
* * * * to * * * *.
K4 rounds. Complete as first finger.
4th finger
Join in yarn to rem sts.
Next round K12, pick up and K 2 sts
from base of 3rd finger. 14 sts.
K 3 rounds. complete as first finger.
Thumb
Using medium-size needles and A,
with RS of work facing K11 sts from
safety pin, then pick up and K11 sts
from cast-on sts. 22 sts.
Complete as first finger.

Left fingerless glove
Work as for left glove, working from
chart 2, completing fingers as for right
fingerless glove.

Beret
Using smallest needles and A, cast on
126 sts and divide onto three
needles. (Mark next st as first of
round.)
Work 11 rounds K1, P1 rib.
Next round *(K2, M1) 27 times,
(K1, M1) 9 times, rep from * once
more. 198 sts.
Change to largest needles and beg
patt form chart 1.
Work 27 rounds.
Shape crown
Cont in A only.
Next round *K2 tog, K2, rep from *
to last 2 sts, K2 tog, 148 sts.
Next round K.
Next round (K12, sl 1, K2 tog, psso)
9 times, K13. 130 sts.
Next round Sl first st onto end of last
needle, K to end.
Next round (K10, sl 1, K2 tog, psso)
10 times. 110 sts.
Next round (K8, sl 1, K2 tog, psso)
10 times. 90 sts.

Cont to dec in this way until the
round "(sl 1, K2 tog, psso) 10 times"
has been worked. 10 sts.
Next round K.
Next round (K2 tog) to end. 5 sts.
Thread yarn through the rem sts,
draw up and fasten off.

Ankle socks
Using smallest needles and A, cast on
72 sts and divide onto 3 needles.
(Mark next st as first of round). Work
4 rounds K1, P1 rib.
Change to largest needles and beg
patt from chart 1.
Work 18 rounds.
Change to smallest needles and cont
in A only.
Next round (K3, K2 tog) 4 times,
(K2, K2 tog) 8 times, (K3, K2 tog)
4 times. 56 sts.
Work in K1, P1 rib for 2in.
Turn work inside out, so reversing
fabric.
K12 rounds.
Divide for heel
Next round K13, sl last 14 sts of
round to other end of same needle.
27 sts.
Divide rem sts onto 2 needles and

Chart 1

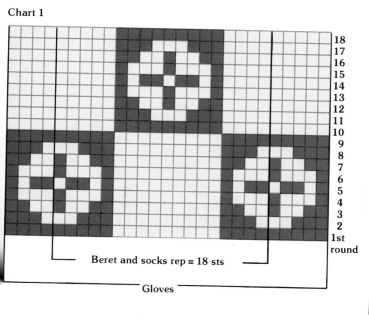

Beret and socks rep = 18 sts

Gloves

Chart 2

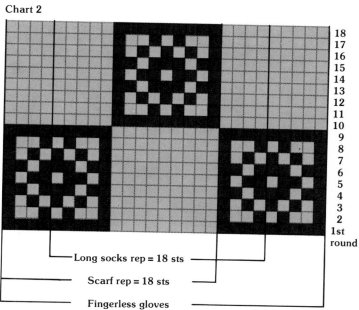

18
17
16
15
14
13
12
11
10
9
8
7
6
5
4
3
2
1st
round

Long socks rep = 18 sts

Scarf rep = 18 sts

Fingerless gloves

▫ = A   ■ = B   ▨ = C   ■ = D

leave for instep.
Cont on 27 sts for heel in rows as
foll:
1st row (WS) Sl 1, P to end.
2nd row Sl 1, K to end.
Rep these 2 rows 15 more times,
then the first row again.
Turn heel
1st row K19, K2 tog tbl, turn.
2nd row P12, P2 tog, turn.
3rd row K12, K2 tog tbl, turn.
Rep 2nd and 3rd rows 5 more times,
then the 2nd row again.
Next row K7 to complete heel (6 sts
rem on LH needle).
Sl all instep sts onto one needle.
With spare needle, K6 sts rem for
heel, pick up and K 16 sts along side
of heel, with 2nd needle K29 instep
sts, with 3rd needle pick up and K
16 sts along side of heel, K7 heel sts.
74 sts.
Shape instep in rounds as foll:
1st round K.
2nd round First needle – K to last 3
sts, K2 tog, K1, 2nd needle – K to
end, 3rd needle – K1, K2 tog tbl, K
to end.
Rep these 2 rounds until 56 sts rem.
Work even for 48 rounds.
(Length of foot may be adjusted here
if necessary.)
Next round First needle – K to end,
2nd needle – K1, K2 tog tbl, K to last
3 sts, K2 tog, K1, 3rd needle – K to
end.

Shape toe
1st round First needle – K to last 3
sts, K2 tog, K1, 2nd needle – K1, K2
tog tbl, K to last 3 sts, K2 tog, K1,
3rd needle – K1, K2 tog tbl, K to
end.
2nd round K.
Rep last 2 rounds until 30 sts rem.
K sts from first needle onto end of
3rd needle. Graft or bind off sts tog
from 2 needles.

Long socks
Using smallest needles and C, cast on
72 sts and divide onto 3 needles.
(Mark next st as first of round.)
Work 4 rounds K1, P1 rib.
Change to largest needles and beg
patt from chart 2.
Work 18 rounds.
Change to smallest needles and cont
in A only.

Next round K.
Next round (K6, M1) 12 times.
84 sts.
Work in K1, P1 rib for 2½in. Turn
work inside out so reversing fabric.
K40 rounds.
Shape leg
1st round K2 tog, K to last 3 sts, K2
tog tbl, K1.
K 5 rounds.
Rep the last 6 rounds until 60 sts
rem.
Work even until work measures 14in
from reversing of fabric.
Divide for heel
Next round K14, sl last 15 sts of
round to other end of same needle.
29 sts.
Divide rem sts onto 2 needles and
leave for instep.
Cont on 29 sts for heel in rows as
foll:
1st row (WS) Sl 1 P-wise, P to end.
2nd row Sl 1 K-wise, *K1, ybk, sl 1
P-wise, rep from * to last 2 sts, K2.
Rep these 2 rows 16 more times,

then the first row again.
Turn heel
1st row K17, sl 1, K1, psso, turn.
2nd row P6, P2 tog, turn.
3rd row K7, sl 1, K1, psso, turn.
4th row P8, P2 tog, turn.
Cont in this way until all sts are
worked onto one needle, ending with
a P row. 17 sts.
Next row K9 to complete heel (8 sts
rem on LH needle).
Sl all instep sts onto one needle.
With spare needle, K8 sts rem for
heel, pick up and K 18 sts along side
of heel, with 2nd needle K31 instep
sts, with 3rd needle, pick up and K
18 sts along side of heel, K9 heel sts.
84 sts.
Shape instep in rounds as foll:
1st round K.
2nd round First needle – K to last 3
sts, K2 tog, K1, 2nd needle – K, 3rd
needle – K1, K2 tog tbl, K to end.
Rep these 2 rounds until 58 sts rem.
Work even for 56 rounds. (Length
may be adjusted here.) Sl first st of
2nd needle onto end of first needle
and last st of 2nd needle onto 3rd
needle.
Shape toe
1st round First needle – K to last 3
sts, K2 tog, K1, 2nd needle – K1, K2
tog tbl, K to last 3 sts, K2 tog, K1,
3rd needle – K1, K2 tog tbl, K to
end.
2nd round K.
Rep these 2 rounds until 26 sts rem,
ending with a 2nd round.
K sts from first needle onto end of
3rd needle. Graft or bind off sts tog
from 2 needles.

Scarf
Using largest needles and C, cast on
144 sts and divide onto 3 needles.
(Mark next st as first of round.)
K one round.
Cont in st st, beg patt from chart 2
until work measures approx 60in
from cast-on edge ending with a 9th
patt row.
Bind off.

To finish
Press scarf flat and join ends.
Cut rem yarn into 14in lengths.
Using 3 strands of C and 3 strands of
D tog make a fringe along the short
ends of scarf.

Guernsey Family Sweaters

This "family group" of sweaters illustrates three traditional
Guernsey styles – including the plain workday garment and
the more decorative versions for Sundays and celebrations.

Sizes

Man's sweater
To fit 38[40:42]in chest
Length 26[26½:27]in
Sleeve seam 18[18½:19]in
Woman's sweater
To fit 32[34:36]in bust
Length 24[24½:25]in
Sleeve seam 16½in
Child's sweater
To fit 26[28:30]in chest
Length 19[20½:22]in
Sleeve seam 12[13½:15]in

Note Instructions for larger sizes are in brackets []; where there is only one set of figures it applies to all sizes.

Gauge

27 sts and 36 rows to 4in over st st on size 2 needles.

Materials

Man's sweater
23[27:30]oz firmly-twisted sport-weight yarn
Woman's sweater
20[23:27]oz firmly-twisted sport-weight yarn
Child's sweater
16[16:20]oz firmly-twisted sport-weight yarn
1 pair size 2 needles
Size 2 circular needle

Man's sweater

Back and front (one piece)
**Using pair of needles, cast on 132 [140:148] sts for front.
Next row Sl 1, *K1 tbl, rep from * to end.
Rep the last row 24 more times.
Break yarn and leave these sts on a spare needle.**
Rep from ** to ** for back.
Using circular needle, join back and front by slipping both sets of sts onto needle, marking first st of back as first st of round. 264[280:296] sts. Work in rounds. Work 6 rounds K2, P2 rib.
Next round (Pick up the loop between last st knitted and next st and knit into the back of it − called M1 −, K132[140:148]) twice. 266[282:298] sts.
Next round (P1, K132[140:148]) twice.
Rep last round until work measures 17[17:17¼]in.
Shape underarm gussets
1st round M1, K1, M1, K132[140:148]) twice.
2nd and every other round K.
3rd round (M1, K3, M1, K132[140:148]) twice.
5th round (M1, K5, M1, K132[140:148]) twice.
Cont to inc in this way until the round (M1, K17, M1, K132[140:148]) twice has been

worked.
Next round (Sl 19 sts onto a stitch holder, K132[140:148]) twice.
Leave the 132[140:148] sts of back on a spare needle and cont in rows on sts for front.
Next row (WS) P5, K5, P112[120:128], K5, P5.
Next row K.
Rep the last 2 rows until front measures 26[26½:27]in, ending with a WS row. Leave these sts on a spare needle.
With WS of work facing, join yarn to sts for back. Complete as for front.
Shape shoulders
With WS of work tog, using one of the pair of needles, beg at left armhole edge, join shoulder as foll: (K1 st from front and 1 st from back tog to make 1 st) 38[41:44] times, turn and bind off these sts. Fasten off. Join yarn to right shoulder and complete to match left shoulder, leaving center 56[58:60] sts for neck opening.
Shape neck gussets
With RS of work facing, using pair of needles, pick up and K 1 st from neck edge of left shoulder, K1 from front, turn.
Next row Sl 1 P-wise, P1, P1 from back, turn.
Next row Sl 1 K-wise, K2, K1 from front, turn.

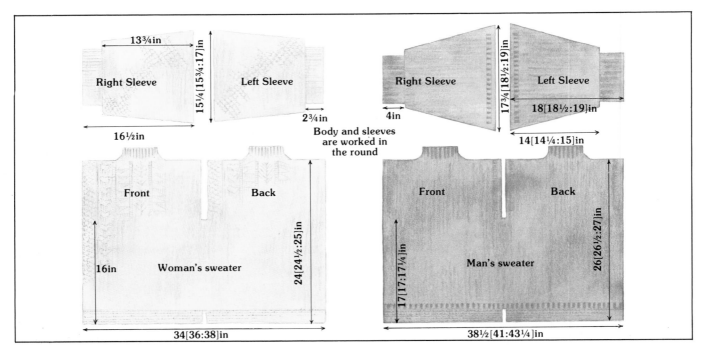

13¾in
Right Sleeve
15¼[15¾:17]in
Left Sleeve
16½in
2¾in

17¾[18½:19]in
Right Sleeve
Left Sleeve
4in
18[18½:19]in

Body and sleeves are worked in the round

14[14¼:15]in

Front
Back
24[24½:25]in
16in
Woman's sweater
34[36:38]in

Front
Back
26[26½:27]in
17[17:17¼]in
Man's sweater
38½[41:43¼]in

Cont in this way until there are 15 sts. Break yarn and leave these sts. Work right neck gusset in the same way.

Neckband

Using circular needle, with RS of work facing, K across back neck sts, inc 1 st at each end, K left neck gusset sts, K across sts on front, K right neck gusset sts. 116[120:124] sts. Mark first gusset st as first st of round. Work 12[14:16] rounds K2, P2 rib. Bind off in rib.

Sleeves

Using circular needle, with RS of work facing, beg at underarm, K19 sts from gusset, pick up and K 104[108:112] sts around armhole edge. 123[127:131] sts. Mark first gusset st as first st of round.
1st round K2 tog, K15, K2 tog tbl, P1, work in K2, P2 rib to last st, P1.
2nd and 3rd rounds K17, P1, rib to last st, P1.
4th round K2 tog, K13, K2 tog tbl, P1, rib to last st, P1.
5th and 6th rounds K15, P1, rib to last st, P1.
7th round K2 tog, K11, K2 tog tbl, P1, K to last st, P1.
8th and 9th rounds K13, P1, K to last st, P1.
Cont as set, dec 1 st at each side of gusset until 105[109:113] sts rem.
Next round P1, K104[108:112].
Next round P1, K2 tog tbl, K to last 2 sts, K2 tog.

Next round P1, K to end.
Rep the last round 4 more times.
Rep the last 6 rounds until 71[73:75] sts rem.
Work even until sleeve measures 18[18½:19]in (sleeve may be lengthened here).
Next round P1, K4[3:3], K2 tog, (K8[6:9], K2 tog) 6[8:6] times), K to end. 64[64:68] sts.
Work in rounds of K2, P2, rib for 4in. Bind off in rib.

To finish

Press lightly on WS if appropriate for yarn used, omitting ribbing and garter st sections.

Woman's sweater

Back and front (one piece)
****Using pair of needles, cast on 117[125:133] sts for front.
Next row Sl 1, *K1 tbl, rep from * to end.
Rep the last row 24 more times.
Break yarn and leave these sts on a spare needle.****
Rep from ** to ** for back.
Using circular needle, join back and front by slipping both sets of sts onto needle, marking first st of back as first st of round.
Beg patt
When working from chart, read each row from right to left.
1st round P1, K2, (P2, K2) 2[3:4] times, work first row from chart, K2 (P2, K2) 5[7:9] times, work first row from chart, K2, (P2, K2) 2[3:4] times, P1.

2nd round As first round, working 2nd row from chart.
3rd round K1, P2, (K2, P2) 2[3:4] times, work 3rd row from chart, P2, (K2, P2) 5[7:9] times, work 3rd row from chart, P2, (K2, P2) 2[3:4] times, K1.
4th round As 3rd round, reading 4th row from chart.
These 4 rounds establish the edge st patt and place the center patt panel. Keeping edge sts and patt panel from chart correct cont until work measures 16in.
Shape underarm gussets
1st round (Pick up loop between last st knitted and next st and knit into the back of it – called M1 –, patt 117[125:133]) twice.
2nd round (K1, patt 117[125:133]) twice.
3rd round (M1, K1, M1, patt 117[125:133]) twice.
4th round (K3, patt 117[125:133]) twice.
5th round (M1, K3, M1, patt 117[125:133]) twice.
6th round (K5, patt 117[125:133]) twice.
Cont to inc in this way until the round "(M1, K15, M1, patt 117[125:133]) twice" has been worked.
Next round (Sl 17 sts onto a stitch holder, patt 117[125:133]) twice. Leave the 117[125:133] sts of back on a spare needle and cont in rows and patt on sts for front until work measures 24[24½:25]in, ending with a WS row.

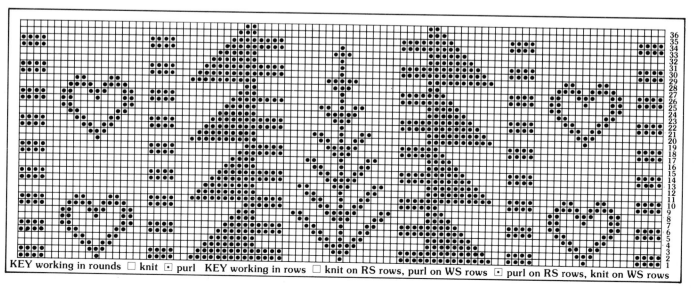

KEY working in rounds ☐ knit ⊡ purl KEY working in rows ☐ knit on RS rows, purl on WS rows ⊡ purl on RS rows, knit on WS rows

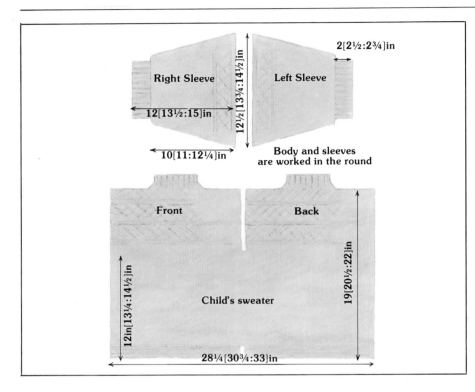

Right Sleeve

Left Sleeve

2[2½:2¾]in

12½[13¾:14½]in

12[13½:15]in

10[11:12¼]in

Body and sleeves
are worked in the round

Front

Back

Child's sweater

12in[13¾:14½]in

19[20½:22]in

28¼[30¾:33]in

With WS of work facing, join yarn to sts for back. Complete as for front.

Shape shoulders
With WS of work tog, using one of the pair of 00 needles, beg at left armhole edge, join shoulders as foll: (K1 st from front and 1 st from back tog to make 1 st) 34[37:40] times, turn and bind off these sts. Fasten off. Join yarn to right shoulder and complete to match left shoulder, leaving center 49[51:55] sts for neck opening.

Shape neck gussets
With RS of work facing, using 3mm needles, K1 st from neck edge of left shoulder, K1 from front, turn.
Next row Sl 1 P-wise, P1, P1 from back, turn.
Next row Sl 1 K-wise, K1 from front, turn.
Cont in this way until there are 13 sts. Break yarn and leave these sts. Work right neck gusset in the same way.

Neckband
Using circular needle, with RS of work facing, K across right neck gusset, K back neck sts, K across left neck gusset sts and front. 100[104:108] sts. Mark next st as first st of round. Work 12 rounds K2, P2 rib. Bind off in rib.

Sleeves
Using circular needle, with RS of work facing, beg at underarm, K17 sts from gusset, pick up and K92[96:104] sts around armhole edge. 109[113:121] sts. Mark first gusset st as first st of round.
1st round K2 tog, K13, K2 tog tbl, P1, K2, *P2, K2, rep from * to last st, P1.
2nd round K15, P1, K2, *P2, K2, rep from * to last st, P1.
3rd round K2 tog, K11, K2 tog tbl, K1, P2, *K2, P2, rep from * to last st, K1.
4th round K14, P2, *P2, P2, rep from * to last st, K1.
Cont in this way, dec 1 st at each side of gusset until 93[97:105] sts rem.
Next round K2 tog, patt to end. Patt 3[3:5] rounds.
Next round Patt 1, work 2 tog, patt to last 3 sts, work 2 tog tbl, patt 1. Patt 7[7:5] rounds.
Rep the last 8[8:6] rounds until 64[68:70] sts rem.
Work even until sleeve measures 13¾in (sleeve may be lengthened here).
Next round K3[5:3], K2 tog, (K6[6:5], K2 tog) 7[7:9] times, K to end. 56[60:60] sts.
Work in rounds of K2, P2 rib for 2¾in. Bind off in rib.

To finish
Press lightly on WS if appropriate for yarn used, omitting ribbing and garter stitch.

Child's sweater
Back and front (one piece)
**Using pair of needles, cast on 97[105:113] sts for front.
Next row Sl 1, *K1 tbl, rep from * to end.
Rep the last row 20 more times. Break yarn and leave these sts on a spare needle.**
Rep from ** to ** for back.
Using circular needle, join back and front by slipping both sets of sts onto needle, marking first st of back as first st of round. Work in rounds.
Next round (Pick up the loop between last st knitted and next st and knit into the back of it − called M1 −, K97[105:113]) twice. 196[212:228] sts.
Next round (P1, K97[105:113]) twice. Rep the last round until work measures 12[13¼:14½]in.
Shape underarm gussets
1st round (M1, K1, M1, K97[105:113]) twice.
2nd and every other row K.
3rd round (M1, K3, M1, K97[105:113]) twice.
5th round (M1, K5, M1, K97[105:113]) twice.
Cont in inc in this way until the round "(M1, K13, M1, K97[105:113]) twice" has been worked.
Next round (Sl 15 sts onto a stitch holder, K97[105:113]) twice.
Leave the 97[105:113] sts of back on a spare needle and cont in rows on sts for front.
Next row (WS) P.
Now work in patt.
1st, 3rd and 4th rows P.
2nd row K.
5th row (RS) P1, *K7, P1, rep from * to end.
6th row P1, *K1, P5, K1, P1, rep from * to end.
7th row K2, *P1, K3, rep from * ending last rep K2.
8th row P3, *K1, P1, K1, P5, rep from * ending last rep P3.
9th row K4, *P1, K7, rep from * ending last rep K4.
10th row As 8th row.
11th row As 7th row.
12th row As 6th row.

13th row As 5th row.
14th–21st rows As 6th–13th rows.
22nd row P.
These 22 rows form the patt.
Cont in patt until front measures 19[20½:22]in, ending with a WS row. Leave these sts on a spare needle. With WS of work facing, join yarn to back sts. Complete as for front.

Shape shoulders
With WS of work tog, using a 00 needle, beg at left armhole edge, join shoulders as foll: (K1 st from front and 1 st from back tog to make 1 st) 27[30:33] times, turn and bind off these sts. Fasten off. Join yarn to right shoulder; complete to match left, leaving 43[45:47] sts for neck opening.

Shape neck gussets
With RS facing, using pair of needles, pick up and K 1 st from neck edge of left shoulder seam, K1 from front, turn.
Next row Sl 1 P-wise, P1, P1 from back, turn.
Next row Sl K-wise, K2, K1 from front, turn.
Cont in this way until there are 11 sts. Break yarn and leave these sts. Work right neck gusset in the same way.

Neckband
Using circular needle, with RS of work facing, K across back neck sts, K left neck gusset sts, K across sts on front, K right neck gusset sts. 88[92:96] sts. Mark first st as first st of round. Work 10[10:12] rounds, K2, P2 rib. Bind off in rib.

Sleeves
Using circular needle, with RS of work facing, beg at underarm, K15 sts from gusset, pick up and K73[81:89] sts around armhole edge. 88[96:104] sts. Mark first gusset st as first st of round.
1st round K2 tog, K11, K2 tog tbl, P to end.
2nd round K13, P to end.
3rd round K2 tog, K9, K2 tog tbl, P to end.
4th round K to end.
5th round K2 tog, K7, K2 tog tbl, P1, *K7, P1, rep from * to end.
6th round K10, *P1, K5, P1, K1, rep from * to end.
7th round K2 tog, K5, K2 tog tbl, K2, *P1, K3, rep from * ending last rep K2.
8th round K10, *P1, K1, P1, K5, rep from * ending last rep K3.
9th round K2 tog, K3, K2 tog tbl, K4, *P1, K7, rep from * ending last rep K4.
10th round K8, *P1, K1, P1, K5, rep from * ending last rep K3.
11th round K2 tog, K1, K2 tog tbl, K2, *P1, K3, rep from * ending last rep K2.
12th round K4, *P1, K5, K1, rep from * to end.
13th round K3 tog, P1, *K7, P1, rep from * to end.
14th round P1, K1, *P1, K5, P1, K1, rep from * to end.
15th round P1, K2, *P1, K3, rep from * ending last rep K2.
16th round P1, K3, *P1, K1, P1, K5, rep from * ending last rep K3.
17th round P1, K4, *P1, K7, rep from * ending last rep K4.
18th round As 16th round.
19th round As 15th round.
20th round As 14th round.
21st round P2, *K7, P1 rep from *.
22nd round P1, K2 tog tbl, K to last 2 sts, K2 tog. 72[80:88] sts.
Next round P.
Rep the last round twice more.
Next round P1, K to end.
Rep the last round 6 more times.
Next round P1, K2 tog tbl, K to last 2 sts, K2 tog.
Rep the last 6 rounds until 52[56:60] sts rem. Work even until sleeve measures 10[11:12¼]in.
Next round K3[2:4], K2 tog, (K5[6:6], K2 tog) 6 times, K3[2:4], K2 tog, 44[48:52] sts. Work in rounds of K2, P2 rib for 2[2½:2¾]in.
Bind off

To finish
Press lightly on WS.

Special technique – shaping underarm gussets

1 Work in rounds to armhole position. On next round begin working right underarm gusset. Make one, knit one, make one. Work across back stitches, then begin left underarm gusset in the same way, then work across stitches for front.

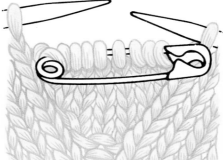

2 Continue shaping gussets by increasing one stitch on each side on every other row until gusset is required width. Slip gusset stitches on to stitch holder and work back and front yokes separately on two needles.

3 When back and front yokes are completed pick up stitches for sleeves and, working in rounds, continue shaping gussets by decreasing one stitch on each side on every other row until one gusset stitch remains.

Hebridean Guernsey

This version of the Guernsey fisherman's sweater comes from the Hebridean islands off the west coast of Scotland. It features lace panels and motifs as well as the more usual cables and textures.

Sizes
To fit 28–30[32–34:36]in chest/bust
Length 23[24:25]in
Sleeve seam 17[17¾:18½]in

Note Instructions for larger sizes are in brackets []; where there is only one set of figures it applies to all sizes.

Gauge
30 sts and 40 rows to 4in over st st on size 3 needles

Materials
450[500:550]g four ply yarn (see page 9) or 19[21:23]oz sport-weight yarn
1 pair size 3 needles
Set of four sizes 2 and 3 double-pointed needles
Cable needle

Panel patt A (worked over 6[10:16] sts)
1st row (WS) K.
2nd row P.
3rd row K1, P to last st, K1.
4th row P1, (yo, K2 tog) 2[4:7] times, P1.
5th row As 3rd.
6th row P1, K to last st, P1.
These 6 rows form panel patt A.

Panel patt B (worked over 8 sts)
1st row (WS) K1, P1, K1, P4, K1.
2nd row P1, K4, P3.
3rd and 4th rows Rep first and 2nd rows.
5th row As first row.
6th row P1, sl next 2 sts onto a cable needle and hold at front of work, K2, then K2 sts from cable needle – called C4F –, P3.
These 6 rows form panel patt B.

Panel patt C (worked over 17 sts)
1st row (WS) P.
2nd row K5, P7, K5.
3rd row P4, K2, P1, K3, P1, K2, P4.
4th row K3, P2, K2, P3, K2, P2, K3.
5th row P2, K2, P3, K3, P3, K2, P2.
6th row K1, P2, K4, P3, K4, P2, K1.
7th row P1, (K3, P3) twice, K3, P1.
8th row As 6th row.
9th row P2, K1, P4, K3, P4, K1, P2.
10th row K7, P3, K7.
11th and 13th rows P8, K1, P8.
12th and 14th rows K8, P1, K8.
15th and 17th rows P3, (K1, P1) twice, K3, (P1, K1) twice, P3.

16th row K4, (P1, K1) 5 times, K3.
18th and 19th rows As 12th and 11th rows.
20th row As 10th row.
21st row P7, K1, P1, K1, P7.
22nd row As 20th row.
23rd row P.
24th row K.
25th and 26th rows (K1 tbl) 17 times.
These 26 rows form panel patt C.

Panel patt D (worked over 8 sts)
1st row (WS) K1, P4, K1, P1, K1.
2nd row P3, K4, P1.
3rd and 4th rows As first and 2nd rows.
5th row As first row.
6th row P3, sl next 2 sts onto cable needle and hold at back of work, K2, then K2 from cable needle – called C4B –, P1.
These 6 rows form panel patt D.

Panel patt E (worked over 11 sts)
1st and 3rd rows (WS) P.
2nd row K1, yo, K3, sl 1, K2 tog, psso, K3, yo, K1.
4th row P1, K1, yo, K2, sl 1, K2 tog, psso, K2, yo, K1, P1.
5th and 7th rows K1, P9, K1.
6th row P1, K2, yo, K1, sl 1, K2 tog, psso, K1, yo, K2, P1.
8th row P1, K3, yo, sl 1, K2 tog, psso, yo, K3, P1.
These 8 rows form panel patt E.

Panel patt F (worked over 17 sts)
1st row (WS) P.
2nd row K8, P1, K8.
3rd row P7, K3, P7.
4th row K6, P5, K6.
5th row P5, K2, P1, K1, P1, K2, P5.
6th row K4, P2, K2, P1, K2, P2, K4.
7th row P3, K2, P3, K1, P3, K2, P3.
8th row K2, P2, K3, P3, K3, P2, K2.
9th row P1, K2, P3, K5, P3, K2, P1.
10th row K5, P2, K1, P1, K1, P2, K5.
11th row P4, K2, P2, K1, P2, K2, P4.
12th row K3, P2, K3, P1, K3, P2, K3.
13th row P2, K2, P3, K3, P3, K2, P2.
14th–17th rows Rep 4th–7th rows.
18th row K7, P3, K7.
19th row P6, K5, P6.
20th and 21st rows As 10th and 11th rows.

22nd and 23rd rows As 2nd and 3rd rows.
24th row K.
25th and 26th rows (K1 tbl) 17 times.
These 26 rows form panel patt F.

Panel patt G (worked over 17 sts)
1st and every other row (WP) P.
2nd row K6, K2 tog, yo, K1, yo, sl 1, K1, psso, K6.
4th row K5, K2 tog, yo, K3, yo, sl 1, K1, psso, K5.
6th row K4, K2 tog, yo, K5, yo, sl 1, K1, psso, K4.
8th row K3, (K2 tog, yo, K1) twice, yo, sl 1, K1, psso, K1, yo, sl 1, K1, psso, K3.
10th row K2, K2 tog, yo, K1, K2 tog, yo, K3, yo, sl 1, K1, psso, K1, yo, sl 1, K1, psso, K2.
12th row K1, K2 tog, yo, K1, K2 tog, yo, K5, yo, sl 1, K1, psso, K1, yo, sl 1, K1, psso, K1.
14th row K3, (yo, sl 1, K1, psso, K1) twice, K2 tog, yo, K1, K2 tog, yo, K3.
16th row K4, yo, sl 1, K1, psso, K1, yo, sl 1, K2 tog, psso, yo, K1, K2 tog, yo, K4.
18th row K5, yo, sl 1, K1, psso, K3, K2 tog, yo, K5.
20th row K6, yo, sl 1, K1, psso, K1, K2 tog, yo, K6.
22nd row K7, yo, sl 1, K2 tog, psso, yo, K7.
24th row K.
25th and 26th rows (K1 tbl) 17 times.
These 26 rows form panel patt G.

Back and Front (worked in one piece)
Using set of four smaller double-pointed needles, cast on 240[264:288] sts. Divide onto three needles, join into a round. Mark first st to denote beg of round. Work in rounds of K1, P1 rib for 2¾[3:3½]in.
Next round (Rib 10[11:12], pick up loop between st just worked and next st on LH needle and work into the back of it – called M1 –) 24 times. 264[288:312] sts.
Change to set of larger double-pointed needles and beg patt.
1st round *Marking next st for side seam, (P2, K4, P1, K4, P1) 11[12:13] times*, rep from * to * again.

2nd round *K1, P1, K5, P1, K3, P1, rep from * to end:

3rd round *P2, K6, P1, K2, P1, rep from * to end.

4th round *K1, P1, K7, P1, K1, P1, rep from * to end.

5th round *P2, K9, P1, rep from * to end.

6th round *(K1, P1) twice, K7, P1, rep from * to end.

7th round *P2, K2, P1, K6, P1, rep from * to end.

8th round *K1, P1, K3, P1, K5, P1, rep from * to end.

These 8 rounds form the patt.

Cont in patt until work measures 16[16½:17]in.

Leave first 132[144:156] sts on a spare needle for front, sl rem sts onto a needle and work in rows as foll for back.

**Next row (WS) *K1 tbl, rep from * to last st, leave rem st on a safety pin for side seam.

Next row K tbl to end, inc[dec:dec] 1 st at each end of row.

133[141:153] sts.

Place panel patts as foll:

Next row (WS) Work first row of panels A, D, C, B, E, D, F, B, E, D, C, B and A.

Next row Work 2nd row of panels A, B, C, D, E, B, F, D, E, B, C, D and A.

Cont in this way until 26 rows of panel patts C and F have been completed *at the same time*, marking each end of 15th row to denote sleeves.

Now cont as set, placing panel patt G instead of C and C instead of F. Work 26 rows.

Now cont as set, placing panel patt F instead of G and G instead of C. Work 26 rows.

Next row (WS) K tbl to end.

Rep last row until work measures 7[7½:8]in from sleeve markers, ending with a RS row.

Shape shoulders

Next 2 rows K tbl to last 5[6:6] sts, turn.

Next 2 rows K tbl to last 10[12:12] sts, turn.

Next 2 rows K tbl to last 15[18:18] sts, turn.

Next 2 rows K tbl to last 20[24:24] sts, turn.

Next 2 rows K tbl to last 25[30:30] sts, turn.

Next 2 rows K tbl to last 30[36:36] sts, turn.

Next 2 rows K tbl to last 35[42:42] sts, turn.

Next 2 rows K tbl to last 44[46:50] sts, turn.

Leave these sts on a spare needle. With WS of work facing, rejoin yarn to sts for front.

Cont as for back from ** until work measures 6[6:6¼]in from sleeve markers, ending with a WS row.

Shape neck

Next row Patt 51[52:57], K2 tog and turn, leaving rem sts on a spare needle. Complete left side of neck first.

Dec 1 st at neck edge on every row until 44[46:50] sts rem.

Work even until work matches back to shoulder shaping, ending with a RS row.

Shape shoulder

Next row K tbl to last 5[6:6] sts, turn.

Next and foll alt rows K tbl to end.

Next row K tbl to last 10[12:12] sts, turn.

Next row K tbl to last 15[18:18] sts, turn.

Next row K tbl to last 20[24:24] sts, turn.

Next row K tbl to last 25[30:30] sts, turn.

Next row K tbl to last 30[36:36] sts, turn.

Next row K tbl to last 35[42:42] sts, turn.

Next row K tbl to end.

Leave these sts on a spare needle. With RS of work facing, return to sts for right side of neck, sl center 27[33:35] sts onto a stitch holder, join yarn to rem 53[54:59] sts, K2 tog tbl, patt to end.

Complete to match first side of neck, reversing shapings.

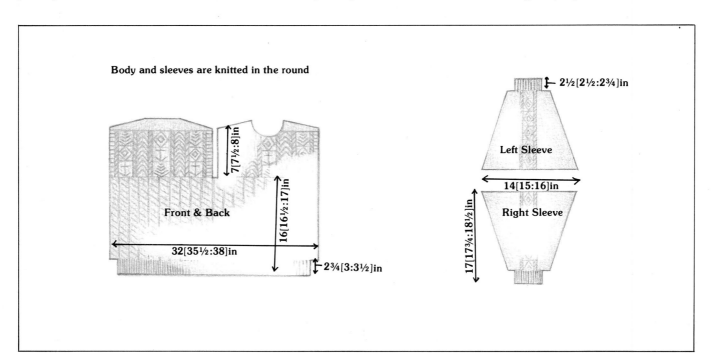

Body and sleeves are knitted in the round

Front & Back

32[35½:38]in

16[16½:17]in

7[7½:8]in

2¾[3:3½]in

2½[2½:2¾]in

Left Sleeve

14[15:16]in

Right Sleeve

17[17¾:18½]in

Gussets

With RS of work facing, using pair of needles, K seam st from safety pin.
Next row Inc 1, P1, inc 1.
Next row K3.
Cont in this way, working in st st, inc 1 st at each end of next and every other row until there are 17 sts. Leave these sts on a safety pin.

Sleeves

Graft shoulder seams.
With RS of work facing, using set of larger double-pointed needles, beg at underarm, K17 sts from gusset, pick up and K 49[54:59] sts from sleeve marker to shoulder, pick up and K1 st at shoulder seam, pick up and K49[54:59] sts down to sleeve marker. 116[126:136] sts.
Mark first gusset st as first of round and cont as foll, noting that WS rows of panel patts will now be worked as RS rows; therefore, read K for P and P for K on these rows.

Next round K2 tog, K13, K2 tog tbl, K31[36:41], P1, K1, work first row of panel patts D, G and B, K1, P1, K to end.
Next round K46[51:56], P2, work 2nd row of panel patts D, G and B, P2, K to end.
Next round K2 tog, K11, K2 tog tbl, K31[36:41], P1, K1, work 3rd row of panel patt D, G and B, K1, P1, K to end.
Next round K44[49:54], P2, work 4th row of panel patts, D, G and B, P2, K to end.
Cont in this way, keeping panel patts correct, dec 1 st at each side of underarm gusset on next and every other row until 100[110:120] sts rem. (1 st rem in gusset.)
Next round P1, patt to end.
Rep the last round 1[5:3] more times.
Next round P1, K2 tog tbl, patt to last 2 sts, K2 tog.
Dec 2 sts in this way on every foll

5th[4th:4th]round until 52[52:58] sts rem.
Work even as set until sleeve measures 14½[15¼:15¾]in.
Change to set of smaller double-pointed needles and work in rounds of K1, P1 rib for 2½[2½:2¾]in.
Bind off in rib.

Neckband

With RS of work facing, using set of smaller double-pointed needles, beg at left shoulder, pick up and K 19[20:21] sts down left side of neck, K across 27[33:35] sts at center front, pick up and K 19[20:21] sts up right side of neck and K across 45[49:53] sts on back neck. 110[122:130] sts.
Mark next st as beg of round.
Work 14 rounds K1, P1 rib.
Bind off in rib.

To finish

Sew underarm gussets neatly in place with a flat seam.

Special technique – grafting garter stitch

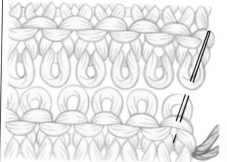

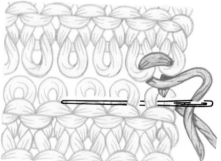

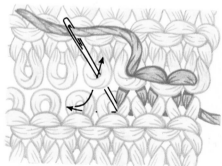

1 The shoulders of the sweater are grafted rather than seamed together. Place the back and front sections together with the loops facing as shown. Thread a needle with matching yarn, or use a long end from one of the sections. Bring the needle through from back to front of first loop on lower edge, then from back to front of first loop on upper edge.

2 Pull the yarn through. Now take the needle from front to back of the second loop on the upper section. Pull the yarn through. Take the needle from front to back of the first loop on the lower section and bring it out from back to front of the next stitch along on the lower section.

3 Pull the yarn through. Continue in this way until all the stitches are grafted together. This produces a much neater joining than a seam and is especially suitable for joining across the shoulders.

Peruvian-patterned Garments

Look elegantly ethnic in this key-patterned alpaca vest, or knit an Inca bird into a pullover for a child. The poncho on page 163 is decorated with another version of the key pattern.

Sizes

Vest
To fit 32[34:36:38]in bust
Length 21[21:22:22]in
Pullover
To fit 25[28:31]in chest
Length 18[20:22]in
Sleeve seam 13[14:15]in

Note Instructions for larger sizes are in brackets []; were there is only one set of figures it applies to all sizes.

Gauge

Vest
30 sts and 32 rows to 4in over patt on size 3 needles
Pullover
25 sts and 26 rows to 4in over patt on size 4 needles

Materials

Vest
6oz fingering yarn such as Jaeger Alpaca in main color (A)
4oz in each of 2 contrasting colors (B) and (C)
1 pair each sizes 1, 2 and 3 knitting needles
6 buttons
Pullover
125[150:150]g double knitting yarn (see page 9) or 5[6:6]oz knitting worsted in main color (A)
100g or 4oz, respectively, in each of 2 contrasting colors (B) and (C)
1 pair each sizes 2 and 4 knitting needles
Set of four size 2 double-pointed needles

Vest

Back

Using smallest needles and A, cast on 90[98:106:114] sts.
Work in K1, P1 rib for 2½in, ending with a RS row.
Next row Rib 13[1:4:8]; *pick up loop between last st worked and next st and work into back of it – called M1 –, rib 2[3:3:3], rep from * to last 13[1:6:10] sts, rib to end. 122[130:138:146] sts.
Change to largest needles and beg patt from chart on page 160, reading K rows from right to left and P rows from left to right.
1st row K1, *K first row from chart, rep from * to last st, K1.
2nd row K1, *P 2nd row from chart,

rep from * to last st, K1.
Cont in this way, keeping patt from chart correct until 80[80:90:90] rows have been worked from chart.
Shape armholes
Keeping patt correct, bind off 8 sts at beg of next 2 rows.
Next row K1, sl 1, K1, psso, patt to last 3 sts, K2 tog, K1.
Next row K1, patt to last st, K1.
Rep the last 2 rows 7 more times. 90[98:106:114] sts.
Cont in patt until 70 rows have been worked from the beg of armhole shaping, ending with a 30th[30th:10th:10th] patt row.
Change to medium-size needles, B and cont in st st.
Work 2 rows.
Shape shoulders
Bind off 7[8:8:9] sts at beg of next 4 rows, 7[8:9:9] sts at beg of foll 2 rows and 7[7:9:10] sts at beg of next 2 rows. Bind off rem 34[36:38:40] sts.
Pocket linings (make 2)
Using medium-size needles and B, cast on 40 sts. Work 40 rows in st st.
Leave these sts on a spare needle.

Left front

**Using smallest needles and A, cast on 50[50:58:58] sts.
Work in K1, P1 rib for 2½in, ending with a RS row.
Next row Rib 1[1:4:4], *M1, rib 3, rep from * to last 1[1:6:6] sts, rib to end. 66[66:74:74] sts.
Change to largest needles and work in patt as for back until 40 rows have been worked from chart.
Place pocket
Next row (RS) Patt 13[13:17:17] sts, sl next 40 sts onto a st holder, patt 13[13:17:17].
Next row Patt 13[13:17:17] sts, patt across 40 sts of pocket lining, patt 13[13:17:17] sts.
Cont in patt until 80[80:90:90] rows have been worked from chart.**
Shape armhole and neck
Next row Bind off 8 sts, patt to end.
Next row Patt to end.
Next row K1, sl 1, K1, psso, patt to last 3 sts, K2 tog, K1.
Next row Patt to end.
Next row K1, sl 1, K1, psso, patt to end.
Next row K1, P2 tog, patt to end.

Next row K1, sl 1, K1, psso, patt to end.
Next row Patt to end.
Rep the last 6 rows again, then the first 4 of them again. 44[44:52:52] sts.
Keeping armhole edge straight, cont to dec at neck edge as before on every foll 3rd[3rd:2nd:3rd] row until 28[31:34:37] sts rem.
Work even until 70 rows have been worked from beg of armhole shaping, ending with a 30th[30th:10th:10th] patt row.
Change to medium-size needles, B and cont in st st.

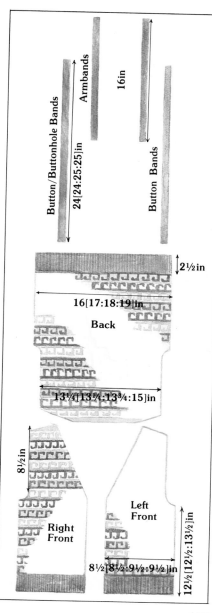

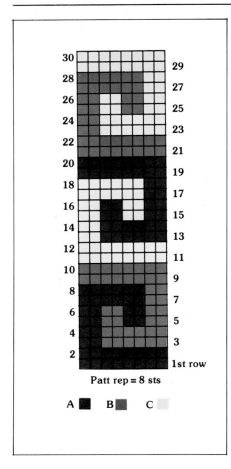

30 29
28 27
26 25
24 23
22 21
20 19
18 17
16 15
14 13
12 11
10
8   7
6   5
4   3
2
1st row

Patt rep = 8 sts

A ■ B ▨ C ☐

Work 2 rows.
Shape shoulder
Bind off 7[8:8:9] sts at beg of next and every other row once. Work 1 row. Bind off 7[8:9:9] sts at beg of next row. Work 1 row. Bind off rem 7[7:9:10] sts.

Right front
Work as for left front from ** to **. Patt 1 row.
Shape neck and armhole
Next row Bind off 8 sts, patt to end.
Next row K1, sl 1, K1, psso, patt to last 3 sts, K2 tog, K1.
Next row Patt to end.
Next row Patt to last 3 sts, K2 tog, K1.
Next row Patt to last 3 sts, P2 tog, K1.
Next row Patt to last 3 sts, K2 tog, K1.
Next row Patt to end.
Rep the last 6 rows again, then the first 4 of them again.
44[44:52:52] sts.
Complete to match left front, working 1 extra row before shaping shoulder.
160

Pocket edgings
With RS of work facing, using smallest needles and A, K across 40 sts on st holder. Work in K1, P1, rib for 1¼in, ending with a WS row. Bind off in rib.

Armbands (make 2)
Using smallest needles and A, cast on 11 sts.
1st row K1, *P1, K1, rep from * to end.
2nd row K1, *K1, P1, rep from * to last 2 sts, K2.
Rep the last 2 rows until work measures 16in, ending with a 2nd row. Bind off in rib.

Button band
Work as given for armbands until band measures 24[24:25:25]in, ending with a 2nd row. Bind off in rib.

To finish
Press as appropriate for yarn used. Join shoulder seams.
Sew button band to left front edge, ending at center back neck.
Mark the position of 6 buttonholes as foll: one ¾in from lower edge, one at 2¾in from lower edge, one slightly below beg of neck shaping and 3 more evenly spaced between.
Buttonhole band
Work buttonhole band as for button band, making buttonholes opposite markers as foll:
1st buttonhole row (RS) K1, (P1, K1) twice, K2 tog, yo, (P1, K1) twice.
2nd buttonhole row K1, *K1, P1, rep from * to last 2 sts, K2.
Cont in rib until band measures 24[24:25:25]in, ending with a 2nd row. Bind off in rib.
Join side seams. Sew armbands to armhole edge. Sew buttonhole band to right front, ending at center back neck, join to button band. Sew pocket linings to WS and pocket edgings to RS. Sew on buttons.

Pullover
Back
**Using smaller needles and A, cast on 82[90:102] sts.
1st row *K2, P2, rep from * to last 2 sts, K2.
2nd row K1, P1, *K2, P2, rep from

* to last 4 sts, K2, P1, K1.
Rep the last 2 rows for 2½in, ending with a 2nd row.
Change to larger needles and B.
Next row K, inc 1 st at each end on 2nd size only. 82[92:102] sts.
Next row P.
Cont in st st, working from chart on page 162 until 58[66:74] rows have been worked from chart.
Shape armholes
Keeping chart correct, bind off 6 sts at beg of next 2 rows.
Next row K1, sl 1, K1, psso, work to last 3 sts, K2 tog, K1.
Next row Work to end.
Rep the last 2 rows 3 more times. 62[72:82] sts.
Cont to work from chart until 76[88:100] rows have been worked. Change to B.**
Work 30 rows st st, ending with a P row.
Shape shoulders
Bind off 5[7:8] sts at beg of next 4 rows and 6[6:8] sts at beg of foll 2 rows. Leave rem 30[32:34] sts on a spare needle.

Front
Work as for back from ** to **.
Work 14[12:10] rows st st, ending with a P row.
Shape neck
Next row Work 22[26:30] sts and turn, leaving rem sts on a spare needle.
Work left side of neck first.
Next row P1, P2 tog, work to end.
Next row Work to last 3 sts, K2 tog, K1.
Rep the last 2 rows twice more. 16[20:24] sts.
Work even for 9[11:13] rows, ending with a P row.
Shape shoulder
Bind off 5[7:8] sts at beg of next and every other row once. Work 1 row. Bind off rem 6[6:8] sts.
With RS of work facing, return to sts on spare needle, sl center 18[20:22] sts onto a st holder, join in B and work to end.
Next row Work to last 3 sts, P2 tog tbl, P1.
Next row K1, sl 1, K1, psso, work to end.
Rep the last 2 rows twice more. 16[20:24] sts.
Complete to match left side of neck.

Sleeves

Using smaller needles and A, cast on 42[42:46] sts.

Work in rib as for back for 2½in, ending with a 2nd row.

Change to larger needles and B.

Next row *K twice into every st, rep from * to last 2[2:0]sts. K2[2:0]. 82[82:92] sts.

Beg patt.

1st row K1B, *4B, 2C, 4B, rep from * to last st, K1B.

2nd row P1B, *3B, 4C, 3B, rep from * to last st, P1B.

3rd row K1B, *2B, 6C, 2B, rep from * to last st, K1B.

4th row P1B, *1B, 8C, 1B, rep from * to last st, P1B.

5th–8th rows Work 4 rows st st in C.

9th–12th rows Work 4 rows st st in A.

13th row K1B, *1B, 8A, 1B, rep from * to last st, K1B.

14th row P1B, *2B, 6A, 2B, rep from * to last st, P1B.

15th row K1B, *3B, 4A, 3B, rep from * to last st, K1B.

16th row P1B, *4B, 2A, 4B, rep from * to last st, P1B.

17th–20th rows Work 4 rows st st in B.

21st–24th rows Work 4 rows st st in C.

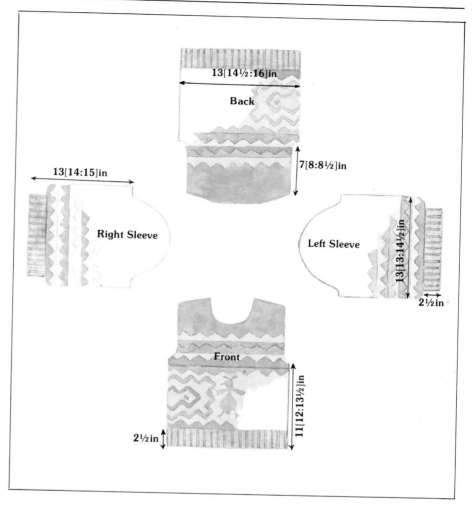

Special technique – holding yarn in left hand

1 When working with two different colors in a row it is often easier to hold one color in the right hand and knit it as usual, and the other color in the left hand and use it to knit as follows.

2 To work knit stitches, use the forefinger of the left hand to hold yarn in position. Insert the right-hand needle knitwise into the first stitch on the left-hand needle. Take the needle behind the yarn and pull a loop through the stitch as usual.

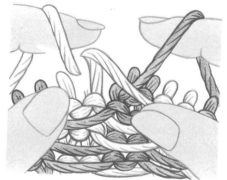

3 To work purl stitches, hold the yarn in position with the left forefinger. Insert the right-hand needle purlwise into the first stitch on the left-hand needle. Move the needle around the yarn making a loop. Take the loop through the stitch.

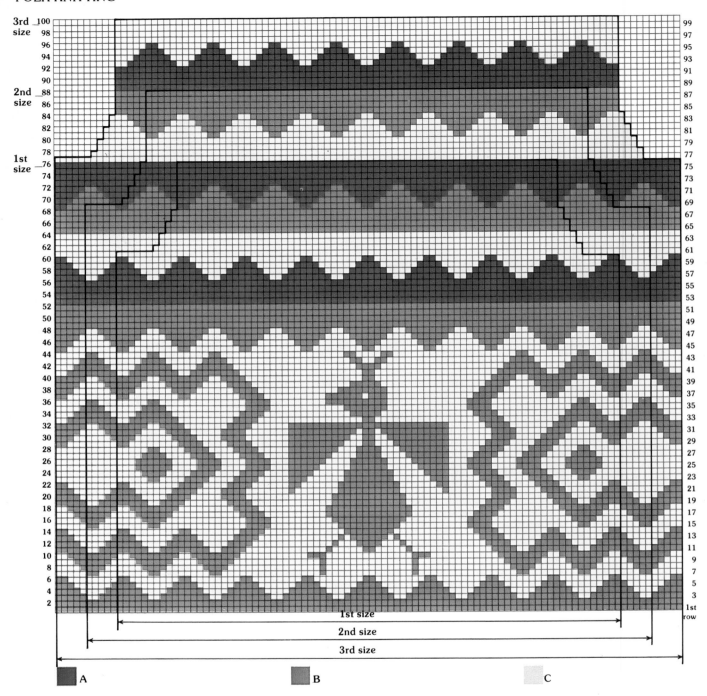

■ A	■ B

□ C

25th row K1C, *4C, 2A, 4C, rep
from * to last st, K1C.
26th row P1C, *3C, 4A, 3C, rep
from * to last st, P1C.
27th row K1C, *2C, 6A, 2C, rep
from * to last st, K1C.
28th row P1C, *1C, 8A, 1C, rep
from * to last st, P1C.
29th–32nd rows Work 4 rows st st in
A.
33rd–36th rows Work 4 rows st st in
B.
These 36 rows form the patt. Cont in
patt until work measures 13[14:15]in,
ending with a P row.
162

Shape sleeve top
Keeping patt correct, bind off 6 sts at
beg of next 2 rows.
Next row K1, sl 1, K1, psso, work to
last 3 sts, K2 tog, K1.
Next row Work to end.
Rep the last 2 rows until 58[48:62]
sts rem, ending with a WS row.
Next row K1, sl 1, K1, psso, work to
last 3 sts, K2 tog, K1.
Next row P1, P2 tog, work to last 3
sts, P2 tog tbl, P1.
Rep the last 2 rows until 30[32:34]
sts rem, ending with a WS row.
Bind off.

To finish
Press lightly. Join shoulder seams.
Neckband
With RS of work facing, using set of
four double-pointed needles and A,
pick up and K 30[32:34] sts from
back neck, pick up and K 16[18:20]
sts down left side of neck, K across
18[20:22] sts at center front, pick up
and K 16[18:20] sts up right side.
80[88:96] sts. Work in rounds of K2,
P2 rib for 2in. Bind off very loosely.
Join side and sleeve seams. Set in
sleeves. Fold neckband in half to WS.
Catch down.

Patt rep = 9 sts

Poncho

Size
To fit 7–8 years
Length 25in
Width 38in at widest point

Gauge
15 sts and 20 rows to 4in over st st on size 9 needles

Materials
25oz bulky yarn in main color (A)
7oz in contrasting color (B)
1 pair each sizes 6 and 9 knitting needles
Size 9 steel crochet hook

Back and front (alike)
Using larger needles and A, cast on 2 sts.
Beg with a K row, work 2 rows in st st. Cont in st st inc 1 st at each end of every row until there are 86 sts.
Now inc 1 st at each end of next and every other row until there are 144 sts, ending with a P row.
Join in B and work first–20th rows in key patt from chart.
Cont in A. Beg with a K row, cont in st st until work measures 24½in, ending with a P row.
Shape shoulders Bind off 51 sts at beg of next 2 rows. 22 sts.
Neck Change to smaller needles and work in K1, P1 rib for 1¼in, ending with a WS row. Join in A and K to end. Bind off loosely in rib.
To finish
Join shoulder and neckband seams. using crochet hook and A, work 1 row sc all around edge of poncho. Mark down 6in from shoulder and catch together at armholes. Fringe edges.

163

Tyrolean Cardigan

A profusion of flowers blooms on this brilliantly patterned cardigan. It has a traditional peplum, pompon ties, and detachable collar. There is also a matching hat and mittens.

Sizes
To fit 32[34:36:38]in bust
Length 21½[22:22½:22½]in
Sleeve seam 17[18:18:18½]in

Note Instructions for larger sizes are in brackets []; where there is only one set of figures it applies to all sizes.

Gauge
29 sts and 31 rows to 4in over patt on size 5 needles
22 sts and 31 rows to 4in over st st on size 5 needles

Materials
Cardigan
850[900:950:1000]g double knitting yarn (see page 9) or 35[37:39:41]oz knitting worsted
Collar
100g double knitting yarn or 4oz knitting worsted
Beanie
100g double knitting yarn or 4oz knitting worsted
Mittens
100g double knitting yarn or 4oz knitting worsted
4 skeins tapestry yarn in red
3 skeins in blue
2 skeins each in yellow and green
1 pair each sizes 3 and 5 knitting needles
9 buttons
Shoulder pads (optional)

Back
Using larger needles, cast on 152[156:160:164] sts.
K 4 rows.
Work peplum
Beg patt.
1st row (RS) P1[3:5:7], *K the 3rd st on LH needle, then K the first and 2nd st – called TW3 –, K1, P2, sl next 3 sts onto cable needle and hold at back of work, K3, then K3 from cable needle – called C6B, K3, sl next 3 sts onto cable needle and hold at front of work, K3, then K3 from cable needle – called C6F, P2, K1, TW3 ***, K1, P5, K tbl 2nd st on LH needle then K first st – called TW2B –, K1, (K1, P1, K1, P1, K1) all into next st, turn, P5, turn K5, sl 4th, 3rd, 2nd and first st over 5th – called MB –, K1, K 2nd st on LH needle, then K first st – called TW2F

–, P5, K1 **, rep from * to *** once, P4, rep from * to ** once, rep from * to *** again, P1[3:5:7].
2nd row K1[3:5:7], *P3, K3, P6 tbl, P3, P6 tbl, K3, P3 ***, K6, P7, K6 **, rep from * to *** once, K4, rep from * to ** once, rep from * to *** again, K1[3:5:7].
3rd row P1[3:5:7], *K4, P2, K6 tbl, K3, K6 tbl, P2, K4 ***, K1, P4, TW2B, K5, TW2F, P4, K1 ***, rep from * to *** once, P4, rep from * to ** once, rep from * to *** again, P1[3:5:7].
4th row K1[3:5:7], *P3, K3, P6 tbl, P3, P6 tbl, K3, P3 ***, K5, P9, K5 **, rep from * to *** once, K4, rep from * to ** once, rep from * to *** again, K1[3:5:7].
5th row P1[3:5:7], *TW3, K1, P2, K6 tbl, K1, MB, K1, K6 tbl, P2, K1, TW3 ***, K1, P3, TW2B, K1, MB, K3, MB, K1, TW2F, P3, K1 **, rep from * to *** once, P4, rep from * to ** once, rep from * to *** again, P1[3:5:7].
6th row K1[3:5:7], *P3, K3, P6 tbl, P3, P6 tbl, K3, P3 ***, K4, P11, K4, **, rep from * to *** once, K4, rep from * to *** once, rep from * to *** again, K1[3:5:7].
7th row P1[3:5:7], *K4, P2, K6 tbl, K3, K6 tbl, P2, K4 ***, K1, P2, TW2B, K9, TW2F, P2, K1 **, rep from * to *** once, P4, rep from * to ** once, rep from * to *** again, P1[3:5:7].
8th row K1[3:5:7], *P3, K3, P6 tbl, P3, P6 tbl, K3, P3 ***, K3, P13, K3 **, rep from * to *** once, K4, rep from * to ** once, rep from * to *** again, K1[3:5:7].
9th row P1[3:5:7], *TW3, K1, P2, K6 tbl, K1, MB, K1, K6 tbl, P2, K1, TW3 ***, K1, P1, TW2B, K1, MB, K7, MB, K1, TW2F, P1, K1 **, rep from * to *** once, P4, rep from * to ** once, rep from * to *** again, P1[3:5:7].
10th row K1[3:5:7], *P3, K3, P6 tbl, P3, P6 tbl, K3, P3 ***, K2, P15, K2 **, rep from * to *** once, K4, rep from * to ** once, rep from * to *** again, K1[3:5:7].
11th row P1[3:5:7], *K4, P2, K6 tbl, K3, K6 tbl, P2, K4 ***, K1, TW2B, K13, TW2F, K1 **, rep from * to *** once, P4, rep from * to ** once, rep from * to *** again,

P1[3:5:7].
12th row K1[3:5:7], *P3, K3, P6 tbl, P3, P6 tbl, K3, P3 ***, K1, P17, K1 **, rep from * to *** once, K4, rep from * to ** once, rep from * to *** again, K1[3:5:7].
13th row P1[3:5:7], *TW3, K1, P2, K6 tbl, K1, MB, K1, K6 tbl, P2, K1, TW3 ***, TW2B, K1, MB, K11, MB, K1, TW2F **, rep from * to *** once, P4, rep from * to ** once, rep from * to *** again, P1[3:5:7].
14th row As 12th row.
15th row P1[3:5:7], *K4, P2, K6 tbl, K3, K6 tbl, P2, K4 ***, TW2F, K15, TW2B **, rep from * to *** once, P4, rep from * to ** once, rep from * to *** again, P1[3:5:7].
16th row As 12th row.
17th row P1[3:5:7], *TW3, K1, P2, K6 tbl, K1, MB, K1, K6 tbl, P2, K1, TW3 ***, K1, P5, TW2B, K1, MB, K1, TW2F, P5, K1 **, rep from * to *** once, P4, rep from * to ** once, rep from * to *** again, P1[3:5:7].
18th row As 2nd row.
19th row P1[3:5:7], *K4, P2, K6 tbl, K3, K6 tbl, P2, K4 ***, K1, P4, TW2B, K5, TW2F, P4, K1 **, rep from * to *** once, P4, rep from * to ** once, rep from * to *** again, P1[3:5:7].
20th row As 4th row.
21st row P1[3:5:7], *TW3, K1, P2, C6F, K3, C6B, P2, K1, TW3 ***, K1, P3, TW2B, K1, MB, K3, MB, K1, TW2F, P3, K1 **, rep from * to *** once, P4, rep from * to ** once, rep from * to *** again, P1[3:5:7].
22nd row As 6th row.
23rd row P1[3:5:7], *K4, P2, K6 tbl, K3, K6 tbl, P2, K4 ***, K1, P2, TW2B, K9, TW2F, P2, K1 **, rep from * to *** once, P4, rep from * to ** once, rep from * to *** again, P1[3:5:7].
24th row As 8th row.
25th row P1[3:5:7], *K4, P2, K6 tbl, K3, K6 tbl, P2, K4 ***, K1, P1, TW2B, K1, MB, K7, MB, K1, TW2F, P1, K1 **, rep from * to *** once, P4, rep from * to ** once, rep from * to *** agian, P1[3:5:7].
26th row As 10th row.
27th row P1[3:5:7], *K4, P2, K6 tbl, K3, K6 tbl, P2, K4 ***, K1, TW2B, K13, TW2F, K1 **, rep from * to

*** once, P4, rep from * to ** once, rep from * to *** again, P1[3:5:7].

28th row As 12th row.

29th row P1[3:5:7], *K4, P2, K6 tbl, K3, K6 tbl, P2, K4 ***, TW2B, K1, MB, K1, MB, K1, TW2F **, rep from * to *** once, P4, rep from * to ** once, rep from * to *** once, P1[3:5:7].

30th row As 12th row.

31st row P1[3:5:7], *K4, P2, K6 tbl, K3, K6 tbl, P2, K4 ***, TW2F, K15, TW2B **, rep from * to *** once, P4, rep from * to ** once, rep from * to *** again, P1[3:5:7].

32nd row As 12th row.

These 32 rows form the patt.

Next row K1[3:5:7], *K2 tog, K1, rep from * to last 1[3:5:7] sts, K to end. 102[106:110:114] sts.

Change to smaller needles and work 3 rows K1, P1 rib.

Next row (make eyelets) Rib 4[2:4:2], *yo, rib 2 tog, rib 2, rep from * to last 2[0:2:0] sts, rib to end. Work 2 rows in rib.

Next row Rib 38[27:16:5], *work

twice into next st, — called inc 1, — rib 12, rep from * 1[3:5:7] times more, rib to end. 104[110:116:122] sts.

Change to larger needles, and recommence patt as foll, working from corresponding rows of peplum.

1st row P1[4:7:10], TW3, work from *** to ** of peplum, then work from * to ***, P4, rep from * to ***, then from *** to ** again, TW3, P1[4:7:10].

2nd row K1[4:7:10], P3, work from *** to ** of peplum, then from * to ***, K4, rep from * to ***, then *** to ** again, P3, K1[4:7:10].

3rd row P1[4:7:10], *K3, work from *** to ** of peplum, then from * to **, P4, rep from * to ***, then from *** to ** again, K3, P1[4:7:10].

4th row As 2nd row.

5th row P1[4:7:10], TW3, work from *** to ** of peplum, then from * to ***, P4, rep from * to ***, then *** to ** again, TW3, P1[4:7:10].

Cont working patt sections in this order, *at the same time*, inc and work

into reverse st st 1 st at each end of the next and every foll 6th row until there are 124[130:136:142] sts. Work even for 10 rows.

Shape armholes

Keeping patt correct, bind off 4 sts at beg of next 2 rows and 3 sts at beg of foll 2 rows.

Dec 1 st at each end of next 3[5:6:8] rows.

104[106:110:112] sts.

Work even until work measures 7¾[8¼:8¾:8¾]in from beg of armhole shaping, ending with a WS row.

Shape shoulders

Bind off 30[30:32:32] sts at beg of next 2 rows.

Leave rem 44[46:46:48] sts on a spare needle.

Left front

Using larger needles, cast on 76[78:80:82] sts.

K 4 rows.

Beg patt as foll, working from corresponding rows of back peplum.

1st row P1[3:5:7], work as for back

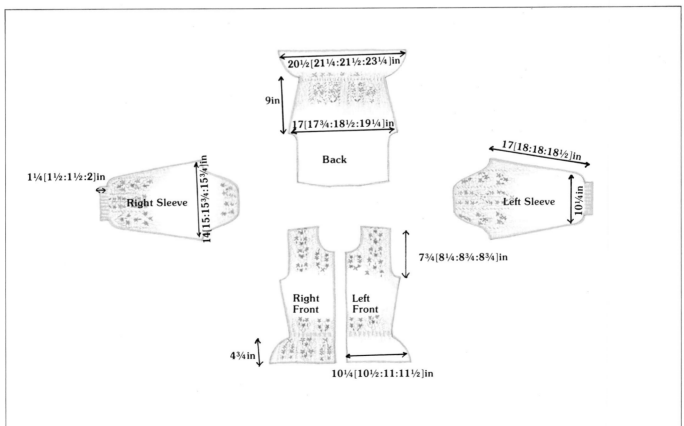

from * to ** once, then from * to *** once, P1, K1.
2nd row K2, work as for back from * to **, then from * to *** once, K1[3:5:7].
3rd row P1[3:5:7], work as for back from * to ** once, then from * to *** once, P1, K1.
4th row K2, work as for back from * to ** once, then from * to *** once, K1[3:5:7].
Cont working in this way, work a further 28 rows.
Next row K1[3:5:7], *K2 tog, K1, rep from * to end. 51[53:55:57] sts.
Change to smaller needles.
Work in K1, P1 rib as foll:
Next row K1, *P1, K1, rep from * to end.
Next row P1, *K1, P1, rep from * to end.

Cont in rib as set. Work 1 more row.
Next row (make eyelets) Rib 4[2:4:2], *yo, work 2 tog, rib 2, rep from * ending last rep rib 1.
Work 3[2:2:2] rows in rib.
2nd, 3rd and 4th sizes only
Next row Rib [26:21:15], *inc 1, rib 12, rep from * [0:1:2] more times, rib to end. [54:57:60] sts.
All sizes
Change to larger needles and recommence patt as foll, working from corresponding rows of back peplum:
1st row P1[4:7:10], TW3, work as for back from *** to ** once, then from * to *** once, K1.
2nd row K1, work as for back from *

to **, P3, K1[4:7:10].
3rd row P1[4:7:10], K3, work as for back from *** to **, then from * to ***, K1.
4th row K1, work as for back from * to **, P3, K1[4:7:10].
5th row P1[4:7:10], TW3, work as for back from *** to **, then from * to ***, K1.
Cont working in this way, *at the same time*, inc and work into reverse st st 1 st at side edge on the next and every foll 6th row until there are 61[64:67:70] sts.
Work even for 10 rows.
Shape armholes
Keeping patt correct, bind off 4 sts at beg of next row and 3 sts at beg of every other row once.
Dec 1 st at armhole edge on foll 3[5:6:8] rows. 51[52:54:55] sts.
Work even until work measures 4¾[5:5:5]in from beg of armhole shaping, ending at front edge.
Shape neck
Bind off 8 sts at beg of next row and 4 sts at beg of every other row once.
Dec 1 st at neck edge on every row until 30[30:32:32] sts rem.
Work even until work matches back to shoulder shaping, ending at armhole edge.
Shape shoulder
Bind off rem sts.

Right front
Using larger needles, cast on 76[78:80:82] sts. K 4 rows.
Beg patt as foll, working from corresponding rows of back peplum.
1st row K1, P1, work as for back from * to ** once, then from * to *** once, P1[3:5:7].
2nd row K1[3:5:7], work as for back from * to ** once, then from * to *** once, K2.
3rd row K1, P1, work as for back from * to ** once, then from * to *** once, P1[3:5:7].
4th row K1[3:5:7], work as for back from * to ** once, then from * to *** once, K2.
Cont in this way, work a further 28 rows.
Next row *K1, K2 tog, rep from * to last 1[3:5:7] sts, K to end. 51[53:55:57] sts.
Change to smaller needles. Work 3 rows K1, P1 rib as for left front.

Next row (make eyelets) Rib 1, work 2 tog, yo, *rib 2, work 2 tog, yo, rep from * to last 4[2:4:2] sts, rib to end.
Work 3[2:2:2] rows in rib.
2nd, 3rd and 4th sizes only
Next row Rib [26:21:15], * inc 1, rib 12, rep from * [0:1:2] more times, rib to end. [54:57:60] sts.
All sizes
Change to larger needles and recommence patt as foll:
1st row K1, work as for back from * to ** once, TW3, P1[3:5:7].
2nd row K1[3:5:7], P3, work as for back from *** to **, then from * to ***, K1.
Complete to match left front, reversing all shaping.

Sleeves
Using smaller needles, cast on 52[54:56:58] sts. Work in K1, P1 rib for 1¼[1½:1½:2]in.
Next row Rib 5[8:11:14]. * inc 1, rib 1, rep from * to last 5[8:11:14] sts, rib to end. 73 sts.
Change to larger needles. Beg patt, working corresponding rows from back peplum as foll:
1st row K1, TW3, work as for back from *** to ** once, then from * to **, TW3, K1.
2nd row P4, work as for back from *** to ** once, then from * to **, P4.
3rd row K4, work as for back from *** to ** once, then from * to **, K4.

4th row P4, work as for back from *** to ** once, then from * to **, P4.

5th row K1, TW3, work as for back from *** to ** once, then from * to **, TW3, K1.

Cont working in this way, *at the same time*, inc and work into reverse st st 1 st at each end of the next and every foll 6th row until there are 103[109:113:113] sts.

Work 34[22:10:10] rows.

Shape top

Bind off 4 sts at beg of next 2 rows and 3 sts at beg of foll 2 rows. Dec 1 st at each end of next and every other row until 45 sts rem. Bind off.

Button band

Using smaller needles, cast on 6 sts. Work in K1, P1 rib until band, when slightly stretched, fits from beg of rib to neck edge of left front, ending at inner edge. Leave sts on a safety pin. Sew band in place. Mark 8 button positions on band, the first 1¼in from neck edge, the last ½in from cast-on edge with the others evenly spaced between.

Buttonhole band

Using smaller needles, cast on 6 sts. Work in K1, P1 rib for ½in.

1st buttonhole row Rib 3, bind off 1, rib to end.

2nd buttonhole row Rib 2, cast on 1, rib to end.

Cont in rib, making buttonholes opposite markers, until band fits up right front edge, ending at outer edge. Do not break yarn. Sew band in place.

To finish

Join shoulder seams.

Neckband

Using smaller needles, rib across sts of buttonhole band, pick up and K 34[36:38:38] sts up right side of neck, K21[22:22:23], K2 tog, K21[22:22:23] across sts on back neck, pick up and K34[36:38:38] sts down left side of neck, rib across button band. 123[129:133:135] sts. Beg with a 2nd row work 3 rows K1, P1 rib as given for left front. Work the 2 buttonhole rows again. Rib 2 more rows. Bind off in rib. Work embroidery using 2 strands of
168

yarn. (See Special Technique.) Join side and sleeve seams. Set in sleeves easing fullness at top. Sew on buttons and insert shoulder pads. Make a twisted cord and thread through waist eyelets. Make two small pompoms and sew to ends of cord.

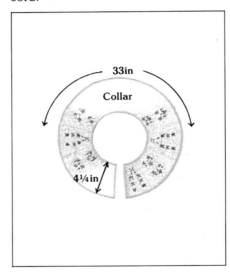

Detachable collar

Using larger needles, cast on 244 sts. K 4 rows.

Beg patt, working from corresponding rows of back peplum.

1st row K1, work as for back from * to ** twice, then from * to *** once, P4, rep from * to ** twice, then from * to *** again, K1.

2nd row K1, work as for back from * to ** twice, then from * to *** once, K4, rep from * to ** twice, then from * to *** again, K1.

Cont in this way. Work a further 30 rows.

Next row (K2 tog) to end.

Next row (K2 tog) to end. 61 sts.

Make edging

1st row K.

2nd row K1, * yo, K2 tog, rep from * to end.

3rd row *K1, (K1, P1) all into yo of previous row, rep from * to last st, K1.

4th row Bind off 1, *insert LH needle into st below yo of 2nd row, draw through a loop and sl previous st over, bind off 3, rep from * to end. Make a twisted cord and thread through at neck edge.

Beanie

Using larger needles, cast on 131 sts. Beg with a K row cont in st st for 2½in, ending with a P row.

Beg patt.

1st row K.

2nd and every other row P.

3rd row *K12, MB, rep from * to last st, K1.

4th row P.

Rep these 4 rows 4 more times. Beg shaping.

1st row *K2 tog, K11, rep from * to last st, K1.

2nd and every other row P.

3rd row *K2 tog, K9, MB, rep from * to last st, K1.

Keeping patt correct, cont to dec in this way on every other row until 11 sts rem.

Next row K2 tog, K to last st, K1. Break off yarn, thread through rem sts, draw up and fasten off securely.

To finish

Embroider flowers in "wedges" between rows of bobbles.

Join seam. Roll brim to RS and tack in place. Make a twisted cord, tie in a neat bow, sew to crown. Make two small pompoms and sew to each end of cord.

Right mitten

**Using smaller needles, cast on 40 sts.

Work 9 rows K1, P1 rib.

Next row Rib 3, * work twice into next st − called inc 1 −, rib 6, rep from * to last 2 sts, rib 2. 45 sts. ** Beg patt and thumb gusset.

1st row *K1, P2, TW3, P2, sl next 2 sts onto cable needle and hold at back of work, then K2 from cable needle − called C4B, sl next 2 sts onto cable needle and hold at front of work, K2, then K2 form cable needle − called C4F −, P2, TW3, P2, K1. P1, *K2, P1, K17.

2nd and every other row K1, P to last 24 sts, P1, K2, P3, K2, P8, K2, P3, K3.

3rd row *K1, P2, K3, P2, K8, P2, K3, P2, K1, P1, * work into front, back and front of next st, K1, P1, K17.

5th row K1, P2, TW3, P2, K8, P2, TW3, P2, K1, P1, K4, P1, K17.

7th row K1, P2, K3, P2, C4F, C4B,

P2, K3, P2, K1, P1, (inc 1, K1) twice, P1, K17.
8th row As 2nd row.
These 8 rows establish the cable patt.
Next row As first row from * to *, K6, P1, K to end.
Next and every other row As 2nd row.
Next row As 3rd row from * to *, inc 1, K3, inc 1, K1, P1, K to end.
Cont in this way inc 1 st at each side of gusset on every foll 4th row until there are 55 sts.
Work even for 5 rows.
Divide for thumb
Next row Patt 37, turn, leaving palm sts on spare needle.
Next row K1, P11, cast on 4 sts, turn.
Next row K16.
Next row K1, P to last st, K1.
Rep last 2 rows 8 more times.
Shape top
1st row (K2 tog) to end.

2nd row K1, P to last st, K1.
Break off yarn, thread through rem sts, draw up and fasten off securely. With RS of work facing, rejoin yarn to palm sts, K to end. 43 sts.
Dec 1 st at each end of next and every other row until 7 sts rem.
Bind off.

Left mitten
Work as for right mitten from ** to **

Beg patt and thumb gusset.
1st row K17, P1, K2, P1, K1, P2, TW3, P2, C4B, C4F, P2, TW3, P2, K1.
2nd and every other row K3, P3, K2, P8, K2, P3, K2, P3, K2, P to last st, K1.
3rd row K17, P1, work into front, back and front of next st, K1, P1, patt to last st, K1.
Cont in this way, inc 1 st at each side of gusset on every foll 4th row until

there are 55 sts.
Work even for 5 rows.
Divide for thumb
Next row K30, cast on 4 sts, turn, leaving back of hand sts on spare needle.
Next row K1, P14, K1, turn.
Complete as thumb of right mitten. With RS of work facing, rejoin yarn to sts for back of hand, patt to end. Keeping patt correct, complete as for right mitten, reversing shaping.

Mitten edging
Using smaller needles and with RS of work facing, pick up K39 sts along rib edge.
K 1 row.
Work edging as for detachable collar.

To finish
Embroider mitten backs (see Special Technique.)
Join thumb and side seam.

Special technique – Tyrolean embroidery

1 Tyrolean embroidery stitches are simple ones like detached chain stitch and French knots. Work floral motifs to follow the lines of the stitch pattern. On the chevron panel work one flower in the point of each "V" and one above it on each side in a different color.

2 On the cable and bobble panel work three flowers and two leaves on each side of the bobbles, and one flower between each pattern repeat, alternating the contrasting colors as shown.

3 The medallion cable running along the center of the mitten backs makes a perfect "frame" for a string of lazy-daisy motifs in alternating contrasting colors.

American Indian Sweater

The brilliant geometric patterns of the American Indians have been used on this long, lean sweater. It looks marvelous with pants, or with boots and a mid-calf skirt.

Sizes
To fit 32[34:36:38]in bust
Length 26in
Sleeve seam 18in
Note Instructions for larger sizes are in brackets []; where there is only one set of figures it applies to all sizes.

Gauge
22 sts and 26 rows to 4in over patt on size 5 needles

Materials
275[275:325:325]g double knitting yarn or 11[11:13:13]oz of knitting worsted in main color (A).
150[150:200:200]g or 6[6:8:8]oz, respectively, in each of two contrasting colors (B) and (C)
100[100:150:150]g or 4[4:6:6]oz, respectively, in each of two contrasting colors (D) and (E)
1 pair each sizes 3 and 5 knitting needles
Set of four size 3 double-pointed needles

Back
**Using smaller needles and A, cast on 97[103:109:115] sts. Work in K1, P1 rib as foll:
1st row K1, *P1, K1, rep from *.
2nd row P1, *K1, P1, rep from *.
Rep the last 2 rows for 2in, ending with a 2nd row.
Change to larger needles and beg with a K row cont in st st working patt as foll: See pages 172–174 for charts.

Work first–22nd rows from chart 1.
Work 23rd–41st rows from chart 2.
Work 42nd–90th rows from chart 3.
Work 91st–106th rows from chart 4.**
Work 107th–143rd rows from chart 5. Work 144th–160th rows from chart 6.
Shape shoulders
Next row Bind off 28[31:34:37] sts, K41 and sl these sts onto a holder, bind off rem 28[31:34:37] sts.

Front
Work as for back from ** to **.
Work 107th–142nd rows color patt from chart 5.
Shape neck
Cont working from chart 5 and chart 6, keeping patt correct.
Next row K40[43:46:49] sts, and turn, leaving rem sts on a spare needle. Work left side of neck first. Bind off 3 sts at beg of next row and 2 sts at beg of every other row 3 times. Now dec 1 st at beg of every other row 3 times. 28[31:34:37] sts. Work even to match back until 160th row has been worked from chart 6.
Shape shoulder
Bind off these sts.
With RS of work facing return to sts on spare needle, sl center 17 sts onto a holder, join yarn to next st, K to end. Work 1 row.
Complete to match first side of neck, reversing shaping.

Sleeves
Using smaller needles and A, cast on 45[49:53:57] sts.
Work in K1, P1 rib as for back for 2¾in, ending with a first row. Inc 12 sts evenly across last row. 57[61:65:69] sts.
Change to larger needles and beg with a P row cont in st st and patt as foll, *at the same time*, inc 1 st at each end of 7th and every foll 6th row.
Work 42nd–90th rows from chart 3. 73[77:81:85] sts.
Work 91st–106th rows from chart 4. 77[81:85:89] sts.
Work 107th–143rd rows from chart 5. 89[93:97:101] sts.
Bind off loosely.

To finish
Join shoulder seams.
Neckband
Using three of set of four double-pointed needles, with RS of work facing and using A, K across 41 sts on back neck, pick up and K20 sts down left side of neck, K across 17 sts at center front and pick up and K20 sts up right side of neck. 98 sts.
Work in rounds of K1, P1 rib for 2¾in. Bind off loosely in rib.
Press as appropriate for yarn used, omitting ribbing.
Place center of bound-off edge of sleeve at shoulder seam, set in sleeves. Join side and sleeve seams.
Fold neckband in half to WS and slip-stitch down.

Special technique – introducing new yarn

1 *Insert right-hand needle into stitch on left-hand needle. Wind new yarn around right-hand needle and pull through the stitch, thus knitting one stitch with new yarn. Leave old yarn at back of work.*

2 *Knit next stitch in the same way but this time wind both strands of new yarn over right-hand needle and knit. This secures the end of the new yarn, as shown.*

3 *Repeat as for second stitch and thereafter leave the end at the back of the work and knit with one strand only.*

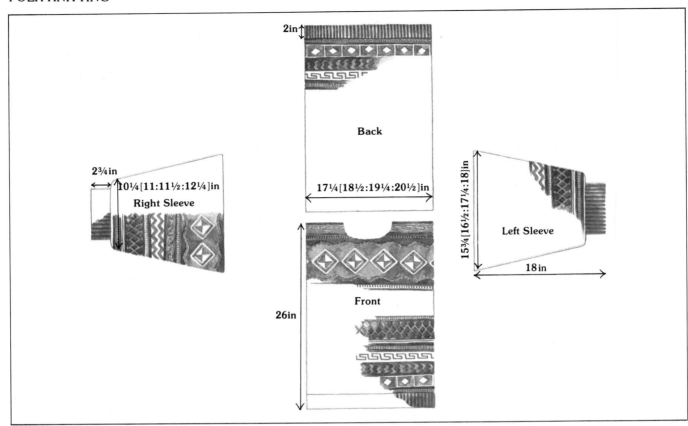

Reading the charts

Work in stockinette stitch, reading K rows (odd-numbered) from right to left and P rows (even-numbered) from left to right.

A

B

C   D

E

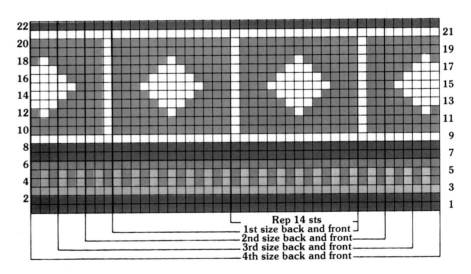

Rep 14 sts
1st size back and front
2nd size back and front
3rd size back and front
4th size back and front

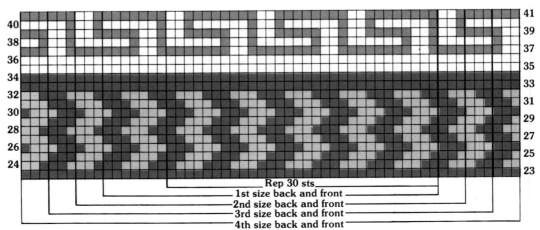

Rep 30 sts
1st size back and front
2nd size back and front
3rd size back and front
4th size back and front

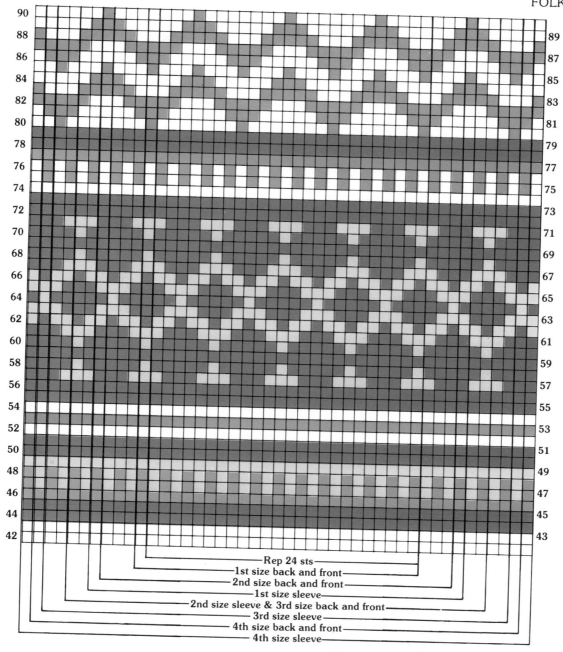

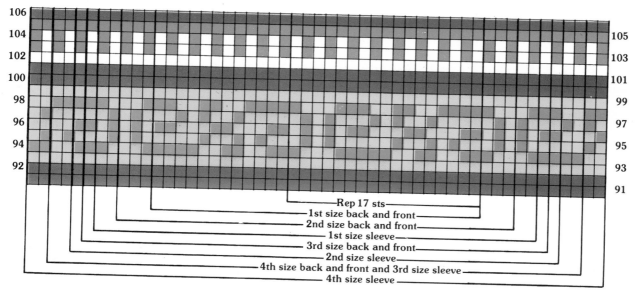

Rep 24 sts
1st size back and front
2nd size back and front
1st size sleeve
2nd size sleeve & 3rd size back and front
3rd size sleeve
4th size back and front
4th size sleeve

Rep 17 sts
1st size back and front
2nd size back and front
1st size sleeve
3rd size back and front
2nd size sleeve
4th size back and front and 3rd size sleeve
4th size sleeve

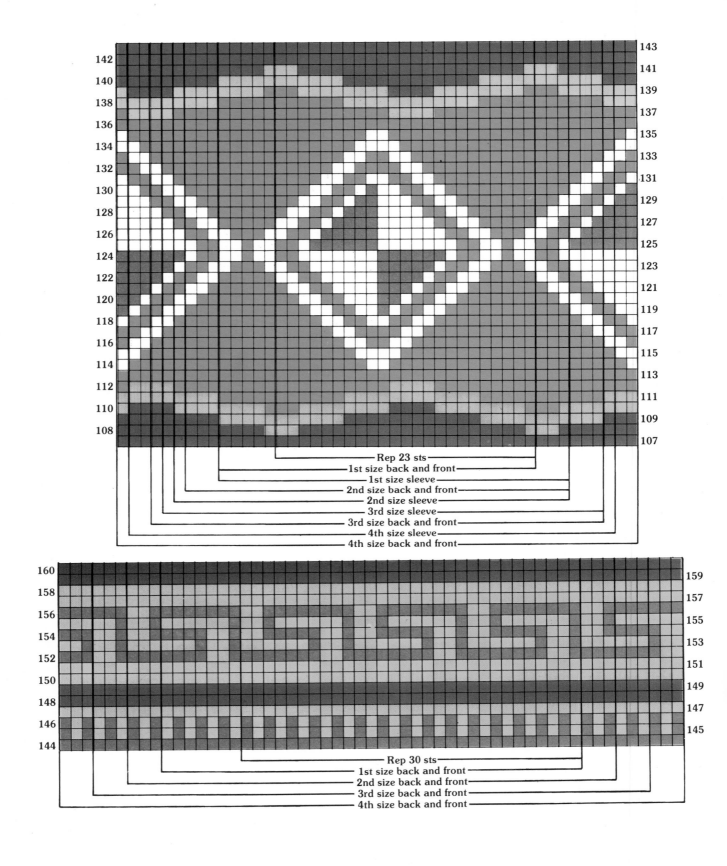

Rep 23 sts
1st size back and front
1st size sleeve
2nd size back and front
2nd size sleeve
3rd size sleeve
3rd size back and front
4th size sleeve
4th size back and front

Rep 30 sts
1st size back and front
2nd size back and front
3rd size back and front
4th size back and front

Finishing Touches

There are many kinds of decorative finishes that can be added to knitted garments. They can be used to add interest to an otherwise plain sweater or dress or to create an entirely original texture or fabric. Pompoms and tassels can be made in matching or contrasting yarns and simply sewn on wherever you like. Use them to trim collars and necklines; add them to cords for ties; tassel an entire edge to make a thick, sweeping fringe.

Beads and sequins can either be sewn on after the garment is finished or knitted in as you go along (they have to be threaded onto the yarn before knitting it). Special techniques for knitting in beads are shown on page 29.

Knitting, like any other fabric, can be embroidered. You can use many of the usual embroidery stitches – chain stitch, cross stitch, back stitch, smocking, stem stitch and so on. There is also duplicate stitch (page 28), which is specially intended for knitted fabrics. With this you can create color patterns and motifs that look as if they have been knitted in.

Tasseled Sweater

Huge fluffy tassels add a light-hearted touch to a soft,
warm sweater with an unusual pointed collar patterned in
a rich combination of contrasting colors.

Sizes
To fit 32[34:36:38]in bust
Length 24½[24½:24¾:24¾]in
Sleeve seam 18in

Note Instructions for the larger sizes are given in brackets []; where there is only one set of figures it applies to all sizes.

Gauge
15 sts and 19 rows to 4in over st st on size 9 needles

Materials
20[20:22:22]oz heavyweight mohair yarn, such as Phildar Vizir in main color (A)
4oz in contrasting color (B)
2oz in each of two contrasting colors (C) and (D)
1 pair each sizes 6 and 9 knitting needles
Set of four size 6 double-pointed needles

Back
**Using smaller pair of needles and A, cast on 62[66:70:74] sts.
1st row *K2, P2, rep from * to last 2 sts, K2.
2nd row *P2, K2, rep from * to last 2 sts, P2.
Rep the last 2 rows until work measures 5in, ending with a 2nd row.
Change to larger needles.
Next row (K2, work into front and back of next st − called inc 1) 2[3:4:5] times, K to last 6[9:12:15] sts, (inc 1, K2) 2[3:4:5] times. 66[72:78:84] sts.**
Beg with a P row cont in st st until work measures 24½[24½:24¾:24¾]in, ending with a P row.
Bind off, marking center 20 sts for back neck.

Front
Work as for back from ** to **.
Beg with a P row cont in st st until work measures 21½[21½:22:22]in from cast-on edge, ending with a P row.
Shape neck
Next row K25[28:31:34], bind off 16 sts, K to end.
Complete right side of neck first.
Dec 1 st at neck edge on next 2

rows. 23[26:29:32] sts.
Work even until work measures 24½[24½:24¾:24¾]in, ending with a P row.
Bind off. With WS of work facing, return to sts for left side of neck. Rejoin yarn to neck edge and complete to match first side.

Sleeves
Using smaller needles and A, cast on 30 sts. Work in rib as for back for 2½in ending with a 2nd row.
Change to larger needles.
Beg with a K row cont in st st. Inc 1 st at each end of every foll 4th row until there are 64 sts.
Work even until work measures 18in, ending with a P row.
Bind off.

Back collar
Using larger needles and B, cast on 2 sts. Beg working from chart on page 178 as foll:

1st row (RS) K.
2nd–5th rows K, inc 1 st at each end of every row.
6th row With B, inc into first st, K3, P2A, K3B, inc into last st.
7th row With B, inc into first st, K3, K4A, K3B, inc into last st.
8th row With B, inc into first st, K3, P6A, K3B, inc into last st.
Keeping chart correct, cont in this way inc 1 st at each end of every row until there are 80 sts.
Work even until 71 rows of chart have been worked, ending with a RS row.
Bind off.

Front collar
Work as for back collar until 57 rows of chart have been worked, ending with a RS row.
Shape neck
Next row Patt 32, turn, leaving rem sts on a spare needle.
Complete right side of neck first.

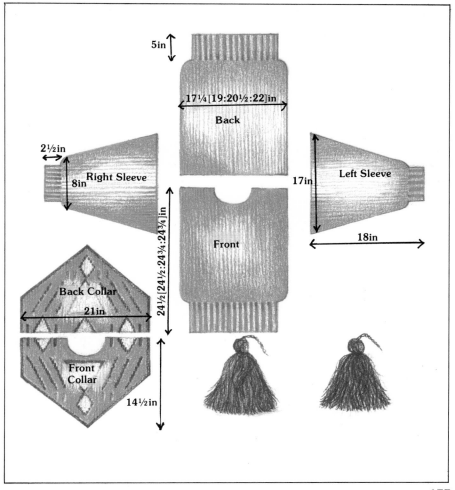

Keeping chart correct, dec 1 st at
neck edge on next 2 rows.
Work even until 71 rows of chart
have been worked, ending with a RS
row. Bind off.
With WS of work facing, rejoin yarn
to neck edge, bind off 16 sts, patt to
end.
Complete to match first side of neck.

To finish
Join shoulder seams.
Neckband
With RS of work facing, using set of
four double-pointed needles and A,
pick up and K14 sts down left side of
neck, 16 sts from front neck, 14 sts
up right side of neck and 20 sts from
back neck. 64 sts.
Work in rounds of K2, P2 rib for
1¼in. Bind off in rib.
Sew front and back pieces of collar
together at shoulders, matching patt
carefully. Neatly sew to neck edge
below neckband.
Placing center of bound-off edge of
sleeve to shoulder seam, set in
sleeves.
Join side and sleeve seams.
Using B, make two large tassels
approximately 8in long and attach to
collar points at front and back with a
corded tie (see Special Technique).

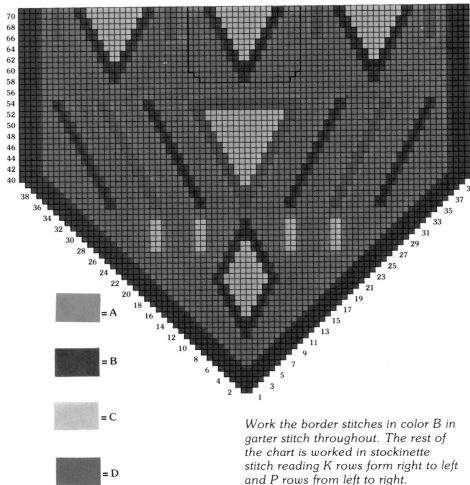

= A

= B

= C

= D

*Work the border stitches in color B in
garter stitch throughout. The rest of
the chart is worked in stockinette
stitch reading K rows form right to left
and P rows from left to right.*

Special technique – making a corded tie

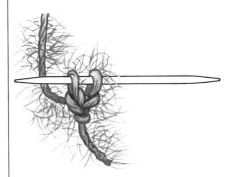

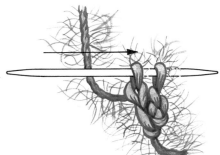

1 *The tassels are attached to the
collar of the sweater with corded
ties. Using double-pointed needles
cast on two stitches onto one of the
needles (three stitches can be cast on
for a thicker tie). Knit these two
stitches as usual.*

2 *Do not turn the work. Push the
two stitches up to the working
end of the needle and knit the two
stitches again, pulling the working
yarn firmly around to the first stitch.*

3 *Do not turn the work. Push the
two stitches up to the working
end again and knit the stitches as
before. Continue in this way until the
cord is the required length. Knit the
two stitches together and fasten off.*

Rose-patterned Sweater

The square collar on this flattering simple sweater makes a
perfect "canvas" for duplicate stitch, whether traditional, like
these soft pink cabbage roses, or more abstract and modern.

Sizes

To fit 34[36:38]in bust
Length 21¾[22½:22½]in
Sleeve seam 17in

Note Instructions for larger sizes are in brackets []; where there is only one set of figures it applies to all sizes.

Gauge

24 sts and 30 rows to 4in over st st on size 5 needles

Materials

650[650:700]g double knitting yarn (see page 9) or 27[27:29]oz knitting worsted
1 pair each sizes 3 and 5 knitting needles
Size 3 circular needle
1 skein tapestry wool in each of light, medium, and dark shades of pink
1 skein in green

Back

** Using smaller pair of needles, cast on 96[102:108] sts.
Work 21 rows K1, P1 rib.
Next row Rib 5[8:11], * work into front and back of next st − called inc 1 −, rib 5, rep from * to last 7[10:13] sts, inc 1, rib to end. 111[117:123] sts. Change to larger needles. Beg with a K row cont in st st until work measures 14in, ending with a P row.
Shape armholes
Bind off 3 sts at beg of next 6 rows.
Dec 1 st at each end of every foll row until 79[81:85] sts rem. **
Work even until work measures 7¾[8½:8½]in from beg of armhole shaping, ending with a P row.

Shape shoulders
Bind off 10[10:11] sts at beg of next 2 rows and 11 sts at beg of foll 2 rows.
Bind off rem 37[39:41] sts.

Front

Work as for back from ** to **.
Work even until work measures 4in from beg of armhole shaping, ending with a P row.
Shape neck
Next row K21[21:22] sts, leave these on a spare needle, bind off next 37[39:41] sts, K to end.
Complete right side of neck first.
Work even until work matches back to shoulder shaping, ending armhole edge.
Shape shoulder
Bind off 10[10:11] sts at beg of next row. Work 1 row. Bind off rem 11 sts. With WS of work facing return to sts on spare needle. Join yarn to neck edge. Complete to match first side, reversing shaping.

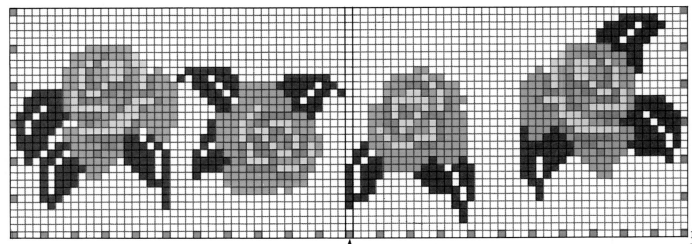

Center stitch

1st row

Sleeves

Using smaller needles, cast on 48[52:56] sts.
Work 21 rows K1, P1 rib.
Next row Rib 9[11:13], (inc 1) 31 times, rib to end. 79[83:87] sts.
Change to larger needles. Beg with a K row cont in st st until work measures 17in, ending with a P row.

Shape top

Bind off 3 sts at beg of next 6 rows.
Dec 1 st at each end of the next and every other row until 53[55:57] sts rem.
Work even until work measures 21¼[21½:21½]in, ending with a P row.
Dec 1 st at each end of every row until 19[21:23] sts rem.
Bind off 3 sts at beg of next 4 rows.
Bind off rem sts.

Collar

Using smaller needles, cast on 97[99:101] sts. Cont in rib as foll:
1st row (RS) K1, *P1, K1, rep from * to end.
2nd row P1, *K1, P1, rep from * to end.
Rep the last 2 rows twice more.
Next row (K1, P1) twice, K to last 4 sts, (P1, K1) twice.

Next row (P1, K1) twice, P to last 4 sts, (K1, P1) twice.
Rep the last 2 rows until work measures 5½in, ending with a WS row.

Shape neck

Next row (K1, P1) twice, K26, leave these sts on a spare needle, bind off next 37[39:41] sts, work to end.
Complete right side of neck first.
Work even until work measures 9½[10:10]in, ending with a WS row.
Break yarn and leave these sts.
With WS of work facing return to sts on spare needle. Join yarn to next st, work to end.
Cont until work matches first side of neck, ending with a P row.
Next row Work 30 sts, cast on 37[39:41] sts, work across sts for other side of neck. 97[99:101] sts.
Cont on sts as set for another 8½in, ending with a WS row.
Rep first–2nd rib rows 3 times.
Bind off in rib.

To finish

Press as appropriate for yarn used.
Join shoulder seams.
With RS of front and back facing WS of collar, place collar in position,

matching neck edges.

Front neck edge

Using smaller needles, beg at left front corner of neck, working through two thicknesses of garment and collar, pick up and K37[39:41] sts.
Rep first–2nd rib rows as for collar 4 times, *at the same time*, dec 1 st at each end of every row.
Bind off in rib.

Back neck edge

Using circular needle, beg at right front corner of neck, pick up and K30[33:33] sts up right side of neck, 37[39:41] sts across back neck, 30[33:33] sts down left side of neck. 97[105:107] sts. Work in rows.
Complete as for front neck edge.
Join corners of edging. Join side and sleeve seams. Set in sleeves.

Duplicate stitch

Using two strands of tapestry yarn duplicate stitch roses on collar following chart. Place pattern by matching center stitch of collar to center stitch on chart and working bottom row on chart on first knit row of collar. Continue working border dots every fifth stitch up the sides of the collar and across lower back edge. Press embroidery under a damp cloth.

Special technique – attaching a square collar

1 Join shoulder seams. Place the collar in position on the sweater with the wrong side of the collar facing the right sides of the back and front. Match the neck edge of the collar to the neckline of the sweater.

2 Pick up the required number of stitches along the front neck edge through the bound-off edges of the collar neck edge and the sweater neckline for each stitch. Work in single rib as instructed decreasing one stitch at each end of every row. Bind off in rib.

3 Pick up the required number of stitches along sides and back neck edge working through both layers as before. Work in single rib for the required depth, decreasing one stitch at each end of every row. Join the lower front corners of the ribbing.

Beaded Cardigan

This beautifully shaped cardigan with ruffled replum has glass beads knitted into a simple textured pattern. If you prefer, you could sew the beads on after the knitting is completed.

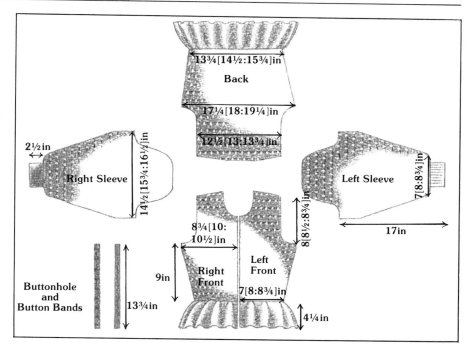

Sizes
To fit 34[36:38]in bust
Length 21¼[21¾:22]in
Sleeve seam 17in

Note Instructions for larger sizes are in brackets []; where there is only one set of figures it applies to all sizes.

Gauge
28 sts and 28 rows to 4in over bead patt on size 5 needles

Materials
700[750:800]g double knitting yarn (see page 9) or 29[31:33]oz knitting worsted
1 pair each sizes 3 and 5 knitting needles
9 buttons
Approx 1000 beads

Back
Before beg work, thread approx 120 beads onto each of 8 balls of yarn. Using larger needles and yarn without beads, cast on 243[253:263] sts.
Beg peplum
**K 2 rows.
Next row (RS) P3, *K7, P3, rep from * to end.
Next row K3, *P7, K3, rep from *. Rep the last 2 rows for 2¾in, ending with a WS row.
Next row P3, *sl 1, K1, psso, K3, K2 tog, P3, rep from * to end.
Next row K3, *P5, K3, rep from *.
Next row P3, *sl 1, K1, psso, K1, K2 tog, P3, rep from * to end.
Next row K3, *P3, K3, rep from *.
Next row P3, *sl 1, K2 tog, psso, P3, rep from * to end.
Next row K3, *P1, K3, rep from * to end. 99[99:107] sts.
Change to smaller needles.
***Next row** *P1, K1, rep from * to last st, P1.
Next row *K1, P1, rep from * to last st, K1.
Next row *P1, K1, rep from * to last st, P1.
Next row K1, *P1, K1, P2 tog, yo, rep from * to last 2 sts, P1, K1.**
1st and 3rd sizes only
Work a further 2[0] rows in rib.
2nd size only
Next row Rib 19, (inc into next st, rib 19) 3 times, inc into next st, rib to end. 103 sts.
All sizes

Now work 0[1:2] rows in rib, inc 1 st at each end of every row. 99[105:111] sts. Change to larger needles and yarn with beads.
Beg bead patt.
1st row (RS) K1, *K4, P2, rep from * to last 2 sts, K2.
2nd row K1, P1, *K2, P4, rep from * to last st, K1.
3rd–5th rows Rep first–2nd rows once, then first row again.
6th row K1, P1, *K2, P1, ybk, push bead up close to RS of work, sl 2, yfwd, – called place bead, P1, rep from * to last st, K1.
7th row K1, *insert RH needle between 4th (K st) and 5th (P st) on LH needle, draw through a loop and sl onto LH needle, K it tog with next st on LH needle, P2, K3, rep from * to last 2 sts, K2.
8th row K1, *P4, K2, rep from * to last 2 sts, P1, K1.
9th row K2, *P2, K4, rep from * to last st, K1.
10th–13th rows Rep 8th–9th rows twice.
14th row K1, *P1, place bead, P1, K2, rep from * to last 2 sts, P1, K1.
15th row K2, *P2, insert RH needle between 4th (K st) and 5th (P st) on LH needle, draw through a loop, sl it onto LH needle, K it tog with next st on LH needle, P2, K3, rep from * ending last rep K2.
16th row as 2nd row.

These 16 rows form the patt.
Cont in patt, inc 1 st at each end of the next and every foll 3rd row until there are 123[129:137] sts, working extra sts into patt.
Work even until work measures 9in from beg of bead patt, ending with a WS row.
Shape armholes
Keeping patt correct, bind off 4 sts at beg of next 4 rows. Dec 1 st at each end of next 4[7:8] rows.
Dec 1 st at each end of every other row until 91[93:97] sts rem.
Work even until work measures 8[8½:8¾]in from beg of armhole shaping, ending with a WS row.
Shape shoulders
Bind off 13 sts at beg of next 2 rows, then 13[13:14] sts at beg of foll 2 rows. Leave rem 39[41:43] sts on a spare needle.

Left front
Using larger needles and yarn without beads, cast on 123[133:143] sts.
Work as for back from ** to **.
Work 2[1:0] rows in rib.
Now work 0[1:2] rows in rib, inc 1 st at each end of every row. 51[57:63] sts. Change to larger needles and yarn with beads.
Beg bead patt as for back. Inc and work into patt 1 st at side edge on the 17th and every foll 3rd row until there are 63[69:75] sts.

Work even until work matches back to underarm, ending at side edge.
Shape armhole
Keeping patt correct, bind off 4[5:5] sts at beg of next row and 4[4:5] sts at beg of every other row once. Dec 1 st at armhole edge on foll 4[7:9] rows and then 1 st on every other row until 47[49:52] sts rem. Work even until work measures 4¾in from beg of armhole shaping, ending at front edge.
Shape neck
Keeping patt correct, bind off 8 sts at beg of next row, then dec 1 st at neck edge on every row until 26[26:27] sts rem. Work even until work matches back to shoulder shaping, ending at armhole edge.
Shape shoulder
Bind off 13 sts at beg of next row. Work 1 row.
Bind off rem 13[13:14] sts.

Right front
Work as for left front reversing shapings.

Sleeves
Using smaller needles and yarn without beads, cast on 48[54:60] sts. work in K1, P1 rib for 2½in.
Next row Rib 9 [12:15], (work twice into next st, rib 13) twice, work twice into next st, rib to end. 51[57:63] sts. Change to larger needles and yarn with beads.
Beg bead patt as for back, inc 1 st at each end of every foll 3rd row until there are 105[111:117] sts. Work even until work measures 17in, ending with a same patt row as back at underarm.
Shape top
Keeping patt correct, bind off 4[5:5] sts at beg of next 2 rows and 4[4:5] sts at beg of foll 2 rows. Now dec 1 st at each end of every row until 59[61:63] sts rem, then at each end of every other row until 33 sts rem. Bind off 3 sts at beg of next 6 rows. Bind off rem 15 sts.

Shoulder pads (make 2)
Using smaller needles and yarn without beads, cast on 38 sts. Work in K1, P1 rib for 26 rows. Bind off in rib.

To finish
Join shoulder seams.
Neck edging
Using smaller needles, with RS of work facing, pick up and K30[33:36] sts up right front neck edge, K across 39[41:43] sts on back neck, pick up and K30[33:36] sts down left front neck edge. 99[107:115] sts.
Now work in rib as for back from *** to **.
Work a further 3 rows in rib.
Work ruffle
1st row (RS), P3, *K1, P3, rep from *.
2nd row K3, *(P1, K1, P1) all into next st, K3, rep from * to end.
3rd row P3, *K3, P3, rep from *.
4th row K3, *(P1, K1) all into next st, P1, (K1, P1) all into next st, K3, rep from * to end.
5th row P3, *K5, P3, rep from *.
6th row K3, *(P1, K1) all into next st, P3, (K1, P1) all into next st, K3, rep from * to end.
7th row P3, *K7, P3, rep from *.
8th row K3, *P7, K3, rep from *.
9th row As 7th.
Keeping patt correct, bind off.
Button band
Using smaller needles cast on 8 sts. Work in K1, P1 rib until band is long enough, when slightly stretched, to fit left front edge from top of peplum to neck edge. Bind off in rib.
Mark the positions of 9 buttons, the first to come ¾in above base of band, the last ¾in below the neck edge, with the other 7 evenly spaced between them.
Buttonhole band
Work to match button band, making buttonholes opposite markers as foll:
1st row (RS) Rib 3, bind off 2, rib 3.
2nd row Rib to end, casting on over bound-off sts of previous row.
Join side and sleeve seams. Set in sleeves. Fold shoulder pads in half diagonally and overcast edges. Sew in position. Sew on bands and buttons. Using 4 lengths of yarn 120in long, make a twisted cord for waist tie, and using 80in long lengths make a neck tie. Thread through eyelet holes, bringing ends out to tie.

Special technique – placing the beads

1 Beads are placed on wrong-side rows. Thread beads onto yarn before knitting. Work in pattern to bead position. Take yarn to back of work, push bead up close to work, slip two stitches, bring yarn forward. Work to next bead position.

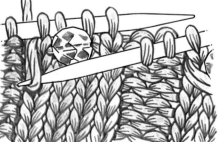

2 On the next row, work to the bead, insert the right-hand needle between the 4th and 5th stitches on the left-hand needle from front to back. Take the working yarn under and over the needle and draw a loop through to the front of the work.

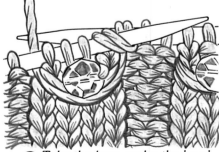

3 Take the loop under the bead and place it on the left-hand needle. Knit the loop together with the next stitch on the left-hand needle. Work in pattern to the next bead position.

Sequined Dress

Make a dramatic entrance to any party in a flouncy
sequined sizzler of a dress that's a lot easier to make than it
looks. The sequins are knitted in as the work progresses
and the ruffles are made separately and sewn on. The
skimpy bodice is fastened with narrow straps
criss-crossing the back.

Size
To fit 34–36in bust
Length at side seam 25½in

Gauge
28 sts and 36 rows to 4in over st st
on size 3 needles

Materials
22oz fingering yarn
1 pair size 3 knitting needles
Approx 8,000 sequins ⅜in in
diameter

Special note The sequins must be
threaded onto the yarn before
beginning to knit. Thread sequins
concave side down.

Front
**Using knitting needles, cast on 184
sts. Beg with a K row cont in st st
until work measures 8¼in, ending
with a P row.
Next row (K2 tog) to end. 92 sts.
Beg with a P row work 3 rows st st.
Beg sequin patt.
1st row K2, *place sequin as foll:
ywfd, move a sequin up close to RS
of work, P1, – called place sequin
–, K1, rep from * to end.
2nd–4th rows Beg with a P row
work 3 rows st st.
5th row K3, *place sequin, K1, rep
from * to last st, K1.
6th–8th rows As 2nd–4th rows.
These 8 rows form the patt.
Work in patt for 2 rows.
Keeping patt correct, beg hip
shaping.
Next row K1, K2 tog, K26, K3 tog,
K28, K3 tog, K26, K2 tog, K1.
86 sts.
Patt 7 rows.
Next row K1, K2 tog, K24, K3 tog,
K26, K3 tog, K24, K2 tog, K1.
80 sts.
Patt 7 rows.
Next row K1, K2 tog, K22, K3 tog,
K24, K3 tog, K22, K2 tog, K1.
74 sts. **
Patt 39 rows.
Beg bodice shaping.
Next row K1, pick up loop between
last st worked and next st on LH
needle and K tbl – called M1 –, K25,
M1, K1, M1, K20, M1, K1, M1,
K25, M1, K1. 80 sts.
Patt 7 rows.
Next row K1, M1, K27, M1, K1,
186

M1, K22, M1, K1, M1, K27, M1,
K1. 86 sts.
Patt 7 rows.
Next row K1, M1, K29, M1, K1,
M1, K24, M1, K1, M1, K29, M1, K1.
92 sts.
Patt 39 rows.
Next row K28, (M1, K1) 5 times,
K26, (M1, K1) 5 times, K28. 102 sts.
Patt 3 rows. Beg neck shaping.
Next row K2 tog, K to last 2 sts,
K2 tog.
Next row P2 tog, P47, bind off 2 sts,
P to last 2 sts, P2 tog.
Complete left side of neck first.
Keeping patt correct, dec 1 st at each
end of every other row until 28 sts
rem. Now dec 1 st at each end of
every foll 4th row until 16sts rem,
ending with a P row.
Next row (K2 tog) to end. 8 sts.

Next row (P2 tog) to end. 4 sts.
Next row (K1, place sequin) twice.
Next row (P2 tog) twice.
Next row K.
Bind off. With RS of work facing,
return to sts for right side of neck.
Complete to match first side.

Back
Work as for front from ** to **.
Patt 18 rows.
Shape back waist
Next row P22, bind off 30 sts, P to
end.
Complete right side of waist first.
Keeping patt correct, dec 1 st at inner
edge on every foll 4th row until 3 sts
rem. Bind off. With RS of work
facing, return to sts for left side of
waist. Join yarn to next st and
complete to match first side.

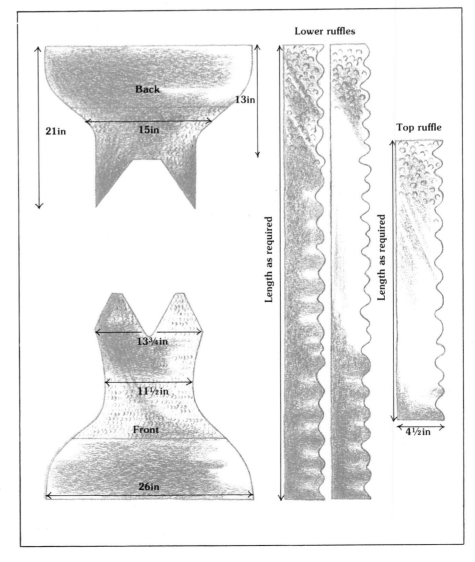

Lower ruffles

Back
13in

21in

15in

Length as required

Length as required

Top ruffle

13¾in

11½in

Front

26in

4½in

Top ruffle
Using knitting needles, cast on 30 sts.
Next row K.
Next row P24, K6.
Rep the last 2 rows once more.
Beg sequin patt.
1st row K2, *place sequin, K2, rep from * to last 3 sts, K3.
2nd, 4th, 6th, 8th, 10th and 12th rows P24, K6.
3rd, 7th and 11th rows K.
5th row K3, *place sequin, K2, rep from * to last 2 sts, K2.
9th row K1, *place sequin, K2, rep from * to last 2 sts, place sequin, K1.
13th row K2, turn.
14th and every other row K to end.
15th row K2, place sequin, turn.
17th row K4, turn.
19th row K3, place sequin, K1, turn.
21st row K6, turn.
23rd row K1, (place sequin, K2) twice, turn.
24th and every other row P to last 6 sts, K6.
25th row K8, turn.
27th row (K2, place sequin) 3 times, turn.
29th row K10, turn.
31st row K3, (place sequin, K2) twice, place sequin, K1, turn.
33rd row K12, turn.
35th row K1, (place sequin, K2) 4 times, turn.
37th row K14, turn.
39th row (K2, place sequin) 5 times, turn.

41st row K16, turn.
43rd row K3, (place sequin, K2) 4 times, place sequin, K1, turn.
45th row K18, turn.
47th row K1, (place sequin, K2) 6 times, turn.
49th row K20, turn.
51st row (K2, place sequin) 7 times, turn.
53rd row K22, turn.
55th row K3, (place sequin, K2) 6 times, place sequin, K1, turn.
57th row K24, turn.
59th row K1, (place sequin, K2) 8 times, turn.
61st row As 57th row.
63rd row As 55th row.
65th row As 53rd row.
67th row As 51st row.
69th row As 49th row.
71st row As 47th row.
73rd row As 45th row.
75th row As 43rd row.
77th row As 41st row.
79th row As 39th row.
81st row As 37th row.
83rd row As 35th row.
85th row As 33rd row.
87th row As 31st row.
89th row As 29th row.
91st row As 27th row.
93rd row As 25th row.
95th row As 23rd row.
97th row As 21st row.
98th and every other row K to end.

99th row As 19th row.
101st row As 17th row.
103rd row As 15th row.
105th row As 13th row.
106th row K to end.
107th–118th rows Rep first–12th rows once.
These 118 rows form the patt. Cont in patt until straight edge fits hipline at beg of sequin patt.
Bind off.

Lower ruffles (make 2)
Work as for top ruffle until straight edge fits lower edge of skirt, ending with a WS row.
Bind off.

Ties (make 2)
Using knitting needles, cast on 4 sts.
Beg with a K row, cont in st st until work measures 47in, ending with a P row.
Bind off.

To finish
Join side seams.
Sew top ruffle to top of skirt at beg of sequin patt, one lower ruffle to hem edge and the second lower ruffle between them. Sew ties to top of bodice. Make a button loop on each inner back edge. Take ties over shoulders, cross over on the back, thread through loops and tie in a bow.

Special technique – placing sequins

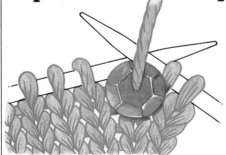

1 The sequins on the dress are placed on right-side rows on the first and 5th pattern rows as follows: On the first row knit the first two stitches: Bring the yarn forward from the back to the front of the work. Push a sequin up close to the right side of the work.

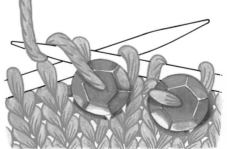

2 Purl the next stitch. The first sequin is now in position. Knit the next stitch, then place the second sequin in the same way. Continue placing the sequins after every other stitch.

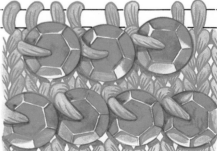

3 On the 5th row the sequins are placed after the third stitch in the row, and then after every other stitch, thus staggering them between the sequins on the first row.

Smocked Sweater

A prettily pointed ruffle and a beaded smocked front
panel give this beautifully shaped sweater a
romantic medieval look.

Sizes
To fit 34[36:38]in bust
Length including ruffle
21¼[21¾:22½]in
Sleeve seam including ruffle 18in
Note Instructions for the larger sizes
are in brackets []; where there is only
one set of figure sit applies to all
sizes.

Gauge
24 sts and 30 rows to 4in measured
over main rib patt on size 5 needles

Materials
650[700:750]g double knitting yarn
(see page 9) or 27[29:31]oz knitting
worsted
1 pair each sizes 3 and 5 knitting
needles
1 size 5 circular needle
approx 110 small beads

Front
Using larger needles, cast on 3 sts.
Beg shaping.
1st row K3.
2nd row (RS) Cast on 4 sts and work
across sts as foll: P2, K1, P4.
3rd row Cast on 4 sts and work as
foll: K2, P1, K5, P1, K2.
4th row Cast on 5 sts and work as
foll: P1, K1, (P5, K1) twice, P2.
5th row Cast on 5 sts and work as
foll: K1, P1, (K5, P1) 3 times, K1.
6th row Cast on 5 sts and work as
foll: K1, (P5, K1) 4 times, P1.
7th row Cast on 5 sts and work as
foll: P1, (K5, P1) 5 times.
Cont in this way, casting on 5[6:6]
sts at beg of next 4[8:6] rows,
working extra sts into patt. Then cast
on 6[7:7] sts at beg of foll 6[8:8]
rows.
1st and 3rd sizes only
Cast on 7[8] sts at beg of next 6[4]
rows.
All sizes
Cont in patt as set on these
129[135:141] sts until work measures
11½[11½:12]in measured at side
edge, ending with a WS row.
**Shape armholes and divide for
neck**
Next row Bind off 4[5:6] sts, patt
58[60:62] including st used in
binding off, K2 tog and turn, leaving
rem sts on a spare needle.
Complete left side of neck first.
Work 1 row.

**Dec 1 st at armhole edge on next
3[5:5] rows, then on every other
row, *at the same time*, dec 1 st at
neck edge on next and every other
row until 40[41:43] sts rem.
Keeping armhole edge straight cont
to dec at neck edge only as before
until 20[20:21] sts rem, ending with a
RS row.
Work even for 3 rows.
Shape shoulder
Bind off 7 sts at beg of next and
every other row once.
Work 1 row.
Bind off rem 6[6:7] sts ******.
With RS of work facing, return to sts
on spare needle. Sl center st onto a
safety pin, join in yarn to rem sts, K2
tog, patt to end.
Next row Bind off 4[5:6], patt to
end.
Complete to match first side of neck,
work from ****** to ******, reversing
shapings, and working 4 rows before
shoulder shaping.

Front lower edge ruffle
With RS of work facing, using circular
needle, pick up and K129[135:141]
sts around lower edge. Work in rows.
1st row (WS) K1[4:1], *P1, K5, rep
from * to last 2[5:2] sts, P1, K1[4:1].
2nd row P1[4:1], pick up loop
between last st and next st on LH
needle and work into the back of it –
called M1 –, *K1, M1, P5, M1, rep

from * to last 2[5:2] sts, K1, M1,
P1[4:1].
3rd row K1[4:1], *P3, K5, rep from
* to last 4[7:4] sts, P3, K1[4:1].
4th row P1[4:1], M1, *K3, M1, P5,
M1, rep from * to last 4[7:4] sts, K3,
M1, P1[4:1].
5th row K1[4:1], *P5, K5, rep from
* to last 6[9:6] sts, P5, K1[4:1].
6th row P1[4:1], M1, *K5, M1, P5,
M1, rep from * to last 6[9:6] sts, K5,
M1, P1[4:1].
7th row K1[4:1], *P7, K5, rep from
* to last 8[11:8] sts, P7, K1[4:1].
8th row P1[4:1], M1, *K7, M1, P5,
M1, rep from * to last 8[11:8] sts,
K7, M1, P1[4:1].
9th row K1[4:1], *P9, K5, rep from
* to last 10[13:10] sts, P9, K1[4:1].
10th row P1[4:1], M1, *K9, M1, P5,
M1, rep from * to last 10[13:10] sts,
K9, M1, P1[4:1].
11th row K1[4:1], *P11, K5, rep
from * to last 12[15:12] sts, P11,
K1[4:1].
12th row P1[4:1], *K11, P5, rep
from * to last 12[15:12] sts, K11,
P1[4:1].
Rep last 2 rows until ruffle measures
2in, ending with a WS row.
Bind off in rib as set.

Back
Using larger needles, cast on
105[111:117] sts. Beg patt.
1st row (RS) P1[4:1], *K1, P5, rep

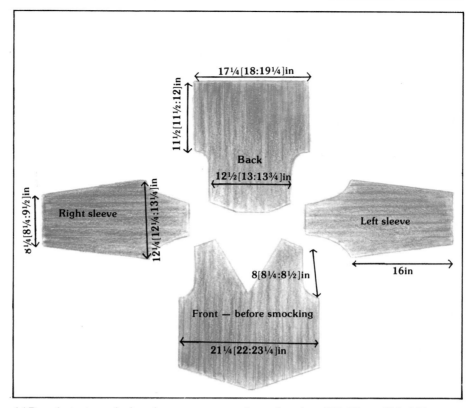

17¼[18:19¼]in

11½[11½:12]in

Back
12½[13:13¾]in

8¼[8¼:9½]in

Right sleeve

12¼[12¼:13¼]in

Left sleeve

8[8¼:8½]in

Front — before smocking

21¼[22:23¼]in

16in

189

from * to last 2[5:2] sts, K1, P1[4:1].
2nd row K1[4:1], *P1, K5, rep from * to last 2[5:2] sts, P1, K1[4:1].
These 2 rows form the rib patt. Cont in patt until work measures same as front to underarm at side seam, ending with a WS row.

Shape armholes
Keeping patt correct, bind off 4[5:6] sts at beg of next 2 rows.
Dec 1 st at each end of next 3[5:5] rows, then on every other row until 77[79:83] sts rem.
Work even until work matches front to shoulder shaping, ending at armhole edge.

Shape shoulders
Bind off 7 sts at beg of next 4 rows, then 6[6:7] sts at beg of foll 2 rows.
Leave rem 37[39:41] sts on a spare needle.

Back lower edge ruffle
With RS of work facing, using circular needle, pick up and K105[111:117] sts around lower edge.
Work as for front lower edge ruffle.

Sleeves
Using smaller needles, cast on 51[51:57] sts.
1st row K1, *P1, K1, rep from * to end.
2nd row P1, *K1, P1, rep from * to end.
Rep the last 2 rows for ¾in, ending

with a 2nd row.
Change to larger needles and beg patt as for back. Inc and work into patt 1 st at each end of the 5th and every foll 8th row until there are 75[75:81] sts.
Work even until work measures 16in, ending with a WS row.

Shape top
Bind off 4[5:6] sts at beg of next 2 rows. Dec 1 st at each end of next and every foll 4th row until 51[45:49] sts rem, then at each end of every other row until 37 sts rem, ending with a WS row.
Next row K2 tog, K2, *(K2 tog) twice, K2, rep from * to last 3 sts, K2 tog, K1. 25 sts.
Bind off.

Sleeve ruffles
With RS of work facing, using larger needles, pick up and K51[51:57] sts along lower edge of sleeve.
Work as for front lower edge ruffle.

To finish
Work smocking over central panel of 55 sts. (See Special Technique.) Join right shoulder.

Neck ruffle
With WS of work facing, using larger needles, K across 37[39:41] sts on back, pick up and K49[54:60] sts down right side of neck, K center st, pick up and K50[55;59] sts up left

side of neck. 137[149:161] sts.
1st row (WS) K2[2:5], *P1, K5, rep from * to last 3[3:6] sts, P1, K2[2:5].
2nd row P2[2:5], M1, *K1, M1, P5, M1, rep from * to last 3[3:6] sts, K1, M1, P2[2:5].
3rd row K2[2:5], *P3, K5, rep from * to last 5[5:8] sts, P3, K2[2:5].
4th row P2[2:5], M1, *K3, M1, P5, M1, rep from * to last 5[5:8] sts, K3, P2[2:5].
5th row K2[2:5], *P5, K5, rep from * to last 7[7:10] sts, P5, K2[2:5].
6th row P2[2:5], M1, *K5, M1, P5, M1, rep from * to last 7[7:10] sts, K5, M1, P2[2:5].
7th row K2[2:5], *P7, K5, rep from * to last 9[9:12] sts, P7, K2[2:5].
8th row P2[2:5], M1, *K7, M1, P5, M1, rep from * to last 9[9:12] sts, K7, M1, P2[2:5].
9th row K2[2:5], *P9, K5, rep from * to last 11[11:14] sts, P9, K2[2:5].
10th row P2[2:5], M1, *K9, M1, P5, M1, rep from * to last 11[11:14] sts, K9, M1, K2[2:5].
11th row K2[2:5], *P11, K5, rep from * to last 13[13:16] sts, P11, K2[2:5].
12th row P2[2:5], *K11, P5, rep from * to last 13[13:16] sts, K11, P2[2:5].
Rep last 2 rows until ruffle measures 2in, ending with a WS row. Bind off in rib as set. Join left shoulder, neck, side and sleeve seams. Set in sleeves.

Special technique – working the smocking

1 *The smocking is worked over the center front ten knit ribs. Begin with center two ribs. Thread needle with matching yarn. Secure yarn at back of work. Bring needle through to front on left of pair. Take it through to back on right, then to front again. Thread bead onto yarn, push it up to work, drawing ribs together.*

2 *Leaving four rows between, draw together the pairs of ribs on each side of the first pair as shown, placing a bead on each one as before.*

3 *Leaving four rows between, draw together the middle pair of ribs and two pairs on each side of the middle pair. Continue in this way smocking alternate pairs of ribs to produce a honeycomb effect, working regularly from right to left on each smocking row.*

INDEX

INFORMATION ON YARNS

If you wish to buy one of the yarns specified by brand name in this book, you can obtain the name of your nearest dealer or of a mail-order source by writing to the manufacturer or importer listed here.

Jaeger
Susan Bates Inc.
212 Middlesex Avenue
Route 9A
Chester
Connecticut 06412

Neveda
Neveda Yarn Company
230 Fifth Avenue
New York
New York 10001

Phildar
Phildar Inc.
6438 Dawson Blvd.
Norcross
Georgia 30093

Pingouin
Pingouin Corporation
PO Box 100
Highway 45
Jamestown
South Carolina 29453

Scheepjeswol
Scheepjeswol USA Inc.
115 Lafayette Ave.
North White Plains
New York 10603